# HARVESTING THE FLAME

# HARVESTING THE FLAME

The history of
Alberta's rural natural gas cooperatives

## BY FAY ORR

REIDMORE BOOKS INC.   EDMONTON, CANADA

**Canadian Cataloguing in Publication Data**

Orr, Fay, 1957 -

   Harvesting the Flame: The history of the Alberta's rural natural gas cooperatives

  ISBN 0-919091-88-1

1. Gas, Natural - Alberta - History.    2. Gas industry - Alberta - History.    3. Cooperation - Alberta - History.
I. Title.
HD9581.C33A46    1989    334'.68573'097123    C89-091482-6

*printed and bound in Canada*

# CONTENTS

# DEDICATION

*Harvesting the Flame* is dedicated to the Natural Gas volunteers
and their spouses who worked so hard
in making the Co-ops a reality.

# FOREWORD

The idea for this book grew out of discussions between directors of the Federation of Alberta Gas Co-ops and Al "Boomer" Adair, the Minister of Transportation and Utilities. "The gasification of rural Alberta is probably one of the greatest success stories that North America has had, but we're not telling anybody about it," Adair told directors. "Friends and relatives in other parts of the country are amazed to the point of envy when they realize nearly every home in Alberta, from the top of the province to the US border, has gas. And when you think of the lay of the land, of the distances and terrain involved, then you have to say that's one heck of an accomplishment."

Indeed, Alberta is the only jurisdiction in the world that has extended natural gas service to most of its rural population. Certainly there is quiet appreciation of this fact among rural Albertans, who have come to regard the clean convenience of natural gas heating as their birthright. But few Albertans, and still fewer other Canadians, are aware of the hard work, personal sacrifice, and government commitment that have made widespread rural gas service a reality. That's why this book has been written.

As the following pages will relate, the dream of rural gas service was born in the 1960s, when small groups of farmers in southern Alberta began forming cooperatives to build and operate gas distribution systems. Using their own money and hands, they laid hundreds of miles of pipeline. The pipeline connected their farms to the big transmission lines which gathered gas from beneath their land for export to other parts of North America. The dream was picked up by the Peter Lougheed Conservatives, who, in 1973, launched the Rural Gas Program to help more cooperatives, along with small towns, counties, Indian bands, and utilities, build even bigger and better systems. By 1988 Alberta's rural gas system was among the biggest gas distribution systems in the world, with more than 57 000 miles of pipe—enough to circle the globe twice—bringing gas to nearly 130 000 customers.

Some of the system was built by major utility companies like Canadian Western, Northwestern Utilities, and ICG Utilities. But by far the biggest portion—roughly 60 per cent—was constructed and is still operated by member- owned cooperatives. In 1989, there were seventy-four gas co-ops in the province bringing gas to nearly 55 000 customers. This book tells the story of those cooperatives and the men and women who overcame formidable odds to make them work.

To date, Alberta's rural gas system has cost about $600 million to build; the provincial government paid for 60 per cent of that, rural Albertans contributed the rest. "It may seem like a lot of money," says Tom Brown, executive director of the Gas Utilities Branch in the Department of Transportation and Utilities. "But already rural Albertans have saved nearly twice that much by using natural gas instead of more expensive fuels like propane and oil."

Moreover, natural gas service has strengthened Alberta's farm industry. "Natural gas is tremendously important to agriculture," says former Utilities minister Lawrence Shaben (1979-82). By providing inexpensive fuel for irrigation, grain drying, green houses, hatcheries, and barn heating, natural gas has helped Alberta farmers become more productive and creative, notes Shaben. "But most importantly, natural gas has helped to keep farmers on the land by improving the quality of rural life."

## A NOTE ABOUT THE APPENDICES

No one book can possibly do justice to the story of every single gas co-op. But readers interested in learning more about individual gas cooperatives should find the appendices at the back of this book useful. Appendix 1 contains an alphabetical list of Alberta's seventy-four gas co-ops, citing the location and size of each one. The four county systems are described in Appendix 2. The names of co-op directors, together with a few words on each co-op's history are also included. Appendix 3 provides the names and a brief description of the achievements of each of the Federation of Alberta Gas Co-ops' directors.

## A NOTE ABOUT MEASUREMENTS

This book uses imperial measurements except in the case of gigajoules, a metric measurement now used throughout the natural gas industry. A conversion to the imperial measurement mcf is given in some historical references.

## PROLOGUE

# *Life Before Gas*

Hauling coal by wagon was a common task in Alberta throughout the early part of this century. This picture was taken in 1923.

Ꭺs many natural gas co-op members will attest, keeping warm in the pre-gas era required hard work and some risk to life and limb. Fred Seely, chairman of the Alder Flats Gas Co-op, recalls how one neighbour nearly killed himself while thawing his propane tank with a blowtorch: "It didn't explode, but it took off like a rocketship. It had flown clear through poplar trees 4 and 5 in. in diameter, and through a hog barn, which was totally destroyed. The guy wasn't killed, but he sure was happy when the gas system came in."

Thawing frozen propane tanks at 3 AM in thirty below weather was among the least of the inconveniences tolerated by rural Albertans in the days before gas. Before propane or "gas away from the mains" came on the market in the late 1940s, rural Albertans spent countless hours chopping wood, mining coal, and scavenging the fields for old fence posts, railroad ties, and cow chips.

"You bet we used cowchips," laughs Jim Musgrove, co-founder of the Atlee Gas Co-op in Jenner, "Lots of 'em. Mostly the kids collected them. They burned with a quiet flame, almost like briquettes. They had a pungent, but not unpleasant odour. We call it farmers' coal." Musgrove and his father would also head out once a year on the family's horse-drawn wagon and scraper to "haul coal" from a nearby strip mine at $5 a load.

Actually, rural Alberta is filled with former do-it-yourself miners. Colin Storch says that anybody living on the coulee banks (a coulee is a deep, narrow ravine) in the Red Deer River Valley north of Drumheller knew where to find exposed seams of coal down on the valley flats. The original chairman of the Big Country Gas Co-op in Morrin, Storch and his neighbours held annual "coal mining bees" until the late 1940s. "Three or four farmers would pick a day in late fall and drive down the coulees on trails they had made for their horses and bobsleighs. Some of the coal was covered with a 5-ft.-thick layer of sandstone that had to be scraped off with a road plow. Then the coal had to be loosened with dynamite and shovelled into the sleigh box. It took a good four days to get enough coal to last the winter," recalls Storch.

With the advent of trucks and better roads, Storch and his neighbours began buying coal from mines near Drumheller. But the demand for the black stuff was huge and often Storch came away empty-handed. "I sat there lots of days from four in the morning until five in the afternoon and still came home with an empty truck—and that don't burn too good."

Mervin Fox, original chairman of the Rockyview Gas Co-op in Crossfield, recalls that buying coal from private mines sometimes entailed back-breaking work. Once, when the owner of the mine he normally bought coal from was sick, Fox and two of his neighbours equipped themselves with helmets, safety lamps, picks, and shovels and went down the mine shaft themselves. "We stayed down there till we had our three truck-loads' worth," says Fox. "I never knew what dark was till I went down there. Never again."

As well as being hard to get, coal was messy to use. Every day ashes had to be cleared from the coal furnace and dumped outside. Moreover, someone had to stoke the furnace several times a day until the invention of automatic stoker furnaces in the 1950s. Sighs Ida Flake, secretary of the Burnt Lake Gas Co-op in Innisfail: "There'll be coal dust and fly ash in our basement forever."

Coal had another annoying trait. It usually ran out when needed most. George Paetkau, manager of the Gem Gas Co-op in southern Alberta, remembers that "Everytime the coal bin was empty, it was forty below and the roads were blocked with snow."

But to Cecil Flake, Ida's husband and the manager of Burnt Lake, stoking coal was a pleasure compared to chopping wood. "Burning wood might be a novelty to the new generation out there now, but to me it was work," he says. "A piece of wood kept you warm many times before you burned it—while chopping it, splitting it, carrying it, and stacking it."

The household coal supply had to be constantly monitored and restored. Sophie Shwetz of Thorhild County is pictured here getting a pail of coal for the house.

Merv Giem, the original secretary/treasurer of the Battle River Co-op, kept quite warm while chopping kindling from the poplar groves surrounding his boyhood home in Ferintosh. But the warmth didn't last. Recalls Giem: "People would bank up fires at night with lumps of coal to keep the chill off the room until the next day. But our furnace was too small to bank up to last all night. So after we nearly froze to death a few mornings, we learned to get a pile of kindling ready the night before."

Burning wood was more than hard work, it was downright dangerous, recalls John Lachowich, original chairman of the Lac La Biche Co-op. A farmer at Rich Lake south of Lac La Biche, Lachowich remembers vividly the days before natural gas:

*You went into the woods, felled trees, and hauled them home. Then you got all the neighbours together with a circular saw attached to a Model T Ford engine and mounted on a sleigh. Then you would spend the whole day sawing logs into short lengths, with five or six men hanging on to one end of the log, and somebody at the other end throwing away the pieces of wood as they fell. We called that blocking.*

*The women were usually cooking while we did this. But my mother, she liked to throw a few blocks away when she came out to call the men in for dinner. Once she slipped her foot under the saw to kick some sawdust away, which you had to do every now and then. But she didn't keep her foot low enough and the saw cut it off.*

Life became somewhat more convenient in the late 1940s and 1950s, when a number of companies and cooperatives sprang up to supply farmers with propane. But like coal, propane tended to let people down in sub-zero weather. Recalls Gem Co-op director Joe Milne: "When it got cold enough, the propane wouldn't vaporize and it would freeze off. You'd have to get up in the middle of the night and light a fire under the propane tank to thaw it out." As mentioned earlier, this sometimes had disastrous results.

Other Albertans began using fuel oil, which was stored in outdoor drums and flowed into an indoor furnace through a small copper pipe. But this had its problems too, remembers Henry Tomlinson, chairman of the Federation of Alberta Gas Co-ops. "When the temperature dropped the oil became too syrupy to flow so you had to carry a bucket of it into the house to warm up. It made the house smell like you had your nose up an exhaust pipe."

Nothing beats natural gas, asserts wood-hater Cecil Flake. "It makes an awful difference now when you get up and drop your feet on the floor and you know you don't have to go downstairs and whittle some shavings off a board and light a fire. And there's no more lifting the lid off the cookstove and finding ice inside it."

Lil Bohmer, secretary/treasurer of the Ankerton Gas Co-op in Bawlf, couldn't agree more: "Gas just made life on the farm so much better. After you got gas on the farm, you had everything."

Many Albertans were still using wood for household fuel during the 1930s and the 1940s. It was extremely hard work to get enough wood, and homemade saws often made this work dangerous.

# CHAPTER *1*

## *The Dream Begins*

This rig drilled for gas and oil in 1903. It was situated in Ross Flats, at the foot of the 101 Street in Edmonton.

For years Bob Hubl ran the Diamond Valley Natural Gas Co-op from the basement of his home. On call twenty-four hours a day, he installed meters, kept the books, billed customers, and repaired gas lines, often at 4 AM and in below zero weather. He bought office supplies with his own money. His wife, Eleanor, answered customers' phonecalls from dawn until midnight, while his sons took over the running of his 800-acre farm south of Red Deer. The most Hubl ever received for his efforts was a monthly stipend of $1 per customer. In 1982, the year he quit, that amounted to $700 a month. Asked years later why he had worked so hard for so little reward, Hubl, then sixty-seven, replied, "It was the only way of making the dream come true."

The arrival of natural gas service was certainly a dream come true for many rural Albertans. Although residents of Alberta's major cities had had natural gas heating since the early 1900s, most of the province's farmers were still using wood, coal, fuel oil or propane by 1973. They would probably still be doing so today if not for the coming together of certain factors: Alberta's status as Canada's principal producer and exporter of natural gas; the development of plastic pipe; the financial commitment of the provincial government to rural gas service; and, perhaps most importantly, the determination and cooperative spirit of rural Albertans like Hubl.

This book tells how Hubl and the hundreds of other men and women in Alberta's natural gas cooperatives made the dream of rural gas service a reality. Chapters 2 to 5 discuss the start of the gas co-op movement, how it spread through Alberta, and how it inspired the provincial government to launch the Rural Gas Program in 1973. These chapters also describe the many financial, material, and geographical obstacles overcome by the co-ops in building one of the largest gas distribution systems in the world. But first, this chapter will look at the circumstances leading up to the formation of the first natural gas co-ops in the 1960s.

## IN THE BEGINNING

The story of how Alberta brought natural gas to most of its rural population really begins during the Paleozoic era when what is now Alberta was covered by the Devonian sea. Dead plants and animals drifted to the sea floor where they were covered by layers of mud and sand and were eventually transformed by heat, decay and pressure into immense quantities of oil and gas.

From here the story of rural gasification leaps some 400 million years to the late nineteenth century and the discovery, by the Canadian Pacific Railway, of natural gas in western Canada.

Natural gas was not on the minds of the CPR crewmen sent to drill along the railroad's right-of-way west of Medicine Hat. The year was 1883, a particularly dry one for the prairies, and the men were after water for their steam engines. Instead, they hit a pocket of natural gas, drilled a couple of wells, and were soon heating and cooking with the gas at their nearby section house. Then, in 1890, the CPR inadvertently stumbled onto gas again, this time while digging for coal on the banks of the South Saskatchewan River in Medicine Hat.

Intrigued by the prospect of a vast fuel supply beneath their streets, the leaders of the then-village of Medicine Hat began to deliberately hunt for more gas. In 1904, they hit a deep and abundant well on Main Street and within the year were lighting Medicine Hat's streets and railway platforms with natural gas, an achievement noted in *Ripley's Believe It or Not*. In 1907, British author Rudyard Kipling visited the city, witnessed a gas-flaring ceremony, and soon after declared Medicine Hat the city "With All Hell for a Basement." Medicine Hat's success sparked other towns throughout the West to search for gas supplies of their own. The dream of

## WHAT IS NATURAL GAS?

*A member of the hydrocarbon family, natural gas is a clean-burning and non-toxic source of heat energy. In its pure state, it is colourless, odourless, tasteless, and lighter than air. Though it will migrate through crevices to the earth's surface, natural gas is generally found trapped beneath the earth. It can only be reached by high-powered drills which bore wells, often through thousands of metres of solid rock.*

*Though primarily a heating fuel, natural gas is also used in the petrochemicals industry, which produces plastics, synthetic fibres, and fertilizers. Currently, Canada's petrochemicals industry consumes 14 per cent of all natural gas produced in this country.*

*Primitive people encountered natural gas seeping and hissing through cracks in the ground. If ignited by lightning, the gas burned until choked off or exhausted. The ancients viewed this as divine. The eternal flame of the Oracle of Delphi in ancient Greece, for example, was likely powered by seeping gas.*

*Natural gas remained largely a mysterious item of worship until the third century AD when the Chinese began using it to light their temples. By the tenth century, the Chinese were lighting the night-time streets of Beijing with natural gas brought from source to lamp through lengths of bamboo—the first natural gas pipelines.*

*Natural gas was not widely used in the rest of the world until the twentieth century, when mining engineers developed the drilling techniques for finding the fuel.*

natural gas service, for urbanites at least, had been born.

## THE EARLY NATURAL GAS COMPANIES

Ontario-born mining engineer Eugene Coste would make the dream come true for urban Albertans. Now considered by some the father of Canada's natural gas industry, Coste was the first person to deliberately discover natural gas in Canada (in Essex County, Ontario, in 1889). In 1905, Coste, accompanied by cable tool drillers W.R. "Frosty" Martin and A.P. "Tiny" Phillips, headed west to drill wells on contract for the CPR.

Canadian Western was one of Alberta's major pipeline builders. This wagonload of pipe was shipped in 1931.

In 1909, his drilling crew brought in the well that would launch Alberta's natural gas industry—"Old Glory." Drilled on the banks of the South Saskatchewan River at Bow Island, the well yielded 9 million cu.ft. of natural gas per day, the largest output of any well then in western Canada.

Convinced enough gas existed to serve every city and town in southern Alberta, Coste approached the CPR about building a 170-mile steel pipeline from Bow Island through Lethbridge to Calgary. When the CPR balked, Coste formed his own Prairie Fuel Gas Company, negotiated control of the CPR wells, and headed to England to raise capital for his venture.

At first, Coste had trouble with British investors who had no idea what the prairies or fuel gas were. Coste changed his firm's name to the more literally descriptive Canadian Western Natural Gas, Light, Heat and Power Company (generally known as Canadian Western). The new name inspired confidence in investors, who soon gave Coste the money he needed. He then purchased the gas franchise rights to the city of Calgary and, on April 22, 1912, began to build his 16-in. diameter pipeline.

Equipped with horses, wooden wagons, tractors, and steam-powered trenching machines, construction crews finished the pipeline—then the third largest in North America—in just eighty-six days. At first, Lethbridge ratepayers, who had access to an ample, local supply of coal, hesitated to join Canadian Western's system. To persuade them, Coste staged a flare-lighting display on the banks of the Oldman River about 8 miles north of town. Suitably dazzled by the giant flame, the townsfolk voted overwhelmingly for gas service three days later.

To celebrate completion of the line, Coste held a second flare-lighting ceremony on July 12, 1912, this time by the CPR tracks in eastern Calgary. More than 12 000 people gathered to watch Mrs. Coste toss lit Roman candles at a gas standpipe in hopes of igniting it. After several wayward throws, she hit the standpipe and set off a flare that leapt with a tremendous roar several hundred yards into the air, sending the crowd scrambling for cover. Amazingly, nobody was hurt in the panic.

Having brought gas to Calgary so spectacularly, Coste soon connected the towns of Nanton, Okotoks, Brooks, Fort MacLeod, Granum, and Claresholm to his system. By 1914, Coste's Canadian Western had 6400 customers and annual sales of more than $600 000.

Inspired by Coste, Edmontonians soon found a gas supply of their own in a field near Viking, 80 miles south of the city. The First World War, rising steel prices, and civic squabbles delayed the building of a Viking-Edmonton pipeline until 1923, when a new company, Northwestern Utilities Limited (known as Northwestern), managed to obtain the required approvals and cash for the job. By 1924, the 80-mile Viking line was serving Edmonton, Viking, Tofield, Ryley, Holden, and Bruce.

In 1925, Canadian Western established a geological department and began exploring for new gas reserves along its pipeline system. It built two pipelines, bringing gas from Turner Valley to its depleting Bow Island reserve. And it added the towns of Stavely, Parkland, High River, and Taber to its system. By 1929 Canadian Western had more than 20 000 customers and annual revenues of more than $2 million. For its part, Northwestern grew more slowly, boasting only 12 000 customers by 1939.

## THE BEGINNINGS OF RURAL SERVICE

Although urban service was their primary concern, both Canadian Western and Northwestern became important links in Alberta's rural gas system. As the province's major pipeline builders during the first half of the century, they helped to assemble part of the vast pipeline network that enabled the Alberta government to launch its Rural Gas Program in 1973. Moreover, under the Rural Gas Program, the two companies extended gas service to a total of more than 42 000 rural customers (about 30 per cent of all people reached under the program) by the end of 1988.

Actually, both companies began providing rural gas service early in their corporate lives. Canadian Western connected its first farm customer in 1915, Northwestern in 1925. However, until the 1960s and the introduction of plastic gas pipe, the companies limited service to farms within a 1/4 mile of their transmission lines, arguing that the high price of steel prevented going any further. Thus, for most rural Albertans, natural gas remained an elusive commodity unless they could negotiate a deal—gas service in exchange for right-of-way—with a company drilling a well or installing a pipeline on their land.

In any event, the rural demand for natural gas was

Although Canadian Western focused primarily on urban services, it had many rural customers. In 1958, a pipeline was laid between Carbon and Calgary.

quite weak until the 1950s. That's when stories about American farmers using natural gas to power irrigation pumps began filtering through the Bow Island/Lethbridge area. The American growers were reportedly cutting their fuel bills in half by switching to natural gas from propane. A few interested Alberta farmers with gas service began experimenting with their own irrigation pumps.

The results were primitive but effective. According to Leo Grudniski, an engineering assistant with Canadian Western's Lethbridge office from 1952 to 1987, "These fellows were so keen to use gas for irrigation, they just hooked a steel gasline right into the carburetor of their tractors and used the power-takeoff on the tractors to run their irrigation pumps. Was it dangerous? To my knowledge nobody ever blew himself up." Risky or not, it worked and an increasing number of farmers began to approach Canadian Western for gas service.

The company served farmers if they lived close enough to its pipeline and if they agreed to pay for equipment and steel pipe. Occasionally, groups of from eight to twenty-five farmers banded together to share the costs of getting gas. Two of these groups or "farmer-owned systems" registered as cooperatives in 1961—the McNally Rural Gas Association and the Sunnyside Rural Gas Association. This was mainly to finance construction with government loan guarantees.

## THE EFFECTS OF PLASTIC PIPE

In 1963, the provincial government approved the use of polyvinylchloride (PVC) plastic pipe in gas distribution systems. Developed in the U.S. in 1945, plastic pipe was cheaper and easier to assemble than steel. While lengths of steel had to be welded by certified tradespeople, the plastic variety was simply glued together with a chemical resin that almost anyone could be quickly trained to use. The new pipe enabled Canadian Western and Northwestern to lower their labour costs and so extend gas service to farms within 2 miles of their transmission lines.

Plastic pipe made it possible for Canadian Western and Northwestern to offer services to rural residents. In most cases, the farmers could install the pipeline on their own land.

Armed with plastic pipe, Canadian Western began encouraging the formation of more farmer-owned systems. The company would lay a steel line from its Bow Island main to the edge of the farmers' land, sell them plastic pipe at cost, and show them how to install it. The average cost per farm ranged from $1000 to $1200. According to Grudniski, Canadian Western had overseen the installation of about thirty-five to forty of these systems by the end of 1963.

Grudniski worked closely with the farmer-owned systems. As a former navy officer, Arctic weather station operator, and seismic crew worker, Grudniski was something of a jack-of-all-trades and certainly appreciated the do-it-yourself fervour of the irrigation farmers: "The farmers easily adapted to building pipelines. Often they held working bees and went from dawn to dusk gluing the pipe and lowering it by hand into trenches made by the company or a contractor. The spirit was wonderful. Personally, I found putting in rural systems much more challenging than urban ones. Nobody had done plastic work in Alberta before, so we had no standards to go by. Specifications for pipe size, depth, type of plastic, type of fittings, the best time of year for construction—all of these things had to be developed as we went along."

At least one future natural gas co-op staffer first learned about natural gas on one of these systems. Doug Dueck, manager of the Birch Hills Co-op in Wanham, about 40 miles north-east of Grande Prairie, belonged to an eight-member farmer-owned system in the 1960s. "I must have helped put in about 3.5 miles of plastic pipe," recalls Dueck, who farmed near Lethbridge until 1983. "That system is still in use today."

Farmers can use natural gas for many purposes other than heating their homes. Doug Dueck is standing in front of a grain dryer which is fueled by natural gas.

Shortly after 1963, Canadian Western stopped installing farmer-owned systems, starting instead to own outright any system it built. The problem, says Grudniski, was legal liability: "With the farmer-owned systems, farmers were personally responsible for anything that went wrong." Most farmers were eventually persuaded to sell to Canadian Western (including the McNally and Sunnyside co-ops), but one or two holdouts still remain.

### "Goliath"

In 1965, Canadian Western unveiled "Goliath," a new device that would help both it and Northwestern quicken the pace of rural gas service. Essentially a modified telephone cable plow, Goliath could "plow in" up to 15 000 ft. of coiled plastic pipe per day. The machine, designed by four Canadian Western employees, consisted of a specialized plowshare mounted on a farm tractor and pulled by a powerful crawler or "cat". Attached to the plow was a trailer carting the pipe, which was fed from a spool through an opening at the top of the plowshare and buried about 36 in. in the ground.

Plowing was much cheaper and quicker than traditional trenching, and by the end of the 1960s, the two utilities were adding a combined average of more than 1000 rural customers a year. (The bulk of Northwestern's rural customers were east of Edmonton.)

But even with plastic pipe and plowing, the utility

Canadian Western unveiled "Goliath" in 1965. This device was a modified telephone cable plow which could plow up to 15 000 ft of coiled plastic pipe per day.

The Alberta Gas Trunk Line Company Limited (later NOVA) assembled a pipeline grid under nearly every part of the province by 1970. Pictured above is Premier Ernest Manning turning on the first leg of AGTL's distribution system.

companies were able to reach only a small portion of Alberta's farms by the 1970s. It would take developments elsewhere in Alberta's energy industry to make widespread rural gas service possible.

## THE BUILDING OF THE EXPORT PIPELINES

When Imperial Oil struck Leduc #1 in 1947, it kicked off the biggest oil boom in Alberta's history. It also tapped a new and plentiful reserve of natural gas, possibly enough to allow exports to other parts of North America. Within months of the find, assorted promoters emerged with plans to build massive pipelines to British Columbia, the American west coast, and eastern Canada. It would take several years and a few more gas finds, however, before the provincial government, finally confident Alberta had enough of the fuel to meet its own needs, would allow companies to export gas.

Finally, in 1954, Westcoast Transmission Ltd. won permission to build a 650-mile transmission line from its reserves at Peace River through some of the world's most rugged terrain to Vancouver and the American border. And, in 1956, Trans-Canada Pipe Lines Limited (TCPL) received the go-ahead—after years of political wrangling—to build a pipeline from Alberta to Winnipeg, Toronto, Montreal, and Ottawa. Both companies completed their transmission lines by 1958.

Meanwhile, on April 8, 1954, the Alberta government, through a special act of the legislature, formed the Alberta Gas Trunk Line Company Limited (AGTL) to gather gas within Alberta for export. On July 10, 1957, then Premier Ernest Manning threw open the valve on AGTL's first leg, running from Bindloss across the Red Deer and Saskatchewan Rivers to the TCPL border gate at Burstall, Saskatchewan. "It is only the beginning of an era in the gas industry that will eclipse anything we ever thought or dreamed of," Manning told some 300 on-lookers. By 1970, AGTL, which became NOVA in 1980, would assemble a pipeline grid underlying nearly every part of the province.

Alberta's emergence as a major exporter of natural gas helped the rural gas movement in two ways. First, it resulted in the creation of AGTL, whose pipeline network would provide the ideal framework for a province-wide rural distribution system. And secondly, it provided the political rationale for a provincially funded rural gas program. After all, how could rural Albertans—who partly owned Alberta's resources—continue to be denied natural gas when it was being transported beneath their very farms to homes thousands of miles away in Toronto, Montreal, and San Francisco?

In the early 1960s, farmers in the Priddis area just south-west of Calgary began to ask precisely this question. Unable to find any good reason why they shouldn't have gas, they set out to build the first member-owned and operated gas co-op in Alberta. Their success would spark a province-wide rural gas movement.

# CHAPTER 2

# The Revolution at Priddis

Harold Webber, pictured in 1975, was a Gas Services Advisory Committee member, as well as the supervisor of Alberta's Co-operatives Activities Branch.

## THE FIRST ATTEMPTS

Shortly after AGTL began building its pipelines, the provincial government set up a Gas Services Advisory Committee to investigate the possibility of distributing gas to rural Albertans living near AGTL pipelines. Gas and pipeline company executives were not encouraging, recalls Harold (Hal) Webber, a committee member and the supervisor of Alberta's Co-operatives Activities Branch from 1953 to 1975: "They said it would cost just as much to bring gas to a farmer's house in Alberta as it would to transport that same gas all the way to Ontario or California." In other words, Alberta's countryside was too sparsely populated to make rural gas distribution a paying proposition.

Nevertheless, AGTL agreed to install "farm taps" on its lines, and Alberta's major utilities promised the government they would provide gas service to anybody living close to a transmission line. The arrangement satisfied the government but a number of farmers, thought the utilities' installation fees much higher than those paid by urban customers.

"I figured if they could get the gas all the way to California, then they could get it to me," remembers Tom Adams, a farmer at Priddis, a few miles southwest of Calgary: "That trunk line lay about 100 ft. from my door. I could throw stones at it." Adams had worked on pipelines for a few oil companies during the 1950s and knew how easy it would be to hook a small line onto the AGTL main. Thus, in 1961,

Adams and several of his neighbours approached the two utilities in the area, Canadian Western and the smaller Valley Gas Company of Turner Valley, about getting gas service.

Unfortunately, the farmers were unable to strike a deal with either company. Recalls Adams: "Valley Gas wanted to charge us $1200 apiece to install the system. And it wouldn't let us pay cash up front, we had to finance through the company at 12 per cent interest, even though the going rate in those days was around 3 per cent. And it wanted to levy a $6 monthly service charge. I remember the fellow from Valley Gas putting the contract down on the table and saying, 'Here, sign that.' I told him no." The quest for gas might well have ended there had it not been for Adams's friend and neighbour, Stan Jones.

Tom Adams and Stan Jones were both instrumental in setting up the Meota Natural Gas Co-operative in Priddis, just outside of Calgary.

Born in England, Stan Jones had arrived in Alberta as a young man in 1929, taken a crash course in farming at the Agricultural College in Olds, and gone to work milking cows for a Priddis area rancher the following year. Eventually he married the rancher's daughter, Edna, purchased land from the CPR, and settled down to a life of raising cows and growing hay. Later he also became the pest control officer for the Municipal District of Foothills, a post he held until his retirement in 1974. As a Municipal District employee, the affable Jones quickly became acquainted with everyone in the area and was, together with Adams, a leading figure in rallying his neighbours to get natural gas.

Shortly after the fruitless meeting with Valley Gas,

## WHAT IS A CO-OP?

Forming a cooperative to obtain a needed service at a fair price is hardly a new idea. It originated in Great Britain and continental Europe during the 1800s, mainly as a reaction to the social upheavals caused by the Industrial Revolution. By joining together to buy and sell goods, urban workers found they could improve their economic well-being.

Though generally formed for commercial purposes, cooperatives differ from traditional businesses. Their primary objective is not to make profits, but to provide services at the lowest possible cost to members. Membership is open to everyone regardless of race, religion, politics, or class. Each member has one share and therefore one vote. Any surplus earnings are considered savings and returned to the members, with those who use the co-op most receiving the biggest return.

In Canada, the cooperative movement has achieved its greatest success on the prairies where grain growers' associations sprang up in the 1900s to counterbalance the power of bankers, grain merchants, implement makers, and storekeepers, not to mention the ill effects of government tariffs. In 1913, Alberta passed the Cooperative Associations Act, the first legislation of its kind in the West. It was under this law that Alberta's first gas co-ops formed in the 1960s.

Support for the cooperative movement grew during the depression, as people, feeling exploited by big eastern companies and banks, searched for ways to alleviate their poverty. By the 1940s, it was quite common for Albertans to found co-ops whenever private enterprise was unable to provide a service at an affordable price. Given Alberta's long-standing cooperative tradition, it's not surprising so many rural Albertans formed co-ops to obtain natural gas in the 1960s. Nor is it surprising that the Alberta government made the cooperative form of organization the backbone of its Rural Gas Program in 1973.

Jones bumped into cooperatives' supervisor Harold Webber at a credit union annual meeting in Calgary and complained about his inability to obtain gas at a reasonable price. Webber, who had grown up on a farm near Vermilion, well understood Jones's desire to switch to natural gas from less convenient fuels like coal or propane. Webber suggested Jones and his friends form a cooperative. As a cooperative utility, they could purchase gas directly from a gas company, hire their own experts to design and make gasline connections, and obtain provincial loan guarantees covering up to 50 per cent of the cost of their distribution system.

## EARLY COOPERATIVES

Rural Albertans had formed cooperatives in the past to obtain everything from food to electrical service at a fair price. Webber saw no reason why they couldn't use cooperatives to obtain gas. In fact, they had already done it. In 1955, a group of owners on the outskirts of Wainwright had formed the Park Natural Gas Association to purchase and distribute gas from that town's gas system. And, noted Webber, the McNally and Sunnyside rural gas associations near Lethbridge had been formed just a few months before. Intrigued, Jones decided to pay Sunnyside a visit.

The president of Sunnyside was Tom Chapman. Born in Hardieville (now part of Lethbridge) in 1911, Chapman had literally grown up with coal. His Scottish immigrant father had been a coal miner, and Chapman himself had worked the mines near Lethbridge since he was sixteen years old. Yet despite his close ties to the fuel, or perhaps because of them, Chapman was as eager as anybody else in his district to switch from coal to natural gas. It was Chapman, an irrigation farmer when he wasn't underground, who had suggested that he and his neighbours form a cooperative to share the costs of getting gas from Canadian Western.

Chapman proudly drove Jones around the small Sunnyside system, which contained about 20 miles of steel pipe. He explained how Canadian Western had dug the trenches, welded the pipe, and installed meters, while he and his neighbours had wrapped protective tape around the pipe and lowered it into the ground. Impressed by the tour, Jones decided to pursue further the formation of a gas co-op in Priddis. Of course, given the recent experience with Valley Gas, neither Jones nor anyone else from Priddis was about to turn to a utility company for help. Instead, Jones called on Jack Fears, a pipeline designer from Calgary he'd met nearly two years before.

## JACK FEARS AND THE FOUNDING OF MEOTA

Born in Medicine Hat, the city with "All Hell for a Basement," Jack Fears had been introduced early to the wonders of natural gas. His association with the fuel became even more intimate when in 1928, at age fourteen, he went to work digging ditches and toting pipe for oil companies in Turner Valley, where Calgary entrepreneur Archibald Dingman had struck an enormous amount of oil and gas in 1914.

Jack Fears designed the distribution system which would be used by the Meota Natural Gas Co-operative Association Ltd.

While some of Turner Valley's gas was sold to Canadian Western to bolster its Bow Island supplies, most of it was flared off as waste or used for free by oil company employees and their families living in the valley. The young Fears marvelled as people laid steel pipe from the heads of wells through the alleyways behind their ramshackle, makeshift homes. "The pipe was just lying exposed on top of the ground," recalls Fears. "People would clamp a valve to the line, drill a little hole, and string a garden hose from the line to the stoves in their homes. These were dangerous contraptions that would never be allowed today. But amazingly few people were annihilated."

Over the next four years, Fears acquired the valley's easy familiarity with gas. He became a pipefitter, studied mechanical engineering in his spare time, and during the depression left the valley to design and install gas pipelines for a variety of companies. In the late 1950s, he was contracted by the Calgary engineering firm Dutton Williams Mannix to work on AGTL's western leg. It was while testing a section of this pipeline that Fears first met Jones.

"I was testing pipe on Stan's property, and he wanted to know about getting gas. I talked to him and his wife for a couple of hours about how they should be able to get gas from the farm taps AGTL had installed on its lines," remembers Fears, who also told the couple it was their right, as citizens of Alberta, to have access to natural gas. Soon after his conversation with the Joneses, Fears finished his job with Dutton Williams Mannix and joined the small Glaholt and Associates

Many of Alberta's farms are located over rich natural gas and oil deposits.

H.H. Somerville was the Deputy Minister of Mines and Minerals in 1962.

engineering firm in Calgary.

"I'd forgotten all about farmers and gas until one evening my doorbell rang in the spring of 1962. It was Stan Jones and about eight other farmers from Priddis," says Fears. The group wanted Fears's help in setting up a cooperative utility and peppered him with questions about the costs of designing and building a system. They invited Fears to a meeting the next day at the Millarville school south of Priddis.

"When I arrived, the school parking lot was plugged with cars and the auditorium was standing room only," remembers Fears. "Figuring I'd walked in on the wrong gathering, I asked somebody to tell me where the small meeting on natural gas was being held. 'This is it,' he told me. Then Stan Jones spotted me and called me up on stage to speak to the crowd. I was shocked. I'm no public speaker. All I had was a pencil in my pocket and no idea of what to say." Nevertheless, the

These pipes are pictured in Tom Adams's backyard. He was hired as serviceman, and paid 10 dollars a month to be on call 24 hours a day.

energetic Fears bounded on stage and was soon drawing diagrams on a blackboard and answering questions about natural gas.

"Now there were utility company representatives in the audience, and they were furious with me," recalls Fears. "One of them stood up and said I was full of horsefeathers, that there was no way the government would allow a co-op to provide gas without working through a utility. We argued until 1 AM."

Finally, the crowd voted to form the Meota Natural Gas Co-operative Association Ltd., Meota being the name of the Anglican parish in the area and the Cree word for "good place to camp." Jones, a devout Anglican, liked to quip that it would be "an even better place to camp with gas in the tent." While the farmers registered their co-op with Harold Webber in Edmonton, Fears designed a distribution system and applied to the Pipelines Division of the Department of Mines and Minerals for permission to build it.

## THE EARLY YEARS OF MEOTA

### *The Fight for Approval*

Normally the division approved pipeline permits within forty-eight hours. But two weeks passed, and the co-op had yet to receive an answer. Years later, in an article for the local history book, *Foothills Echoes* (published by the Millarville Historical Society, Millarville, Alta., 1979), Jones would write: "While we had the whole-hearted support of the Co-operatives Activities Branch, the support of the Department of Mines and Minerals was less enthusiastic. In fact, we got the distinct impression that somewhere behind the scenes there were forces at work determined to see the demise of Meota before it got off the ground."

Unseen forces or not, Fears and Jones drove to Edmonton to personally confront division officials. As it turned out, their application was still sitting on somebody's desk while one submitted several days later by Valley

Gas to serve some people in the same area had been approved. Recalls Fears: "I think they were scared stiff at the prospect of farmers running their own natural gas system."

Furious at the turn of events, Fears phoned Premier Ernest Manning's office the next day to complain. "I got his secretary and told her the story. Twenty minutes later Premier Manning phoned me back, asked me where I was going to be the next morning and promised to send H.H. Somerville, the deputy minister of Mines and Minerals, to Calgary to review the co-op's file.

"Sure enough, the next day a planeload of about twelve officials, including the deputy minister, flew down to my little office and met with an equal contingent of farmers from Priddis. I had to clear the furniture to make room for everybody." According to Jones's report in *Foothills Echoes*, "After an hour or so, Mr. Somerville appeared quite satisfied that we knew what we were doing, and told us to re-submit our applications for permits and he would approve them the same day." Meota was on its way.

## Building a Co-op

It was late October, however, and the farmers had to rush to install their system before the winter of 1962. Fears devoted most of his time over the next few weeks to the co-op, commuting between Calgary and Priddis every day. He purchased steel pipe and meters, made gas supply arrangements with the Alberta and Southern Gas Company and AGTL (Alberta and Southern supplied the gas, AGTL delivered it), and obtained the required government permits. Additionally, he connected the co-op's pipeline to AGTL's taps. He was paid $1.50 an hour, barely enough to meet his expenses. Years later Fears would explain the cause of his devotion: "I was angry at the way these people had been treated. If I didn't help them get gas, nobody else would. They would be out in left field."

At the same time, Jones sold gas contracts, obtained easements (permission to cross farmers' land with pipeline), collected money from co-op members, and obtained a $2130 provincial government loan guarantee to help finance construction. For his part, Tom Adams assembled a group of volunteers to wrap black, corrosion-fighting tape around nearly 3 miles worth

Government inspectors from the Pipelines Division and Gas Protection Branch are pictured pressure testing pipe.

Trenches for the pipeline had to be dug across fields, roads, a river, and several creeks.

of 2-in. steel pipe. Adams's brother-in-law welded the pipe, and Jones's son, who owned a backhoe, dug the pipeline trenches. Recalls Adams: "From first daylight to midnight for seven days a week we worked."

The co-op was not without its detractors, even though government inspectors from the Pipelines Division and Gas Protection Branch oversaw key stages of the work. Utility officials continued to warn of the

Many people in the district helped install pipe. Polly Anna Powell is shown gluing two lengths of pipe together.

The members of the Meota Gas Co-op celebrated their 25th anniversary in 1988. Tom Adams (far left) and Jack Fears (second from right) are pictured with other founding members of the co-op.

dangers of co-op gas service. Sceptics insisted it was impossible for a group of farmers to build a gas system. "They said we'd blow ourselves up," remembers Adams. "I told them if anything exploded I would eat pipe."

Even Fears had to admit the undertaking had an air of unreality. "The operations were hilarious. I was used to working on major transmission lines for AGTL. Now here I was in a backyard operation employing grandmothers and high-school kids." But he agreed wholeheartedly with Jones who liked to note that if farmers could run complicated farm machinery, "they could keep gas running through a pipe."

But installing the system was hard work. Adams and his crew had to trench across miles of farmland, several gravel roads, a river, and a number of creeks. "The river was 60 ft. wide and about 2 ft. deep. We had to dig

a trench on the river bottom, sandbag the pipe, lay it down, and cover it over," recalls Adams. "We weren't always sure what to do, but we learned as we went along, by trial and error." By Christmas 1962, gas was flowing to five Priddis households.

The next fall, the co-op installed another 15 miles of pipe, this time the plastic polyvinylchloride (PVC) variety, which had just been approved by the Alberta government and ordered by Fears from a Vancouver pipe manufacturer. Six volunteers, including grandmother Polly Anna Powell, painstakingly glued the 30-ft. lengths of pipe together. By Christmas 1963, another thirteen Priddis farmers were burning gas. The Meota Natural Gas Co-operative Association Ltd. was firmly established.

To keep overhead costs down, Jones managed the operation from his home and refused a salary. Adams, later nicknamed Mr. Meota Gas, was hired as service-man and paid a token $10 a month to be on call twenty-four hours a day to repair damaged pipe or meters. Adams's wife Jessie looked after customer accounts. Another local woman, Eunice Park, kept the books. Customers were entrusted with reading their own meters and mailing in the results. "It was and remains very much a kitchen table operation," Jessie Adams would remark nearly twenty-eight years later.

Meota was the first in what would become a long line of farmer-owned and operated gas cooperatives, a fact foreshadowed in this rather prophetic passage from the October 1962 issue of the *Daily Oil Bulletin*, a Priddis-area publication: " . . . this group of south-western Alberta farmers and ranchers have [sic] formed a gas distribution set-up that is unique. The foundation laid by the Meota Gas Co-operative Association Ltd. will be copied throughout many districts of the province in years to come."

The next chapter looks at the some of the key individuals involved in spreading the rural gas revolution at Priddis throughout southern and central Alberta.

# CHAPTER 3

# The Revolution Spreads

It didn't take Meota long to spawn imitators. In 1964, a group of irrigation farmers near Tilley and Rolling Hills, neighbouring villages north of Medicine Hat, formed the Tirol (TI—lley and ROL—ling Hills) Gas Co-op Ltd. with the help of Jack Fears and Tom Adams from Meota.

## THE TILLEY GAS COMPANY LTD.

Tilley and Rolling Hills were no strangers to natural gas, the area having been generously endowed with the stuff by Mother Nature. In fact, farmers commonly saw the fuel bubbling up through water-filled ditches from pockets of porous rock below. Moreover, the CPR had drilled wells in the vicinity in the early part of the century. And in 1939, Tilley hotelier Fred Hankel, weary of hauling coal from a mine 24 miles away, paid a Medicine Hat company $4500 to drill a gas well on land he leased from the local improvement district.

Originally intending to serve only his home and hotel, the Nebraska-born Hankel was soon deluged with requests for gas from nearly everyone in Tilley. He formed the Tilley Gas Company Ltd., made his three young children shareholders, bought a supply of used steel boiler tubing from a Calgary firm (regular steel pipe was scarce because of the Second World War), and, with the help of a local welder, connected about 150 village homes to his well. In fact, gas sales were so brisk, Hankel left the hotel business and ran his utility full-time until his death in 1952. At that time his son

Leo and Elsie Skanderup worked to set up a gas co-op in Tilley. They are pictured here with their son, David, in 1967.

Much of the PVC pipe originally laid by Tirol Gas Co-op had to be replaced. This yellowjacket steel line was installed in 1964.

Tom took over the company, which still exists today.

Although most of Hankel's customers lived in the village, he did serve about eleven farmers living on Tilley's outskirts. Their obvious pleasure with natural gas spurred a handful of other farmers to have small gas wells drilled on their land and to install their own steel distribution lines. Eventually, most farmers in the area began to dream of the day they could afford to do likewise. Among the dreamers was Leo Skanderup.

## THE BEGINNINGS OF TIROL

The son of a Lutheran preacher from Denmark, Skanderup had moved to Tilley with his family when he was eight years old. A Canadian army private first class during the Second World War, he lost his left leg below the knee when he triggered a land mine in Germany's Black Forest. After the war he returned to Tilley, married Elsie, a Danish immigrant he'd met at a Lutheran Bible camp near Red Deer, and settled down to raising a family and farming.

Unable to afford a new well, Skanderup began in the early 1960s to talk to his brother and a few neighbours about hooking up to an existing one. "The idea spread like wildfire," remembers Skanderup. "The more people I talked to, the more wanted in on the idea."

Unsure what to do next, the Skanderups visited the local office of Alberta's Gas Protection Branch in Medicine Hat. Branch employee Sid Handley invited the couple home, cooked them dinner, and suggested that a capped CPR well near Rolling Hills would provide a sufficiently large gas supply.

The Skanderups relayed this information to the next meeting of the local chapter of the Farmers' Union, an agricultural organization to which most people in the area belonged. The group dispatched farmer Halvar Rosedahl to ask Canadian Western to connect them to the well; economically unfeasible, insisted the utility. The Skanderups then went to the Department of Mines and Minerals office in Calgary; use propane, advised an official, adding that if they were determined to get gas they should talk to an engineer named Jack Fears.

The Skanderups phoned Fears immediately and arranged to meet at a Calgary lunch counter. Remembers Elsie Skanderup: "Jack was so excited about the possibilities offered by natural gas. We could irrigate with it, heat our pig barns with it . . . he gave us a glowing picture of the Meota co-op and urged us to form one of our own." On April 30, 1964, the Skanderups and their neighbours did exactly that. Leo was elected co-op president, Elsie secretary/treasurer, and Fears was hired as project engineer.

As with Meota, Fears designed Tirol's distribution system, obtained required permits, ordered supplies, and negotiated a gas sales contract with the well's owner, Canadian Pacific Oil and Gas (CPOG), a subsidiary of the CPR. Fears's plans called for a 14-mile, high-pressure steel transmission line to bring gas from the CPOG well at Rolling Hills to Tilley, plus another 130 miles of plastic PVC pipe to carry gas from the steel line to about seventy-five farms. A provincially guaranteed loan and small downpayments from members financed construction.

## PROBLEMS AT TIROL

The co-op tried hard to keep costs down. Local contractors installed the pipeline at reasonable rates. The Skanderups saved on office rental by running the co-op from their kitchen. And Fears donated much of his time. Recalls Leo Skanderup: "Jack stayed at our place, worked eighteen hours a day, and never charged more than $650 a month. He said the co-op couldn't afford to pay him more, and besides, no man was worth much more than that."

Additionally, many members volunteered to glue and lay PVC plastic pipe. Indeed, about ten women regularly gathered in the Skanderups' backyard for day-long pipe gluing bees. "The women did a neater, cleaner job than the men," reports Roy Pritchard, an area handyman who would eventually work on several co-ops throughout Alberta. "To prove it, they put yellow colouring in their glue so that if a leak occurred, we could tell by the colour that it wasn't their fault." (A few years later women at the Burnt Lake Gas Co-op would do the same.)

Unfortunately, most of the PVC pipe did leak while being pressure tested (through no fault of the women or men) and had to be replaced. This nearly doubled construction costs, plunged the co-op into serious debt,

Helmut Entrup farmed near Tilley and he was a director of the Tirol Gas Co-op during the difficult first few years.

and forced Harold Webber and the Co-operatives Activities Branch to take over the co-op for several months until its financial troubles were resolved.

At one point during the takeover, the members considered selling their system to Canadian Western. But Tilley farmer and co-op director Helmut Entrup, who would later become one of the gas cooperative movement's most ardent promoters, persuaded members to reject a sale. Recalls Entrup: "We held a hot and heavy meeting at the Tilley community hall. I pleaded with the people to hang in there. We had a good deal going. We were buying gas at 10 cents per mcf [0.948 mcf = 1 gigajoule] from Canadian Pacific Oil and Gas and selling it for 30 cents, enough of a margin to run the system and retire our debt. We took a vote and—by a majority of three votes—we decided to give the system one more year." The members, who had already agreed to pay $1500 apiece for gas service, each agreed to contribute another $700 to help retire the co-op's debt.

## THE GEM GAS CO-OP

The problems at Tirol did not discourage other rural Albertans from joining the gas cooperative movement. Indeed, Tirol was barely two months old when a third co-op surfaced in Gem, about 40 miles north of Tilley.

Farmers at Gem had been talking about getting gas ever since AGTL installed its Ontario-bound transmission line in the late 1950s. Finally, in 1963, a group of ten landowners approached AGTL, which directed them to Canadian Western. But there were more farmers in the area wanting gas than Canadian Western was able to serve economically. So the farmers, on the suggestion of an oil company landman, went to see Stan Jones from Meota.

Jake Doerksen was the first chairman of the Gem Gas Co-op. In 1979 he received the Federation of Alberta Gas Co-ops Ltd. award in appreciation of 15 years of service to the Co-op.

"He told us to form a co-op. He said, 'It works. It pays. We'll help you get started,'" recalls Jake Doerksen, the first chairman of the Gem Gas Co-op. "We hired Jack Fears, met with Harold Webber, and by June 1964 were ready to go. We held about twenty meetings that summer, even though it was haying and irrigation time and we were busy. But this was pioneering work we were doing and none of us felt sure about it. I was elected chairman of the board. I was the youn-

gest guy on it, and I was scared. Would this thing work? There were some people who were pretty sure it wouldn't."

## JOINING FORCES: THE FEDERATION OF ALBERTA GAS CO-OPS LTD.

However, Fears was certain Gem and the cooperative movement as a whole would continue to succeed. As he would reflect years later, "By Gem, the process was routine and I was getting approvals from the Pipelines Division almost overnight." Still, even Fears worried that the "unseen forces" which had nearly thwarted Meota, might halt the young movement yet. Thus he called a joint meeting of the Meota, Tirol, and Gem co-ops in the basement of a seed-cleaning plant in Brooks. Also on hand were farmers from the nearby towns of Scandia, Rainier, and Bow City who were about to form a fourth co-op—S.R. & B.

Farmers from the areas surrounding the towns of Scandia, Rainier, and Bow City formed the S.R. & B. Co-op. In 1969 they had the "lighting up" ceremony.

"I told them each co-op was politically weak on its own. There were people pressuring the government to stop this silly nonsense of farmers distributing gas. I urged them to get together, to form a federation," recalls Fears. As usual, the farmers took Fears's advice. On July 20, 1964, the Federation of Alberta Gas Co-ops Ltd. was born. Art Larson of Scandia was elected its first president, Leo Skanderup its vice-president.

Eventually the federation would become an influential lobby organization consisting of member counties,

Art Larson was the first president of the Federation of Alberta Gas Co-ops Ltd. He is pictured here in 1977 receiving an award of appreciation from the federation.

towns, villages, Indian bands, and co-ops, altogether representing tens of thousands of rural Albertans. But for the first year, the federation was mainly a central ordering house for co-op supplies. Like the Tirol Co-op, it operated from the Skanderups' busy kitchen. "I had two full-time jobs really," laughs Elsie Skanderup. "Running the co-op and federation, and trying to raise four young children at the same time."

## THE CO-OP'S COMPETITION

Even with the federation's low profile, word of the farmer-operated co-ops began to spread throughout southern Alberta. As mentioned in chapter 1, Canadian Western had begun to promote rural gas service in 1963, when the advent of plastic pipe allowed it to reach farms up to 2 miles from its Bow Island line. Once happy to sign on with Canadian Western without question, farmers now wondered if, perhaps, they could get gas service more cheaply if they provided it themselves.

In June 1965, a group of farmers near Lethbridge formed the Turin-Iron Springs Rural Gas Association to investigate the merits of cooperative ownership. Canadian Western quickly sent sales representatives to meet with association directors. According to a retrospective article in the July 1967 issue of *The Courier*, a newsletter published by Canadian Western's parent company, Canadian Utilities Limited (CUL), "The

big stumbling block was to convince the directors that Canadian Western would be able to give their area better service and lower rates than any cooperative." The utility won. The Turin-Iron Springs Rural Gas Association continued to exist, but its system was installed, operated, and owned by Canadian Western.

Back in Tilley, federation director Helmut Entrup was not amused by developments like the one at Turin-Iron Springs. "Farmers were being asked to play Santa Claus—to pay for the building of a system and then to turn it over to the utility," remarked Entrup years later. "That's when I got my back up and started to travel rural Alberta."

From 1965 to 1968 Helmut Entrup, Leo Skanderup, and Art Larson drove throughout southern Alberta "in sunshine and blizzard, at our own expense" to, as Entrup liked to say, "spread the cooperative gospel." Recalls Entrup: "We kept our ears close to the ground and whenever we heard a rumour that a group of farmers was interested in gas, we'd ask the community leaders to call a meeting and we'd go there to explain our position. Often the utility company representatives would be there too. They would entice the people to go one way. We would entice them to go the other. I would remind farmers they had a God-given responsibility to look after their own affairs."

### Ernie Poetschke and the CUD

But utilities weren't the only ones vying for the farmers' business. In 1965, an Edmonton-based company called Canadian Utilities Development (CUD) appeared on the gas scene. It was owned by Ernie Poetschke, a heavy-set entrepreneur who'd moved to Canada from Berlin after the Second World War.

Poetschke began his life in Alberta as a pipe salesman for an American company with offices in Edmonton. Among his major clients were the Gem and Tirol gas co-ops. According to CUD handyman Roy Pritchard, Poetschke, who died in the mid-1980s, was "always looking for new ways to make money. He came up with the idea of forming a company to install and run co-ops and hired me to help build them."

Poetschke put together a package whereby his company would build, maintain, and operate a gas system, and carry liability insurance, in return for about $1000 to $1200 per co-op member. The co-op board would retain control over such decisions as gas price increases and system expansions, and be given the option to buy

## FREEING THE COAL STOKERS

*A large crowd came to the North Edmonton Co-op's incorporation meeting, sponsored by the local Chamber of Commerce and featuring co-op promoter Ernie Poetschke. However, most people left when Poetschke told them gas service would cost $1800 apiece. Unwilling to give up, directors continued to meet with Poetschke who eventually made a new offer: $1600 per contract with $160 down, the rest financed by lien note. This was an offer members could not refuse. Recalls original director Mike Serink: "About eleven of us were determined to get natural gas. Granted some of us had efficient coal stokers, which though dusty were cheap. But the prospect of getting away from stoking those fires in the milk house, the pig barn, and the potato shed was very appealing."*

the system after about ten years. By December 1966 Poetschke had his first customer—the North Edmonton Gas Co-op in Gibbons.

Pritchard, who'd learned the gas business from Fears and assorted government inspectors, supervised North Edmonton's construction. The co-op was barely finished before CUD took on several more, including East Leduc, Kneehill, Notre Dame, and one at Namao.

The Burnt Lake Co-op was among CUD's customers. In 1969 area farmer Earl Grimson asked the United Farmers of Alberta Co-operative Limited (UFA) if it would help build a province-wide, rural gas distribution system. When the UFA said no (it thought such a system impossible without government financing and political support), Grimson turned to CUD to bring gas to his farm and about fifty-two others.

Ernie Poetschke (front, facing camera) was the founder of the Canadian Utilities Development company, which ran gas systems for co-ops. The first customer was the North Edmonton Gas Co-op in Gibbons.

## AN ACCIDENTAL EXPERT

*Roy Pritchard stumbled into the rural gas business quite by accident. Born and raised in Calgary, the lanky, former army sergeant joined Calgary Power in 1945 as an installer of power poles. Forced to quit a few years later because of an ulcer, Pritchard, with no income and a stack of doctor's bills, put his Calgary house up for rent and moved to Gem on a friend's invitation. He set up house with his wife, Dixie, and two young children in a remodelled granary and made money doing odd plumbing and painting jobs for local farmers. "When the Gem co-op started I was the logical choice for serviceman even though I didn't know a valve from a regulator," he laughs.*

*He learned quickly from the steady stream of engineers and pipe suppliers who used his kitchen, nicknamed the "café," to test pipe and refuel on Dixie's coffee and cooking. By the time Pritchard went to work for Ernie Poetschke at the North Edmonton Gas Co-op in 1966, he was a natural gas "expert."*

*Among his more memorable acquaintances at North Edmonton was a government gas inspector always nattily dressed in a crisp white shirt and bow tie. "One day I had just repaired a gas leak in some pipe buried in a sewage lagoon. The inspector offered to turn the pipe valve on for me so I could let the air out of it and turn the gas back on. Well, he opened the valve, and out came a thick spray of black goo from the lagoon. It covered him from head to toe. I wiped the slime off him with some hay, put a canvas down on his car seat, and away he went, smelling like a septic tank."*

*In 1971, Pritchard left Poetschke's financially troubled company to manage the Ste. Anne Gas Co-op in Onoway, about 20 miles west of Edmonton. Says Pritchard: "The job offer came the day after I'd been up until 4 AM sorting out problems at two different co-ops. I took the offer right away." Of course, life at Ste. Anne, then the biggest co-op in Alberta and the prototype for the Rural Gas Program, wouldn't be easy either. Nonetheless, Pritchard remained there until his retirement in 1984.*

all the while using funds from CUD to pay for his other ventures. Pritchard, who operated as well as built the co-ops, drove a new Chevrolet company car and Poetschke always wore the finest in suits and shoes. "CUD had no money," remembers Pritchard. "It was costing us too much to build the gas systems."

But Poetschke, whom Pritchard remembers as one of the best salesmen he's ever met, still believed a fortune could be made from building co-ops. In 1968, he sold East Leduc and Namao to Plains Western Utilities (since taken over by the Inter-City Gas Corporation, or ICG) to raise cash and formed a CUD subsidiary, Anchor Pipelines, to build more co-ops. The new company, again with Pritchard, built the Battle River, Gull Lake, Leduc West, Wetaskiwin West, and Burnt Lake Co-ops, all in central Alberta.

Battle River bought their system from Anchor Pipelines when the company went into receivership. Pictured here are members of the board.

But Anchor lost money too, and by 1970 was in receivership. Pritchard, retained by the receiver at $700 a month to operate the company, advised the remaining co-ops to exercise their option and buy themselves out. Most of them did, but it took several years and considerable legal wrangling.

"There was a lot of excitement on the board of Battle River when Anchor went under," remembers

Unfortunately, Poetschke overextended himself. In addition to gas pipe, he began selling sewer and water lines. Then he formed a company called Water Care and began selling water purifiers in British Columbia,

founding director Merv Giem, adding that people in the community had been reluctant to invest in a co-op in the first place. "Battle River was a good name for us at the time. A lot of people would have liked to tie us up in a tree someplace. But we had money in the bank and we finally bought our co-op for $54 000."

In 1973 Burnt Lake Co-op members contributed an extra $625 apiece to buy out their Anchor system. Directors then contracted Northwestern Utilities to operate the co-op, but in 1976 terminated the contract and hired their own servicepeople instead.

Despite Anchor's rather messy demise, the company made valuable contributions to the rural gas movement. It brought gas cooperatives to central Alberta and it introduced several more people to the rural gas business—men like Cliff Fenske, Bob Bell, and Glen Skocdopole.

### Bell and Fenske

An employee with Plains Western, Fenske was sent to learn the rural gas business from Pritchard after the company took over two of CUD's systems. "He followed me around to see how things worked," says Pritchard. "Plains Western didn't know anything about the rural gas business, and Fenske had never even seen a piece of plastic pipe." Fenske passed on his knowledge to fellow Plains Western employee Bell, and soon the two left the utility to form their own co-op building company, Bell and Fenske, which would build a number of gas systems in central and southern Alberta over the next few years. In 1972, the company would contribute to the development of the Rural Gas Program.

### Skocdopole's Plow

Glen Skocdopole was working for his family's construction company near Eckville when he first heard of Poetschke and CUD in 1967. Eager to find a new line of work after several years in the oil patch, Skocdopole phoned Poetschke to offer his services. "Of course, I didn't know anything about plastic pipe, but I was sure I could install it for him," recalls Skocdopole. Poetschke contracted Skocdopole to install the Kneehill system at Linden. It was while building this system that Skocdopole perfected a new method for plowing plastic pipe.

Although Canadian Western had introduced its Goliath plow to the fields in 1966, natural gas co-ops were still using the more time-consuming and costly

Glen Skocdopole perfected a new method for plowing plastic pipe while building the Kneehill system. He designed and ran a pipe plow which would be used to install many rural systems.

trenching method of installing pipe. Eager to gain a foothold in the new and growing rural gas industry, Skocdopole decided to design a pipe plow of his own. He flew to Texas and Colorado, studied plows in use there, and soon built a modified version. Test-driven at Kneehill, the plow worked like a charm. Soon Skocdopole was installing rural systems, not only for CUD, but for cooperatives throughout Alberta. Even Canadian Western hired Skocdopole and his plow for some of its bigger rural projects.

### Bruce Palmer and Tom Christie

While Skocdopole was refining his new plow, two other individuals were emerging on the rural gas scene—engineer Bruce Palmer and construction contractor Tom Christie. Both men had built and designed pipelines for Mobil Oil in the 1950s, and in the early 1960s had formed their own company, Palmer

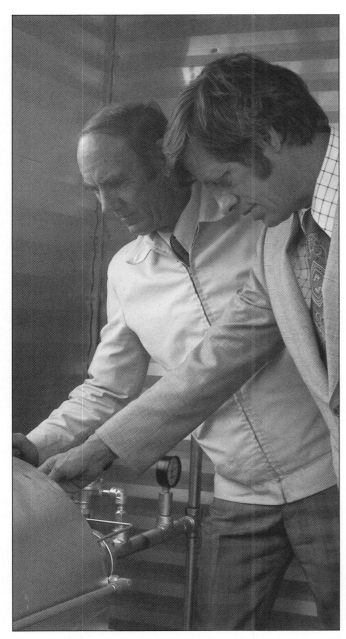

Palmer Engineering began to oversee the construction of rural gas systems in the mid-1960s. Bruce Palmer (right) founded the company with Tom Christie.

Engineering, to install steel gas distribution systems for small Alberta towns and villages. Their first town was Smoky Lake, about 42 miles north-east of Edmonton.

In the mid-1960s the duo began suggesting to farmers that they form gas cooperatives and hire Palmer Engineering to oversee construction of the systems. In 1966, they persuaded a group of farmers about 48 miles north of Calgary to form the Three Hills Gas Co-op (which still existed in 1989, with more than 200 members and nearly 120 miles of pipe). But otherwise Palmer and Christie had few takers. Recalls Christie: "We'd get a few farmers together, then a couple would drop out, driving the price up for everybody else. The higher price would cause a few more to back out, then we wouldn't have enough people to finance a system." To Palmer the problem was one of scepticism on the part of farmers. "Some didn't believe it was possible to bring gas into the country and they weren't willing to risk their money. So we decided to finance the systems ourselves."

In 1968, the men formed the Superior Natural Gas Co. with borrowed funds and designed a distribution system for farmers in the Radway area north of Edmonton. (Palmer contracted North American Road Ltd., an Edmonton construction company which had also developed a pipe plow, to install lines.) The following year the pair borrowed more money, formed a second company, the Superior Natural Gas Distribution Co., and—again with North American Road—brought gas to Strome, Heisler, Bawlf, and Rosalind, farming communities about 48 miles south-east of Edmonton.

The two Superior companies operated like small utilities, building, operating, and maintaining the systems. Now convinced of the feasibility of rural gas, a group of about twenty-six farmers near Strome formed the Ankerton Co-op, on Palmer's advice. (In 1979, Ankerton purchased the Superior Natural Gas Distribution Co., thus adding about 315 customers to the co-op virtually overnight.)

## THE ONE THAT GOT AWAY

*In 1972 a group of acreage owners and farmers north of Edmonton were about to vote to have one of the Superior Natural Gas companies build and operate a gas system for them when fate intervened in the form of Helmut Entrup. Then still with Unifarm, the stocky Entrup strode to the front of the room and in his thick German accent argued passionately in favour of forming a member-owned co-op. "I delivered a speech that was fire and brimstone," recalls Entrup. "I picked up the stack of contracts which were about to be passed out and signed and threw them on the floor." As was his wont, Entrup won his point—his audience immediately voted to form the Coronado Gas Co-op.*

## THE POLITICAL REACTION

By 1968 farmers throughout Alberta were talking about natural gas. Sixteen gas co-ops were incorporated that year, bringing the total formed since 1962 to twenty-one. Despite the burgeoning activity, vast areas of the province remained without service and likely would remain so because they were either too sparsely populated or too far from a gas source, or both.

Premier Ernest Manning headed the Social Credit government which established the 1968 "Rural Gas Distribution Policy."

This fact was drawn to the attention of Dr. Hugh ("Doc") Horner, then the rookie Conservative Opposition MLA for Lac Ste. Anne. What, he demanded of Mines and Minerals Minister Russell Patrick, did the Social Credit government intend to do about extending rural gas service? The minister's response, a two-page document entitled "Rural Gas Distribution Policy," was tabled in the legislature a few days later.

Essentially, the policy said persons interested in forming a gas cooperative could do so provided they obtained proper approvals from the Supervisor of Co-operative Activities and the Superintendent of Pipelines. Although it offered no grants, the government did offer loan guarantees covering up to 50 per cent of a co-op's construction costs. In addition, said the policy paper, pipeline operators could serve rural consumers near their lines, and anybody with natural gas rights could certainly drill a well to meet his or her personal requirements.

In other words, the government had no plan to extend gas service to all rural Albertans.

To be fair to the Social Credit government, its rural gas policy had not served farmers too badly. After all, several hundred farmers had managed by 1968 to form cooperatives and build gas systems that worked reasonably cheaply and well. Moreover, few Albertans were demanding that the government do anything more. Thus it was understandable that when the fiery Tilley co-op director and farmer Helmut Entrup broached the idea of a more wide-ranging rural gas program with Socred ministers, they dismissed him as a well-meaning, but misguided zealot. However, the tiny, but energetic Conservative Opposition was not so dismissive. Instead, it embraced the concept of widespread rural gas service as part of its strategy to win the hearts, minds, and votes of Alberta's farmers.

### A DISCOURAGING WORD

*In 1963 Rosemary farmer Eric Dick wrote to his MLA, William Delday, about the possibility of obtaining natural gas service. Delday in turn wrote to then Mines and Minerals Minister A. Russell Patrick who sent this unencouraging reply:*

*In reference to your note regarding farmers in the Rosemary district inquiring about natural gas, this is a somewhat involved situation...*

*In the case of Mr. Dick...if he were to take gas at the pipe line of Sun Oil Company near his home, at least two regulators would be necessary to knock the pressure down to the normal distribution pressure of from 15 to 30 pounds and then another regulator would have to be installed close to his home to reduce the pressure to about 4 ounces. In addition, of course, a unit would have to be installed to remove the natural gasoline and condensate because with any rapid drop in pressure, the liquids condense creating a serious safety hazard unless removed.*

*Consequently, the cost involved in converting a small amount of gas to domestic use would be very high and in addition, an experienced supervisor would be essential to make a periodic check of the equipment...*

*Despite the answer, Dick kept trying and by 1970 had rounded up enough farmers to form the Rosemary Co-op.*

# CHAPTER 4

## The Lougheed Conservatives Take Up the Cause

Dr. Hugh Horner headed the rural development committee in the late 1960s. He was made Minister of Agriculture when the Lougheed Conservatives came to power in 1971.

In the late 1960s, more and more young people began leaving the farm for the comforts of urban life. Assorted experts predicted that eventually 90 per cent of Albertans would live in cities, news greeted with indifference by the long-reigning Socreds. The Peter Lougheed Conservatives, however, eager to bolster their support in the country, seized the issue. Led by Lougheed's rural lieutenant Dr. Hugh "Doc" Horner, the Conservatives vowed to fight "rural de-population" by raising the quality of farm life to urban standards. Roads, government offices, better schools, better health care, natural gas at reasonable rates, these were all part of the rural development platform with which the Conservatives won the farm vote and the 1971 provincial election. By the end of April 1973 the multi-million dollar Rural Gas Program was solidly underway.

Rural development was the subject of Horner's maiden speech to the legislature in March 1968. Low educational standards, poor roads, and high energy costs were among the hardships being endured by rural Albertans and ignored by the government, he argued. After noting that 45 per cent of Albertans still lived in the country, Horner made an impassioned plea for rural equality. "Give us the opportunities in rural Alberta, and we will show you that our people can do as good a job as those in urban areas. But we need equalization in economic opportunity."

Determining precisely how to equalize rural and urban life was the job of Horner and his rural develop-

## HUGH "DOC" HORNER

*Rural gas service was only one of many ideas put forth by Dr. Hugh M. Horner to improve the lot of the Alberta farmer. As Premier Peter Lougheed's first lieutenant and provincial Minister of Agriculture from 1971 to 1975, Horner pushed for more farmer loans, agricultural society grants, and new markets for Alberta's farm products. He decentralized the Agriculture department by moving several of its branches from Edmonton to places like Lethbridge, Wetaskiwin, Stettler, and Barrhead. He sparked the building of alfalfa plants and encouraged the canola industry. "He was the idea man without equal," colleague Roy Farran once remarked "He knew rural Alberta as few others have known it."*

*Widely credited with winning rural Alberta for the Conservatives, the Saskatchewan born Horner was a formidable politician from a formidably political family. His father was the late Canadian Senator Ralph Byron Horner; his siblings include former members of parliament Jack and Norval, and sisters Jean Horner Roen, Kathleen Horner McCorkell, and Ruth Horner Flannigan, all former Conservative party workers. Horner's cousin Harold Horner was a Saskatchewan MP.*

*Hugh Horner graduated from the University of Western Ontario medical school in 1949, set up general practice in Barrhead in 1950, and later became a town councillor. In 1958, he was elected MP for Jasper-Edson, a seat he held until 1967 when he quit Ottawa to join Lougheed's fight against Alberta's waning Social Credit dynasty. He was forty-six when appointed to Lougheed's cabinet. Horner resigned from cabinet in 1979 after being appointed to the Federal Grain Transportation Authority.*

*As Minister of Agriculture, Horner once said his goal was to create recognition for the farmer as a "vital and integral part of Alberta, doing one of the world's most vital jobs, feeding people." One of his most gratifying moments in politics occurred when he overheard one farmer say to another, "That Horner fellow, he's got lots of programs and some are crazy. But he sure makes the farmer feel like he's somebody."*

ment committee, which hit the road in 1968. "We did a lot travelling during our years in opposition," remembers Horner. "The legislature only sat about five weeks a year, then Premier Manning would pat us on the head and out we'd go."

## THE "DOC" TALKS TO RURAL ALBERTANS

Accompanying Horner on his rural travels was Dr. Allan Warrack, a professor of rural economy at the University of Alberta who would run for the Conservatives in the 1971 election and eventually in 1975 become the minister responsible for the Rural Gas Program. After workshops and meetings with farmers throughout the province, the two men constructed their party's agricultural platform. Its aim was to stop the

Dr. Allan Warrack became the minister responsible for the Rural Gas Program.

farm exodus by improving farm productivity, broadening the rural economy, and bringing rural living standards up to urban ones.

Rural natural gas service was a key platform plank. Recalls Horner: "Warrack and I thought it would be a real coup if Alberta could become the first province to bring natural gas service to every farm. Surely if any province could do it, it was Alberta, which owned and controlled 80 per cent of the natural gas production in Canada."

The men drew their inspiration partly from talks with groups like Unifarm and the Alberta Association of Municipal Districts and Counties. (Unifarm is a political lobby group made up of individual farmer members and farm commodity groups. Essentially, it develops agricultural policies and lobbies government to implement them.) But personal experience influenced Horner and Warrack too. Horner had been a general practitioner and rancher in the Barrhead area since the 1950s. Remembers Horner: "In the early days, when we still made house calls, I was struck by the lack of comfort in farm homes. I delivered a baby in a home heated with a coal oil lamp. I had to put the baby in the oven of the wood-burning stove to keep it warm. Most people had coal- or wood-burning stoves. Some had oil furnaces that were always banging, smelling, or exploding. I had been aware for a long time of the farmers' desire for natural gas."

For his part, Warrack had grown up on a farm 15 miles south-east of Calgary and so knew firsthand the challenge of rural living. Moreover, his introduction to the rural gas issue had been direct and graphic. "I was talking with a farmer in his field, looking at a nearby producing gas well. He asked me why most of Alberta's gas was being marketed outside the province, while he, a citizen and part owner of the gas, was being denied access to it. I didn't have an answer for him."

## LOUGHEED GIVES HIS SUPPORT

The plan to bring natural gas to every farm delighted Lougheed, a city dweller with implicit faith in Horner's ability to understand rural Alberta. "From the first moment I heard of it, I was taken by the idea," he recalls. "I thought it was one hell of a proposal." Lougheed and Horner realized rural gas service would dovetail nicely with their party's pro-export gas policies.

Peter Lougheed on the campaign trail during the election of 1971.

"Natural gas exports were and are the major engine of economic activity in the province," says Lougheed. "Horner anticipated that we wouldn't be able to count on the support of all Albertans for the need to export gas if we didn't make the fuel widely available to rural areas."

While the Conservatives were developing their agricultural strategy, Unifarm director Entrup continued to urge the Social Credit government to extend rural gas service. Finally convinced his words were having no effect, Entrup invited Lougheed to his Unifarm office. "I asked him to give us [Unifarm] some support in the legislature. Lougheed was sitting across from me at my desk and he said, 'Helmut, we'll do better than that. We'll make rural gas service part of our election platform.' "

True to their word, the Conservatives undertook to "expand the provision for natural gas to Alberta farms at reasonable cost" in their campaign document, *New Directions for Alberta, 1971.* The promise was as brief as it was vague. But it was enough to win the support of Entrup and Alberta's premier farm organization. On August 30, 1971, the Lougheed Conservatives won the provincial election.

## THE CONSERVATIVES TAKE OVER

Once in power, it would take the Conservatives more than a year to fulfill their rural gas pledge. First they had to determine if widespread rural gas service was a fiscal and physical possibility. Thus, in early 1972, Horner, now deputy premier and Minister of Agriculture, commissioned Bell and Fenske, Cancrude Engineering, and Palmer Engineering to conduct studies. The companies divided the province among themselves and, as Bruce Palmer recalls, "drove up and down all the roads, counting the farms, locating gas supplies, designing a distribution system, and calculating costs."

With preliminary studies underway, Horner trans-

ferred the Co-operatives Activities Branch from Industry and Tourism to Agriculture, where he could keep a close eye on it, and instructed Harold Webber to continue incorporating gas co-ops as per the old Socred gas policy. Meanwhile, the government set up a new department of Telephones and Utilities to, among other things, develop and later implement a new rural gas policy.

## SETTING UP TELEPHONES AND UTILITIES

Headed by Calgary MLA Leonard Frank Werry—a member of the original Lougheed "six-pack" elected in 1967—the new department was tiny, with only a

The Conservatives, under Premier Peter Lougheed, came to power in 1971. Lougheed and his cabinet are shown in this photo on the steps of the Legislature.

Leonard Frank Werry, a member of the original Lougheed "six-pack", headed the department of Telephones and Utilities. This department was set up in 1972, and one of the first tasks was to develop a new rural gas policy.

secretary, a special assistant, a clerk, and Doug Brooks, an engineer on loan from Alberta Government Telephones (AGT). Brooks became the assistant deputy minister of the Utilities Division of the Ministry of Telephones and Utilities. He oversaw the implementation of the Rural Gas Program. Brooks would never return to AGT, instead spending the next fifteen years until his retirement overseeing Horner's rural gas "coup." It would be the most challenging period of Brooks's life.

Born in Sherbrooke, Quebec, Brooks studied electrical engineering at the University of Toronto in the 1940s before taking a job with Bell Canada. In 1966, he moved to Edmonton to join the small Gamma Engineering Ltd. and, five years later, went to work for AGT. Brooks freely admits he knew "absolutely nothing" about natural gas when Werry hired him in May 1972. "To me, gas was something you pumped into cars. But in my years at Gamma I had gained a lot of confidence in doing things without too much knowledge at the start. So I approached rural gas as a real challenge." Luckily, Brooks was an easy-going individual with an amazing capacity to work long hours and to absorb complaints, qualities that would serve him well during the early years of the program.

While Brooks settled into his "cubby hole office"

down the hall from Werry, Horner was in the legislature fielding a growing number of questions about rural gas. To some Socred MLAs, the government was courting economic ruin with its rural gas notions. "There are many cases where it simply is not within the realms of common sense to pipe natural gas to isolated farm buildings . . . Coming up with public money to subsidize rural gas installation systems could prove quite a financial disaster ten or fifteen years from now," one MLA said. But most other MLAs simply wanted assurances the coming program would eliminate some of the gas supply and financial problems experienced by existing co-ops, especially the ones built by Anchor Pipelines.

Doug Brooks was the engineer hired by Werry in 1972 to oversee the implementation of the Rural Gas Program. He was named the assistant deputy minister of the Utilities Division of the Ministry of Telephones and Utilities.

## THE CO-OPERATIVES ACTIVITIES BRANCH

Before 1973 Albertans wanting to form a gas co-op called on Harold Webber, supervisor of the Co-operatives Activities Branch in the Ministry of Industry and Tourism. Born on a farm near the town of

Vermilion, about 96 miles east of Edmonton, Webber had grown up with coal oil lamps and wood stoves and so sympathized wholeheartedly with the early gas co-ops. "I was quite enthusiastic about them. I knew there was no hidden mystery to gas, as long as you worked with it properly," he said in 1989.

Webber's branch officially incorporated the co-ops and helped them obtain loan guarantees from the Alberta Treasury. Meanwhile, pipeline approvals and inspections were handled by the Pipelines Division of the Ministry of Mines and Minerals. When the Rural Gas Program came in, Webber's branch kept its responsibilities, while the new Telephones and Utilities ministry oversaw the financial and administrative aspects of the program. For its part, Mines and Minerals—this time through the Energy Resources Conservation Board—oversaw the technical part.

Since the co-operatives branch was so intricately involved in the gas program, two of its employees—economist Herb Warner and Les Collins—were seconded to the Utilities ministry to help out. Over the next few years, Collins and Warner attended meetings throughout the province to explain co-op-hood and to set franchise boundaries. Recalls Warner: "I doubt you could find a farm in Alberta that I haven't been within 12 miles of."

Another co-operatives branch employee, John Mann, became heavily involved with gas co-ops, too. A credit union examiner for nearly five years, Mann was appointed supervisor of cooperative activities in 1973. "I attended about four or five meetings per co-op to help them set up, figure out financing, and learn how to obtain easements. I spent so much time on the road in the first year of the program it almost cost me a marriage."

In 1975, Webber retired while the co-operatives branch split into three sections—credit unions, co-op development, and rural power and gas co-ops—and moved from the Agriculture ministry (where it had been shuffled in 1971) to the Ministry of Consumer and Corporate Affairs. Then, in 1977, the rural power and gas co-op section was transferred, along with John Mann, to the Utilities ministry.

## THE RURAL GAS TASK FORCE

In May 1972, Palmer Engineering, Cancrude Engineering, and Bell and Fenske submitted their reports estimat-

ing that natural gas could be delivered to more than 90 per cent of rural Albertans at roughly $2000 per customer. In July, Werry set up a task force to determine how to best organize such a widespread distribution of gas. Chaired by University of Alberta business administration professors Boyd Harnden and Seha Tinic, the task force consisted of about twelve utility and government representatives, including Co-operatives Activities Branch supervisor Harold Webber. The group held its first meeting on July 25, 1972, in the AGT tower's thirty-first floor boardroom; a month later it submitted its report.

The report outlined three alternatives: a) continue with the rural gas policy inherited from the Socreds; b) promote the continued development of member-owned co-ops with more financial assistance and the establishment of a rural utilities branch; or, c) form one giant rural gas cooperative or crown agency.

Professors Tinic and Harnden recommended alternative c, but Werry disagreed. Forming a quasi-crown agency would be too costly, time-consuming, and contrary to the government's free enterprise ethic. Furthermore, a strong, independent co-op movement had already developed and Werry reasoned that the government should tap into its enthusiasm and demonstrated ability to get the job done. Since Meota, not a single gas co-op had experienced a serious failure or accident. Werry chose alternative b.

Recalls Brooks, who recommended the co-op option to Werry: "Co-ops had been able to put in systems more cheaply than utilities by using their own labour. The engineering may not have been as good, but the systems worked. Plus a community of interest had developed. People were willing to work together."

## THE RURAL GAS CRITICS

At least one of Horner's colleagues denounced the idea. In a memo to Horner, one cabinet minister insisted studies done to date were "an inadequate basis for making a policy decision." Unconvinced that many farmers even wanted gas, he suggested co-ops already received enough provincial assistance and that farmers without gas could use alternative fuels. Opined the minister: "Clearly a program of this magnitude would strain the financial resources of the Province."

In a reply memo, Horner bluntly observed that the minister had "failed to understand the problem

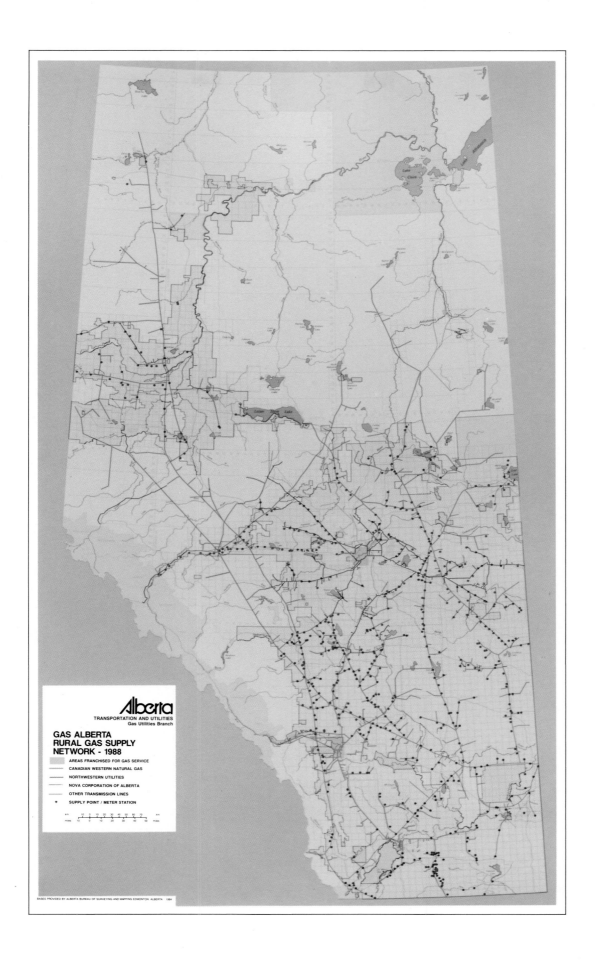

**Alberta**
TRANSPORTATION AND UTILITIES
Gas Utilities Branch

## GAS ALBERTA
## RURAL GAS SUPPLY
## NETWORK - 1988

AREAS FRANCHISED FOR GAS SERVICE

CANADIAN WESTERN NATURAL GAS

NORTHWESTERN UTILITIES

NOVA CORPORATION OF ALBERTA

OTHER TRANSMISSION LINES

• SUPPLY POINT / METER STATION

BASES PROVIDED BY ALBERTA BUREAU OF SURVEYING AND MAPPING EDMONTON, ALBERTA. 1984

completely." Alternative fuels were more expensive and less convenient than natural gas, pointed out Horner, who then wondered if, perhaps, utility companies weren't "bringing some pressure to bear on the government because of the loss of this lucrative [rural gas] business." Concluded the deputy premier: "We are talking about doing something for rural development. This is the way to do it."

Horner brought the recalcitrant minister on side easily enough. But Alberta's major utility companies would be a tougher sell. They were frankly aghast at the prospect of farmers installing gas lines throughout the province and fiercely lobbied the government to change course.

Northwestern and Canadian Western submitted their own report to Werry, urging him to launch a "thorough and detailed multi-million dollar economics/design, engineering/cost study to specifically design and cost a total system" before proceeding any further. The rural demand for gas was being more than adequately met by the marketplace, argued the companies. Nevertheless, a few weeks later the two companies' parent firm, Canadian Utilities Limited (CUL), had proposed yet another alternative for gasifying the countryside.

The suggestion came in a letter to Werry from CUL senior vice-president D.B. Smith. He advised the government to set up three organizations: a rural gas advisory board consisting of customer, government, and utility representatives to supervise engineering and gas costs; a farmer-owned gas distribution company

Egerton King, president of Canadian Utilities Ltd., was a detractor of the Rural Gas Program.

to finance the system with the help of low interest government loans; and, a new CUL subsidiary to operate and maintain the system.

Meanwhile, Anthony Rooney, president of Great Northern Gas Utilities Ltd., insisted it was impossible to "provide reasonably priced natural gas to rural areas and hamlets which are not currently being supplied." Despite this view, he too later submitted a rural gas proposal urging the government to carve rural Alberta into gas service areas and assign them to the major utilities. Farmers would finance the building of gas systems, while the utilities retained ownership of everything (steel pipe, regulators, meters) but the plastic pipe. Said Rooney in a letter to the minister: "We believe that rural gas distribution systems can better serve the long term public interest through a general policy of utilizing the experience, background and existing facilities of the established utility companies in Alberta."

When Werry remained resolutely in favour of co-ops, the utilities stepped up their letter writing. "We question any policy which discourages participation of private enterprise," wrote Rooney. Egerton W. King, president of CUL, exhorted the minister to abandon the co-op scheme and predicted Werry's gas policy would "beset the government with innumerable administrative and political headaches..." and, ultimately, fail. Both he and Rooney beseeched Werry to allow the utilities to control the distribution of gas to rural Alberta. King demanded a meeting with the premier and cabinet to push his position.

But Werry wouldn't budge, his resolve no doubt inspired by Horner, who knew the government would pay a political price if it handed rural Alberta to the utilities. The simple fact was that a lot of farmers didn't like the big gas companies.

## FIGHTING THE CREAM SKIMMERS

As mentioned in chapter 1, the major utilities generally served only those farms within a few miles of their pipelines. Although dictated by sheer economics, this practice created resentment among farmers, who were either denied service or offered it at seemingly exorbitant rates. The practice rankled member-owned gas co-ops, too. As far as they were concerned, the utilities were "cream skimming"—draining the countryside of all the lucrative customers, and leaving the hard-to-reach ones for them.

### RURAL ELECTRIFICATION PROGRAM

*The Rural Gas Program had a precedent of sorts in the Rural Electrification Associations (REAs) set up under the Social Credit government. In fact, many gas co-op directors also belonged to REA boards. Recalls co-op financial supervisor Herb Warner: "Some REAs and gas co-ops held their annual meetings at the same time and place because they shared so many directors." The two types of organization had more than people in common, however. Both followed cooperative principles and both had been created because major utilities couldn't afford to extend service into rural areas.*

*The Socreds launched their rural electrification program in 1948, when few Alberta farms had power. Under the plan, farmers formed cooperative associations—REAs—to finance the cost of electrification. For their part, the power companies set up non-profit subsidiaries to install the systems. Even so, farmers contributed hours of volunteer labour digging holes and tamping poles.*

*The REAs paid for 50 per cent of their systems up front with member contributions collected by directors; they paid the rest with ten-year loans guaranteed by the government. In 1953, the province set up a $10 million revolving fund to finance REA construction with loans at 3.5 per cent interest. The associations, which averaged 300 members, also set up reserve funds to pay for repairs and replacements. In all, 416 REAs were formed, the bulk by 1955, the last in 1967. By 1960 most Alberta farms had power.*

*In the 1970s, member interest in the associations waned and all but 186 were sold to TransAlta Utilities and Alberta Power. Explains Warner: "Rightly or wrongly, a lot of farmers resented the power companies because they felt they had too much control over the REAs. In setting up the Rural Gas Program we made sure the gas co-ops had autonomy."*

Horner also understood the importance local control and ownership held for many farmers, especially those raised during the Depression, when mistrust of big companies was rife and the cooperative movement took deep root in western Canada. To these farmers, the co-op was a tried and true way of doing business that had brought telephones to the countryside in the 1940s, and electricity in the 1950s. As Warrack would remark years later, "The co-op approach was the first thing

## THE JOY OF EASEMENTS

*Before construction crews could begin to roll, directors had to obtain signed right-of-ways from every landowner whose property would be crossed by pipe, including those who had refused gas. "Getting easements was the real fun and games part," says George Shemanko, a director and former chairman of the Central Peace Co-op in Spirit River. "You would think you had the whole system set down, then one guy in the middle who didn't want gas would refuse to let you bring the pipe across his land to his neighbour. A refusal often meant re-routing, which usually meant the need to get even more easements. Sometimes it could mean redesigning the system, which meant higher engineering costs."*

*Fortunately, most people were willing to grant easements in exchange for a token $1 payment. But there were exceptions who made life difficult. Directors of the Alder Flats Co-op encountered one farm couple reluctant to let pipe across a back quarter to their own son's land. Phil Lane, manager of the Lac La Biche Co-op, says his construction crew once had to detour over a mile around a farmer's land because "he felt his neighbour, the gas customer, wasn't a good enough Christian." Lane recalls another character, an aging bachelor and pig farmer, who granted an easement only after the construction crew agreed to clean his yard and corrals.*

*Mervyn Meers, chairman of the Dry Country Co-op in Oyen, played on cherished memories to convince one stubborn farmer. "I reminded him that when I was fifteen years old I used to feed buckets of oats to his horses. He said, 'Yeah, I remember. Where is that damn paper anyway? I'll sign it.' "*

*The only problem easement for the Pekisko Co-op in High River was that of Senator Harry Hayes, who already had gas from Canadian Western. Recalls a Pekisko director: "He wanted pages of details in his easement spelling out every little detail we were responsible for. He didn't refuse, he was just finicky."*

*A high profile holdout in the Crossroads Co-op area was future MLA Connie Osterman. Then embroiled in a long-running dispute with TransAlta Utilities over high voltage transmission lines crossing her land, she was not about to give a gas co-op blanket right-of-way. A leading figure in the community, Osterman was backed by about thirty of her neighbours, who also refused to sign easements. Finally the government dispatched Farmers' Advocate Helmut Entrup to persuade Osterman to relent. Once she understood the nature of the gas program, she readily signed.*

*Many co-op directors say getting easements would have been tougher still if not for Laurie Walker (nee McCormick). As the head of Easement Administration for the province, Walker visited nearly every co-op to explain easements and oversaw the processing of up to 30 000 easements a year during the gas program's peak. By July 1989, 190 000 easements had been signed, each for $1. Says Henry Tomlinson, chairman of the Federation of Alberta Gas Co-ops: "The granting of easements for $1 is in large part the reason for the program's success."*

older farmers, guys like my dad who were still the community leaders when we brought in the program, thought about. If we were bringing in the program today, with a new and different generation out there, we might have gone another route."

The co-op approach made sense for another big reason—easements. Traditionally, oil companies and utilities had paid farmers up to several hundred dollars each for the right to cross their lands with pipeline. To keep the costs of the Rural Gas Program within reason, farmers would have to be persuaded to grant easements for a token $1. (The law required they pay something.) No doubt farmers would be more willing to grant essentially free right-of-way to a co-op owned by their neighbours than to a big, impersonal utility.

## GETTING THE GO-AHEAD

By January 1973, cabinet had blessed Werry's cooperative approach and technical advisor Doug Brooks had assembled a team of experts to thrash out a detailed policy. The team included AGTL senior engineers Jim Wong and Bob Buchanan, and Hal Webber, supervisor of the Co-operatives Activities Branch. Wong was to develop regulatory procedures, while Buchanan drew up plans for a gas broker to negotiate supply contracts on behalf of the co-ops. For his part, co-op veteran Webber was to help flesh out the program's financial aspects.

Says Brooks: "I brought aboard people who could work out in more detail how the program would work, how much financial assistance would be required. I

Bob Buchanan drew up plans for a gas broker to negotiate supply contracts on behalf of the co-ops.

Despite its deep sorrow, the government had little time to mourn. A detailed rural gas policy had to be presented to cabinet in March to make it into the upcoming year's budget. With nearly forty co-ops on hold pending further details and Opposition MLAs beginning to talk of broken campaign promises, the government had no intention of delaying its much vaunted policy another year. Increasingly, rural Conservative MLAs were receiving letters like this one to Gordon Stromberg (Camrose) from Bob Moffatt of Forestburg: "If you have anything on a rural gas policy I would suggest you get in touch with Carl Mallett as soon as possible. It wouldn't hurt to contact him in this regard at any rate as he and some of the other farmers were going at it quite strongly in the coffee shop on this subject. As a matter of fact I believe Carl will go N.D.P. in the next election if something concrete is not given him on this matter. Since he seemed to swing a pretty large stick in the Coulee area last time, a little pacification would seem to be in order."

didn't have the background, so I hired people with experience in natural gas, the oil patch, and utilities. We had to look at the program's probable costs, the economical size of co-ops, the size of grants, the regulatory and technical aspects."

Wong and Buchanan, who normally lived in Calgary, rented apartments in the same highrise during their five-month Edmonton sojourn. Recalls Wong: "We lived and breathed natural gas. I remember sitting with Bob in the pool or steam room late at night discussing the program. We were trying to work out something that had never been done before, anywhere. We had no models to go by."

The intense concentration within Werry's department was shattered on February 25, 1973, when he was killed in a car accident, his vehicle crushed by a truck on a sharply curved stretch of Highway 16 near Edson. Recalls Brooks: "We were stunned. Suddenly we had no leader and everything came to a halt."

Jim Wong, another senior engineer from AGTL, was responsible for developing regulatory procedures.

Roy Farran (far right) was selected to replace Leonard Frank Werry in 1973. He is pictured here with Jim Wong (centre) and Henry Tomlinson.

Within three days of Werry's death, Lougheed had selected his replacement—Calgary North Hill MLA Roy Farran. The premier gave the new minister two weeks to present a full-fledged rural gas policy to cabinet.

A pipe-smoking, British-born gentleman with a penchant for adventure, Farran was more than equal to the task. After all, he'd been tested under more harrowing conditions. He'd driven tanks through the African desert in the Second World War and blown up bridges behind enemy lines in Greece and Sicily. He'd been strafed by German machine guns, and nearly killed by a letter bomb while serving with the British anti-

terrorist police in Palestine in the late 1940s. This, together with his experiences as a Calgary alderman and the publisher of thirty-five weekly Alberta newspapers, had more than prepared Farran for the challenges of rural gas. Still, the coming weeks would not be easy ones.

Hugh ''Doc'' Horner was instrumental in the establishment of the rural gas policy.

# CHAPTER 5

# *The Rural Gas Program*

The Lougheed Conservatives made rural gas service part of their election platform in the 1971 election. Premier Lougheed, pictured here with directors of the Lamco Gas Co-op, was a strong supporter of the program.

When Farran arrived on the rural gas scene, 21 per cent or roughly 82 000 of Alberta's households were without natural gas. Despite their best efforts, Alberta's utilities and gas co-ops had managed to bring gas to less than a quarter of rural Albertans. Still, the need for a Rural Gas Program wasn't obvious to everybody, especially to city dwellers who thought a 79 per cent domestic gas penetration rate province-wide was an excellent record. Thus, Farran's mission on assuming the helm at the Department of Telephones and Utilities was twofold: assemble a multi-million dollar program and, persuade urban and rural Albertans alike that it was necessary.

For his part, Farran needed no convincing. Although a Calgary MLA, he considered himself to be a rural Albertan. He had farmed in England and since coming to Calgary in the early 1950s had always maintained some cattle near the city. "I understood rural Albertans and the need for natural gas," says Farran. "On my own farm I used fuel oil. My wife still tells stories about all the black soot we had in our kitchen."

Excused from all other legislative duties for two weeks, Farran hunkered down with staff in his department's downtown Edmonton boardroom. Expecting to find only a "few loose ends," Farran was surprised to learn his predecessor "had not progressed much beyond the program's broad concept." In other words, Farran had a lot of work to do.

"We worked night and day going through several models for the program on a blackboard," remembers

Farran, who talked extensively with Horner. "I did nothing else." Neither, of course, did Doug Brooks and his team. Laughs Jim Wong: "Farran was a tyrant." But the circumstances demanded a hard taskmaster and by mid-March Farran was ready to present his program to cabinet. "I made my pitch with little charts and wands. This was a complicated project. Nowhere in the free world had anybody buried such a great mass of plastic pipe."

## THE PROGRAM HIGHLIGHTS

Finally, on April 30, 1973, Roy Farran unveiled his Rural Gas Program, the first of its kind, to anyone's knowledge, in the world. Summarized in *Position Paper No. 11—A Rural Gas Policy for Albertans*, the program had several major points:

1. Every effort would be made to make gas available to all Albertans who could be reached for $3000 or less.
2. The farmers would pay for the first $1700 cost of installing gas; the government would provide up to a $1300 grant to cover the rest.
3. Eighty-five per cent of the farmer's contribution could be financed by a fifteen-year, government guaranteed loan at prime plus 1 per cent.
4. A government gas broker—Gas Alberta—would buy bulk gas from producers and sell to the co-ops at a uniform rate to secure steady, good supplies of gas at the best possible price.
5. The government would provide special grants to cover the costs of lengthy, high pressure steel lines to transport gas to remote areas.
6. Rural Alberta would be divided into gas franchise areas with limits determined by population density, municipal boundaries, and natural obstacles.

### The Franchise

Franchise boundaries were made large enough for efficient construction and operations, yet small enough for a high degree of local control and personalized service. Franchises were issued by the government to an approved rural gas distributor. In most cases, this was a co-op, but Indian bands, privately owned utilities, and municipalities also received them. "One of the strengths of the Rural Gas Program has been the working together side by side of private-enterprise distributors

with non-profit cooperatives and municipalities," said Tom Brown, executive director of the Gas Utilities Branch, in 1989. "It is a unique Alberta solution to providing the best possible service at reasonable cost."

Each natural gas distributor was responsible for offering service to all potential customers within its franchise area, except for large, usually industrial, consumers or those living beyond economic reach. In return for fulfilling this responsibility, distributors were given the exclusive rights to serve customers within their franchise.

Another important feature of the gas program was that it exempted gas co-ops from regulation by the Public Utilities Board, which governs rates set by major utilities. In later years, county systems were also exempted from the PUB. This allowed co-op boards and county councils freedom to set their own rates. "If customers are unhappy with rate increases, they can vote their co-op board or county council out of office," notes Federation of Alberta Gas Co-ops chairman Henry Tomlinson.

## THE GRANT FORMULA

*Rural Gas Program grants are issued by the government directly to the distributor, who uses the monies to reduce the customer's share of costs. The size of government grant and customer share varies from franchise to franchise.*

*Over the years, the Rural Gas Program grant formula has changed several times, but for the last ten years it has operated as follows:*

*On first $1700 — no grant*
*On next $1300 — 100 per cent grant*
*On next $1500 — 75 per cent grant*
*Over $4500 — 90 per cent grant*
*Over $8500 — no grant*

*Says Tom Brown, executive director of the Gas Utilities Branch: "So many government programs run on a flat percentage. This program is based on cost-sharing. We direct the grant money where it is needed most." Typically, it now costs about $5500 for a distributor to extend service to a new customer, adds Brown. "Thanks to the Rural Gas Program, the farmer's share is only $2200. The government grant is $3250, or 60 per cent of the total cost. Some distributors are able to invest in a portion of the construction costs, which lowers the farmer's share even further."*

## GAS ALBERTA

*According to NOVA engineer Jim Wong, the establishment of a gas broker was one of the most ingenious aspects of the Rural Gas Program. A steady, reliable source of clean gas was of course essential to a co-op. But, in the past, securing supplies had proven difficult. In 1971, Meota and Trans-Canada Pipe Lines argued for months over the details of providing a new customer with gas. The dispute was finally settled by the intervention of Social Credit Mines and Minerals deputy minister Somerville, who later noted in a memo that it would be nice if co-ops could buy their gas from one entity instead of negotiating contracts with several companies.*

*Meota was not alone in its supply problems. In a letter to Peter Lougheed, Paintearth Co-op chairman George Ekman, then also president of the Federation of Alberta Gas Co-ops, reported that several co-ops were "stranded and bewildered in their attempt to obtain suitable natural gas contracts from the Gas Producers and Pipeline Companies..." Co-ops with supplies were sometimes plagued by "bad" gas containing hydrogen sulphide. Some North Edmonton Co-op customers once accused manager Roy Pritchard of trying to poison them when sour gas leaked into their lines from a nearby gas plant.*

*By negotiating bulk contracts with suppliers, Gas Alberta is able to secure good quality gas at a reasonable price for the co-ops. "Individually, co-ops are small and don't use enough gas to interest a gas producer," explains Tom Brown, executive director of the Gas Utilities Branch in the Department of Telephones and Utilities. "But because Gas Alberta buys gas for about seventy co-ops, it can negotiate a good price. It can obtain special rates from Canadian Western and Northwestern, whereas co-ops buying gas individually from these utilities would have to pay the regular domestic rate. If it wasn't for Gas Alberta, co-ops wouldn't be able to compete with utility prices. Furthermore, NOVA would have to deal with each co-op individually, and that could turn into an administrative nightmare." The brokerage section of "Gas Alberta" was managed very ably by Stu Elder, then Wayne Brown and presently by Randy O'Hara.*

*In addition to buying bulk gas, Gas Alberta manages the rural gas supply network. "At the start of each month we tell NOVA how much gas the system will use and from which suppliers," says Brown. "Gas Alberta also hires operators to look after the rural gas system's 700 RMO (Regulating, Metering, Odorizing) stations." NOVA operates 435 of these RMOs; utilities, oil companies, and some co-ops handle the rest.*

Although Farran wouldn't introduce actual legislation for several months, he allowed co-ops and utilities to proceed immediately under the program. Aware that the inclusion of utilities could spark controversy, Farran was careful to explain his rationale: "The problem of bringing natural gas to the greatest number of rural Albertans is so great as to require the harnessing of all Alberta's resources in the field, including the considerable expertise of the private utility and pipeline companies."

Generally, Farran's sentiments towards the utilities were far kinder than colleague Horner's. Indeed, Farran's position paper praised the utilities for having "taken considerable financial risk to serve marginally economic areas with gas." Later Farran would remark that it was "unfair to criticize the private utilities for only serving with natural gas those who are easiest to serve. It was the system that beat them. They were not allowed to spread the butter more evenly on the bread, to cross-subsidize in the manner of AGT. Utilities weren't allowed to increase the rates paid by urban consumers in order to subsidize the rates paid by rural users. They did their best within a limited distance of main pipelines, and that was all they could cut." Farran's conciliatory attitude was no doubt one reason the utilities, once outspoken program foes, now pledged their full cooperation.

By 1989 the major utilities—Canadian Western, Northwestern, and ICG—would serve nearly half of Alberta's rural gas customers. "There's no doubt the utilities played a key role in the program," observes Brown. "While the co-ops brought much of the enthusiasm that made the program such a success, the utilities made a quiet but significant contribution by developing the service areas in which they already had a strong presence as well as many new areas where residents apparently didn't want to pursue the co-op option."

Alan Dixon, in charge of Canadian Western's rural distribution program during the 1980s, says company engineers, landmen and crews found the rural projects rewarding. "They allowed much more personal contact with customers than urban ones. Sometimes customers cheered on plow crews." Other utility officials say the program benefited their companies by engendering a "can-do, pioneer" attitude among their engineers and crews. Additionally, some rural gas innovations have since been applied to urban systems, most notably the use of PE plastic pipe for gas distribution. Moreover, rural Albertans have turned out to be the utilities' best customers, burning, on average, 50 per cent more gas than urban users.

## PUBLIC REACTION

Although obviously delighted co-ops soon stampeded the fledgling Rural Utilities Branch to take advantage of his program, Farran had his critics. An editorial in the May 3, 1973, *Calgary Herald* wondered why Farran had bothered with his expensive program since farmers could use propane. "Although the motives may be noble, the economics and the ultimate benefits [of the program] may be questionable."

New Democratic Party leader Grant Notley, who lived in rural Alberta, wholeheartedly welcomed natural gas but argued the government should have set up a crown corporation to distribute it. One Socred MLA warned that co-ops would fall into financial ruin as the rural population dwindled, a demographic prediction rejected by the government. Socred leader Werner Schmidt denounced the program as a subsidy to natural gas producers. Jim Armstrong, the editor of *Propane Canada Magazine*, bemoaned the propane dealer's bleak future—"a marginal existence at best."

Meanwhile, in Balzac, a few miles north of Calgary, a group of acreage owners who had been quoted a gas price of $850 by Canadian Western were infuriated at the prospect of now having to pay nearly double. Farran let the landowners off on a technicality, but deplored their attitude. "What they are saying is 'the hell with my neighbour, let's skim the cream.' If they are going to live in the country they must understand it is the only way to reach the maximum number of people. It's the same principle under which rural electrification operated. We can't let cozy little groups near gas pipelines benefit just because they live near the pipelines."

For his part, Horner painted program critics as anti-rural elitists who thought propane was good enough for "country bumpkins" who insisted on staying on their farms rather than moving into nice, convenient cities. "Well, that's the attitude of the former government to everybody who lived outside the Calgary-Edmonton corridor," fumed Horner in the legislature. "It was: well, you know, you poor fellows really, we can't understand why you are living out there; we'd really like to help you, but if you'll just move in here . . ."

Possibly fearful of the famous Horner wrath, most Socreds welcomed the program. Sedgewick-Coronation MLA Ralph Sorenson was downright ecstatic. "Mr. Speaker, I'm an Alberta farmer first, and a Sedgewick-Coronation farmer second. And oh, how I enjoy getting things for my constituency. We're getting the gas. Thank goodness we are on the same plane as PC constituencies here. We have the money and we are getting the gas."

Conservative MLA James Miller (Lloydminster) pointed out the program would aid the agricultural industry, as well as bring comfort to rural homes:

> The producer will find many uses for this utility. He will heat his hog houses, resulting in greater feed efficiency and less loss of young pigs; heated chicken houses will produce more eggs; heated sheds for the cows which are having their calves will result in less loss in calving. We will have heated hothouses, so that the farmers can produce their own vegetables. We will have heated machine shops to enable farmers to work in their shops during the cold winter months. But Mr. Speaker, by far the most tremendous benefit for the farmers . . . is that of being able to dry their grain.

Soon irrigation farmers would gain from the program, too.

## THE PROTOTYPE: STE. ANNE

The government's confidence in the co-op approach was based partly on the experience of Onoway's Ste. Anne Co-op, which began delivering gas in late 1972. Prior to Ste. Anne, the median size of Alberta's co-ops was only ninety-three members, far too small to economically bring gas to all rural Albertans. Co-ops would have to be able to reach up to ten times that number for the Rural Gas Program to succeed. With its 730 customers and 343 miles of plastic pipe, enough to stretch

## THE NOVA LINCHPIN

Without NOVA, formerly the Alberta Gas Trunk Line (AGTL), there would be no Rural Gas Program. The company's nearly 9000 miles of pipeline, once likened by Roy Farran to a "heap of spaghetti," made it possible to transport gas into all but the most northerly parts of Alberta.

But the company did more than carry gas for the program. Its engineers helped design the program and later set up the Rural Utilities Branch to oversee it. Throughout the years, company experts trained co-op staff, produced instruction manuals, and provided valuable help in emergencies.

Tom Brown, executive director of the Gas Utilities Branch, says NOVA has been a "tremendous corporate citizen." For example, recalls Brown, "We'd finished building our steel line to High Level and were about to put the line into operation, when a beaver dam flooded part of the right-of-way, which was solid muskeg, and caused the pipeline to float. We asked NOVA for help, which it provided without hesitation. It sure got us out of a potential mess."

In 1988, NOVA was under contract by the government to design and build pressure regulating stations, and to operate 426 meter stations, 5 gas wells, and 8 high pressure steel lines ranging in length from 5 miles at the Deer Creek Co-op south of Edmonton to 101 miles at the Northern Lights Co-op near High Level. Also in 1988, NOVA supplied Alberta's gas co-ops with 9 billion cu. ft. of gas, roughly 60 per cent of the co-op system's total requirements. (NOVA regularly transports that much gas every day.) Says NOVA division vice-president Ben Kromand: "Other jurisdictions have said they can't do what Alberta did because they don't have a NOVA."

NOVA was and continues to be a key contributor to all aspects of the Rural Gas Program. Often NOVA undertook the most difficult projects, such as installing a steel line through the Crowsnest Pass-Chief Mountain area.

to Lethbridge, Ste. Anne was positive proof that big co-ops could be built, and in record time. Said Farran in introducing his program: "It was on their [Ste. Anne's] actual experience in the field that many of our guidelines were based."

Of course, Onoway hog farmer Henry Tomlinson had no intention of building a $1 million prototype when he voted to form the Ste. Anne Co-op in April 1972. He just wanted gas. Indeed, he'd been trying to get gas ever since the 1960s when Northwestern laid a pipeline within 3 miles of his 640-acre farm. Every year from 1965 to 1970, Tomlinson and a handful of his neighbours trekked to Northwestern and asked to be connected. Each time the answer was, "economically unfeasible."

The Ste. Anne Co-op was tangible proof that large co-ops could be built. This picture shows the installation of line in 1972-73, eventually putting in enough line to stretch from Onoway to Lethbridge.

Ste. Anne co-op was the first large co-op to exist in Alberta, and Roy Farran used their experience in the field to form many of his guidelines. Farran and Henry Tomlinson are shown here on Tomlinson's farm.

Finally, in early 1972, with the temperature stalled at forty below, Tomlinson and his friends tried a new tack. They asked everyone they knew within 14 miles if they wanted gas and plotted the location of the more than 200 who said "yes" on a map. They delivered copies of the chart to Northwestern and the small Palmer-Christie utility, the Superior Natural Gas Distribution Co. Northwestern didn't reply, but Superior offered to hook everybody up for $1450 apiece. Tomlinson and company called a public meeting for April 19, 1972, in the Onoway Community Hall to discuss the proposal. Among the 200 who showed up was co-op enthusiast Entrup.

"Entrup took the floor for fifteen minutes and proceeded to expound on the virtues of co-ops," recalls Tomlinson. "I thought to myself, 'Who invited this guy?' Well, he talked about Meota, Tirol, and Gem, and the farmer's God-given duty to look after himself. He was convincing. He changed everybody's mind about going with Superior. We voted right away to form a co-op and we elected a provisional board of directors. People just kept nominating people and soon we had twenty-four directors. I was made chairman."

Over the next several months the Ste. Anne directors pioneered a course that would be followed by more than seventy co-ops over the next ten years. First they met with Co-operatives supervisor Harold Webber who explained the basics of "co-op-hood" and who officially incorporated them. Next they hired Palmer Engineering to design a system and oversee construction. Third, they fanned out through the countryside signing up members, who each paid $1 for a membership and $25 to cover an engineering feasibility study. When the study was finished, the directors headed out again, this time with contracts for members to sign. Says Tomlinson: "I remember one director telling me about walk-

ing into one really run-down place with a dirt floor where the farmer still burned wood. 'I figured there was no way this fellow could afford service. But he just pulled a roll of bills from his pocket and peeled off $1450 and paid me right then and there.' "

The directors also had to obtain easements from everybody whose land would be crossed by pipe, including those who didn't want gas. Sighs Tomlinson: "Easements were the hardest job of all." Although most people gladly granted them within fifteen to twenty minutes, many balked, especially absentee

The directors of the Lamco Co-op hired Palmer Engineering to design the system and oversee construction. Bruce Palmer (far right) is shown here at a flare-up ceremony.

landowners from Edmonton who were advised by their lawyers not to sign. One farmer refused because he didn't want the pipe to reach his neighbour with whom he'd been feuding for thirty years. In some cases, the co-op simply detoured around the obstinate farmers; mostly, directors spent hours, even days persuading them to relent.

By June the co-op had run into some major obstacles: the 50 per cent loan guarantee then available through the Co-operatives Activities Branch wasn't large enough for many people; Northwestern was beginning to connect some co-op members to its pipeline, thus depriving Ste. Anne of lucrative contracts; and, all of the pipeline companies in the area had refused to sell gas to the co-op. Tomlinson and Palmer paid Horner a visit.

Recalls Palmer: "Horner saved the day. I told him we needed at least an 85 per cent loan guarantee. He phoned Webber, hung up and said, 'You got it.' He did

that for every proposal or problem I brought up—he'd get on the phone to the appropriate person and solve the problem. Within five minutes he'd removed every road block in our way." From now on co-op franchises would be sacrosanct and pipeline companies would have to sell to co-ops.

Construction began in September 1972. Palmer, aware of the anti-co-op pressures being put on the government, knew it was "absolutely vital" to finish Ste. Anne that winter. "We had to prove we could deliver and prove the doubters wrong," he says.

"I fast-tracked by starting to construct before we had all our customers. I built it like a railroad, the surveyors up front staking a course for the pipe, the plow following behind. When they saw that plow coming over the horizon, farmers who'd refused contracts came running out, some in stocking feet, shouting 'Hook me up.' Later some people accused me of designing the system on the back of a cigarette pack, but I knew we'd get more customers that way. I did it deliberately."

For his part, Henry Tomlinson and the other direc-

The installation of the Ste. Anne line had to proceed as quickly as possible. Much of the line was built in the freezing winter months.

By the spring of 1973, the largest rural gas distribution system was in operation. Roy Farran turned on the gas in a triumphant ceremony.

Palmer Engineering developed a new type of pipe with Alcan. Tom Christie (front, in white coat) felt the aluminum pipe would be more cost-efficient for the co-op. Also shown is the late Oscar Dahl, contractor (with camera).

tors were either on the phones or in the fields selling contracts, getting last-minute easements, and calming irate farmers whose land and fences had been damaged by heavy equipment. Every week the directors met once or twice from 8 PM to at least 2 AM. Says Tomlinson: "We promised people gas and we were determined to deliver. We had to. Some people had gotten rid of their coal furnaces in anticipation. One neighbour sold early and went without heat until mid-November." Whenever the directors wavered, Horner would "egg them on, tell them they had to finish," says Palmer.

Construction continued all through the bitterly cold winter. At any one time, forty men, divided into several crews, were in the fields with their bulldozers, backhoes, cats, and plows. They burned coal and straw to thaw impassable frozen ground. In November, one of Palmer's main subcontractors, frustrated by the thirty below temperatures, announced he was quitting until spring. Says Palmer: "Christie and I took over a

## THE ALUMINUM PIONEERS

*Speed wasn't the only priority for Ste. Anne. Reducing costs wherever safely possible was another. Engineers Bruce Palmer and Tom Christie knew large co-ops would have trouble paying for the labour-intensive and awkward lengths of steel pipe required for transporting gas over long distances and for crossing roads, rivers, and railways. Palmer had worked with aluminum pipe in the oil patch during the 1950s and knew it was more pliable, cheaper, and could hold pressures rivalling steel. He called an acquaintance at Alcan Aluminum Limited. Could the company develop a coiled pipe for gas that could be plowed like plastic? A few months later Alcan phoned back. Its interest had been piqued.*

*Alcan senior engineer James F. Whiting headed a special team that worked day and night to produce the new pipe. In December 1972, Alcan shipped several coils of the stuff to Ste. Anne and flew out several experts from its Kingston, Ontario, headquarters to supervise installation. Among the contingent were several vice presidents who followed the plow and greased the pipe to protect it from scratches. Alcan staff argon-welded the ends of the coils together. Later Alcan developed a method of welding in which explosives were used to join pipe ends together. In all, Ste. Anne plowed about 6 miles of aluminum coil into its system in 1972.*

*By 1989 Alberta's rural gas system would contain more than 3840 miles of coiled aluminum, including 61 miles in Ste. Anne alone. Moreover, Alcan would be marketing its new product not only to gas co-ops, but to pipeline companies throughout North America.*

James F. Whiting and Alcan worked very hard to develop and produce the new pipe. Huge spools of aluminum pipe were delivered to the Ste. Anne Co-op in December of 1972.

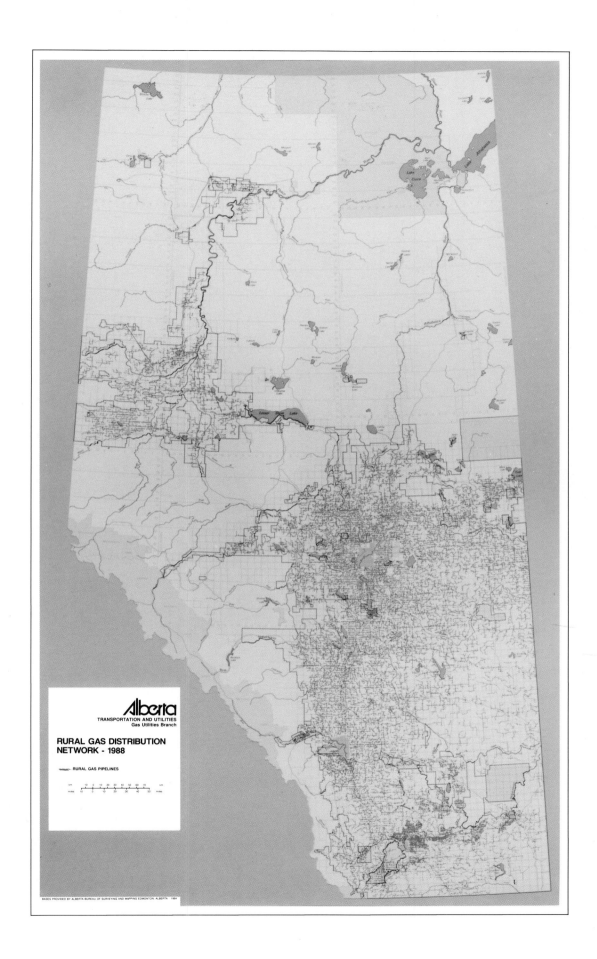

*Alberta*
TRANSPORTATION AND UTILITIES
Gas Utilities Branch

**RURAL GAS DISTRIBUTION
NETWORK - 1988**

RURAL GAS PIPELINES

BASES PROVIDED BY ALBERTA BUREAU OF SURVEYING AND MAPPING EDMONTON, ALBERTA   1984

100-mile section and shamed him into staying on." By February 1973, the biggest rural gas distribution system in Alberta history was complete. Says a proud Palmer: "No system that size would ever be built that quickly again. Building Ste. Anne was the hardest work of my life."

## PROMOTING THE PROGRAM

At times during Ste. Anne's construction, a weary Tomlinson silently cursed himself for ever getting entangled in such a time-consuming project. But his involvement with the rural gas movement only increased upon Ste. Anne's completion. In late February, Farran began inviting the co-op chairman to his office for a play-by-play recounting of the building of Ste. Anne. Usually Doug Brooks and Jim Wong sat in, and sometimes the whole group headed to Tomlinson's home for pork chop suppers. Impressed by Tomlinson's affability and hard-won co-op knowledge, Farran hired him as a consultant for the Rural Gas Program. Farran also hired Ste. Anne director Bill Dixon. As one of Ste. Anne's co-founders, Dixon had devoted countless hours to getting the co-op off the ground, and knew as much about it as Tomlinson.

Soon after Farran announced the rural gas policy in April, he sent Henry Tomlinson, Helmut Entrup, and Bill Dixon, along with several other civil servants to co-op organizational meetings throughout Alberta. Says Tomlinson: "Whoever the person was who set our schedule didn't seem to know the province too well because we'd often be given just two hours to attend a meeting 300 miles away." In any event, says Tomlinson, "We would promote co-ops, then the utilities would make their pitch. Then the farmers would vote on whether to go with a utility-owned or member-owned co-op."

Entrup accompanied the threesome in his new role as Alberta's first Farmers' Advocate. Appointed to the post by Horner on January 1, 1973, Entrup's first job as advocate was to promote the Rural Gas Program. This he did with such uncommon zeal that the NDP passed a resolution at its 1974 convention condemning the government's "pressure tactics" in "coercing" farmers to form co-ops. But Entrup did not coerce; he persuaded like a sledgehammer.

However, Entrup made no apologies for style. A firm believer in self-determination and pride of ownership,

Helmut Entrup (far left) was appointed Alberta's first Farmers' Advocate by Hugh "Doc" Horner in 1973. He used a hard-sell approach all over Alberta to encourage farmers to form co-ops.

he thought it his duty to persuade the reluctant "with all the powers of persuasion," which in Entrup's case included shouting, arm waving, backslapping, table thumping, and the staccato repetition of forceful arguments. Farran once observed that Entrup "talked like a machine gun."

A hard-sell approach was needed, believed Entrup, to overcome many farmers' fears and lack of confidence. Recalls Entrup: "What really scared the hell out of these guys was the thought of taking responsibility for a system worth a million dollars. They thought, 'Okay. We are farmers. What do we know about running a utility company?' I told them to expose themselves, to become better businessmen and managers. Sure the utilities would do a good job. But they could do it too. It was simple. Why give away the profits to a utility company?" Observed Herb Warner of Entrup's approach:

"You needed to be a strong individual to resist Helmut's arguments. I think Helmut is the reason there are so few company-owned co-ops today."

Farran also travelled the province to promote his program, usually showing up for construction start-up ceremonies when he and the local MLA would drive a plow through a brightly coloured ribbon. Sometimes crowds of up to 150 residents would be on hand to cheer the arrival of the plow, recalls Farran. "It was a little like the coming of the railroad in some places."

As for Brooks, he was meeting daily with co-ops and handling from twenty to twenty-five calls a day. "Boom, the co-ops were on our doorstep. There was a lot of activity."

But the joyful enthusiasm with which rural Albertans first greeted the coming of gas would soon fade as many problems beset the program. Rampant inflation, skyrocketing gas prices, a shortage of engineers and materials, faulty plastic pipe, all of these things would threaten to bring the program to a crashing halt and prompt NDP leader Grant Notley to one day label the program "a political powderkeg."

Some difficulties were worldwide and beyond Alberta's control; others were the result of perhaps undue haste on the part of the government and farmers. How Alberta's gas co-ops overcame these obstacles to become strong and respected organizations is the most fascinating part of the whole rural gas story.

# CHAPTER 6

# *The Great Gas Rush*

The first few months of the Rural Gas Program ran fairly smoothly, according to the 1973-74 annual report of the Alberta Department of Telephones and Utilities. Although most activity centred on forming co-ops and canvassing franchise areas for customers, a large amount of construction occurred, thanks partly to $2.88 million in government grants. In all, ten co-ops installed a total of 1200 miles of pipe, bringing gas to some 4200 new rural customers. The report called the period from April to December 1973 a "trial run" which had proven the program to be "feasible and practical." However, the report did hint at a darker side, noting in gentle bureaucratese that the program had "encountered problems which were not evident in the initial planning stages." Still, for the first few months at least, the program was off to a good, although hasty, start.

## SETTING UP A CO-OP

The procedure for setting up a gas co-op was outlined in *Natural Gas for Rural Alberta*, a document issued by the provincial government in May 1973. Interested farmers were to:

- appoint a provisional board of directors
- set franchise boundaries in consultation with the Rural Utilities Branch
- survey area residents to establish the degree of interest

Within the first few months of its establishment, the Rural Gas Program was able to initiate quite a bit of construction. Here, a line is being plowed in for the Benjamin Natural Gas Co-op in the mid-1970s.

- hire an engineer to design a system and estimate a per customer price
- call a meeting of interested farmers and government representatives to decide whether to proceed with a co-op, join an existing one, or delay the project until more interest was shown, and
- elect a permanent board of directors to sell contracts, obtain easements, arrange financing, apply for grants, supervise construction, and generally oversee co-op operations

The Cochrane Lake Co-op was one of the many co-ops established in the early 1970s. In this picture, a director of the co-op is unloading pipe for the beginning of construction.

Alex Onody is shown in the early 1980s with an irrigation pump fuelled by natural gas. His frustration with the cost of propane-fuelled irrigation prompted him to gather a group of his neighbours, and form the Forty Mile Co-op.

## SPRINGING INTO ACTION

As mentioned in chapter 5, several government representatives travelled the province publicizing the Rural Gas Program in the months following its introduction. But for many farmers, the program required little promotion. Cochrane rancher Garnet Ovans had been trying to start a gas co-op since 1971. "I felt we were being skinned [by propane dealers] and had talked to some of the boys about getting an engineer and building a gas system like Meota or Gem." He welcomed the program as just the right vehicle for getting the Cochrane Lake Co-op, incorporated in 1972, off the ground.

Bow Island grain farmer and rodeo calf roper Alex Onody was another to jump at the program. Tired of spending an outrageous $80 a day on propane for his irrigation pump and unable to buy gas from Canadian Western, Onody corralled eighty of his neighbours for a meeting in 1973 with Herb Warner and Al Stanford from the Rural Utilities Branch. (Both Herb Warner and Al Stanford worked in the financial and business organization section of the branch, Warner as supervisor and Stanford as co-ordinator.) They incorporated the Forty Mile Co-op and by 1976 would have 500 members spread over a staggering 4778 sq. miles, the largest co-op in area in the province.

Sam Alberts was the second to try bringing gas to farmers in the Brooks area lying beyond the reach of the Gem, Tirol, and S.R. & B. co-ops. The first attempt in the mid-1960s failed because the farmers were too far apart from one another. As soon as he heard of the Rural Gas Program, Alberts realized it offered the financial help to bridge the distances. Having spearheaded the local telephone and electricity associations in earlier decades, Alberts was no stranger to the cooperative movement and promptly took the lead in forming the Dinosaur Gas Co-op in July 1973.

Throughout the province co-op movement veterans urged their neighbours to avail themselves of the gas program's benefits. In High Prairie, Edmo Peyre resigned from the board of the seed-cleaning co-op he'd formed in the 1960s to establish the Prairie River Gas Co-op. Born and raised in nearby Grouard, the genial and talkative Peyre had rallied local farmers in the late 1940s to install electricity and later telephones. Recalls Prairie River chairman Arnie Cowell: "Edmo was so outgoing, he could talk to the Lord himself. He knew more people in the community than anybody else. He

### STARTING AT THE CROSSROADS

*Directors credit John Moran for getting Crossroads, the first co-op incorporated under the Rural Gas Program, off the ground. Says one director: "John Moran handpicked our board and got us up and running. He was a great ramrod, to use his own word. He would push and shove and get us doing something. It wasn't always the right thing, but it was always something. Maybe we floundered around sometimes, but at least we weren't sitting around."*

*Like many other co-ops, Crossroads had its share of problems. It had to re-plow 450 miles of bad 3306 pipe, which meant redoing several thousand easements. "Most people were understanding, but those who weren't made life pretty rough. It put the credibility of the board to a supreme test," observes one Crossroads director. On top of its re-plow woes, the co-op had money problems during its early years. "In hindsight we made the mistake of amortizing some of our loan into the gas rate and charging people only $1400 per service," says one director. "That became a terrible burden to us for a few years because of high interest rates, but we struggled through."*

*To reduce overhead, the co-op operated from the home of Leon and Marian Layden. "It was fantastic the amount of work that came out of Leon's basement," marvels a director. "I think the success of the program depended on the amount of work individuals like Leon and Marian were willing to do to make sure we all got gas. It was incentive to the rest of us to keep our noses to the grindstone."*

was like an unofficial councillor, holding court and dispensing advice in the Park Hotel coffee shop on weekends with the mayor and Larry Shaben, our MLA [and future Utilities and Telephones Minister]." When Peyre called a community meeting at the local Elks Hall and suggested forming a gas co-op in late 1973, people readily followed his lead.

The Sunshine Co-op in Blackie was another to benefit from a veteran's experience. In 1973, Milt Ryan, a founding director of the Gem Co-op, and of the Federation of Alberta Gas Co-ops, moved to Blackie where he found it a "disappointment to start using oil again after ten years burning gas." But Ryan didn't suffer for long. Once his neighbours learned of his involvement at Gem they called a co-op organizational meeting and appointed Ryan to the provisional board.

Veterans from other co-op programs became involved with the establishment of gas co-ops. Edmo Peyre worked to establish the Prairie River Gas Co-op.

## SOME "NAYSAYERS"

But the past success of Alberta's utility co-ops was not enough to make all rural Albertans embrace Farran's program. Among the sceptics was Cardston propane dealer Gerald Beazer. "My first thought was it's ridiculous to think natural gas could ever be piped to every farm in the country. My second thought was I might lose customers." Not one to block the popular will, however, Beazer soon joined with local gas proponents—who were led by his own brother—in forming the Chief Mountain Co-op in September 1973. Eventually, Beazer would become the co-op's manager.

Not all program doubters were as congenial as Beazer. In DeBolt, a farming community near Grande Prairie, somebody called a meeting to protest the formation

of the East Smoky Co-op. The dissident—the brother of a co-op director—told farmers they were being somehow duped by the large gas companies. Luckily, director and future chairman Arthur Dievert managed to persuade people otherwise and East Smoky was officially incorporated on December 18, 1973.

This is the first load of pipe delivered to the Chief Mountain Co-op in 1974.

Detractors notwithstanding, the Rural Gas Program generated immediate interest in virtually every part of the province. But there were exceptions. When Farran visited the town of Milk River in 1973 as part of a southern Alberta cabinet tour, residents had something else on their minds: getting a road paved. "It was a hot, dry, dusty day and we drove Farran out to see the road. He couldn't have cared less about it. Instead he urged us to get natural gas. 'Get organized for gas, we've got money for that,' he told us," recalls Milk Riverite Ken Welsh. "None of us had a clue about gas, but the local Chamber of Commerce directed us to investigate and in November we formed the Chinook Gas Co-op." Welsh was its first chairman.

Farmers near Wainwright were interested in gas, but less enthused about running a co-op. Recalls Ralph Patterson, an original director of the Wainedge Co-op: "A good crowd turned out to discuss a co-op, but as soon as the chairman called for nominations to the board of directors, 90 per cent of the people got up and left. The ones who remained became directors."

Those "who remained," not only at Wainedge, but at all new and expanding co-ops were about to embark on the most challenging undertaking of their lives. Even those who had participated in other types of

Gas pipelines were installed across Alberta in a flurry of construction throughout the 1970s. This plow is being lifted for a road crossing during the installation of the Chinook Gas Co-op's line.

cooperatives before were unprepared for the immense challenges that lay ahead. What was supposed to be a commitment of only a few hours a week soon turned into an unpaid, full-time job for scores of directors. Recalls Forty Mile's Alex Onody: "I ate, drank, and slept gas co-op for the next five years."

## SIGNING UP CUSTOMERS

Armed with government-prepared canvasser kits containing fuel price comparisons and answers to common questions, directors fanned out through their franchise areas to survey residents. This was a huge job, requiring several visits to every home and considerable salesmanship. On their first swing through an area, directors asked those interested in gas to pay a $1 co-op membership fee and a small deposit. Once a co-op had signed enough customers to make building a gas system possible, either for the whole franchise area or a

significant portion of it, directors went out again, this time to sell contracts and to encourage residents who had said "no" the first time to reconsider. Some co-ops completed their canvassing within months. Others took years.

Sheer distance turned canvassing into a Herculean task for many of the larger co-ops. George Shemanko, former chairman of the Central Peace Co-op in Spirit River, remembers spending "evenings and afternoons, all at our own expense, driving thousands of miles from the Rocky Mountain foothills to the Peace River trying to drum up customers." Similarly, Forty Mile's Alex Onody and his fellow directors covered lots of ground. "An average of 1.5 miles separates the farms in our area," says Onody.

Despite government promotion and the interest of most community leaders, many rural Albertans had yet to hear of the Rural Gas Program, a fact which often slowed canvassers down. "Some people thought natural gas was a recent discovery and had no idea it had been used for years in the cities," recalls Bill Alcorn, who canvassed for the South Flagstaff Co-op in Alliance. "Nobody knew anything about gas," concurs Coreen Bilawchuk, former manager and current secretary of Central Peace. "The hardest part was convincing people you could really get gas through a small plastic pipe and that it was safe."

Canvassing would likely have been harder still if today's billing methods had existed in 1973, says former Birch Hills Co-op director Wallace Tansem. "I'm glad I didn't have to explain the billing formula used now: metered difference x billing factor x heat value x metric conversion. It was simple in those days to do a comparison of fuel costs in selling the program. Still, it was difficult to convince some people to change. It seemed so easy for them to stay with their particular method of heating."

## THE PACK RAT

*Easily the most unusual landowner encountered by Rocky Co-op directors was a horse rancher who lived alone in a one-room shack. His tiny home was strewn with books, magazines, and newspapers, and his yard filled with scrap iron and second-hand trucks purchased at local farm sales.*

*People rarely saw the rancher, although he could sometimes be glimpsed at night splitting wood for his stove, his figure eerily outlined by lamplight.*

*Most obliging when approached by directors about stringing pipe across his land, the rancher became enraged when a plow crew rumbled through an old, unused waterhole on his property. He insisted the pipeline would ruin his trees and hurt his horses, and even wrote the provincial government a letter to this effect, before co-op directors could calm him.*

Directors of co-ops often drove thousands of miles to canvass new customers. Pictured are Forty Mile's directors who personally covered their area explaining the Co-op to farmers. Back row: J. Kolody, H. Haugan, N. Bauer, T. Noga, E. Mudie, L. Nelsen. Front row: A. Onody, A. Mack, P. Biemans, M. Klaiber.

## Pockets of Resistance

Chinook's first chairman Ken Welsh had difficulty selling the cooperative concept to some people who thought he represented a major oil company. "I had to talk to people late into the night trying to explain, 'You are the Chinook Gas Co-op. There is no big company behind this.' " George Comstock of the Rosebud Co-op, says some people thought his co-op was just another utility company. "One woman said, 'Natural gas! I've heard that before. I've signed up with CWNG [Canadian Western] five times and they've always returned my money. You're going to do the same thing. So why sign up?' "

Battle River directors were almost unable to overcome the stigma of the Anchor Pipelines bankruptcy when signing new members for their expansion in 1973. "It took us two years," recalls original director Merv Giem.

"Edmonton thought we must be doing something wrong and sent someone to show us how to canvass. He toured with us for three days, never signed up one member, returned to Edmonton and told his superiors we were probably doing it right after all."

Mervin Fox, original chairman of the Rockyview Co-op in Crossfield, well understands the scepticism encountered during the early days of the program. "Here we were a company with no funds trying to set up a $1.4 million operation, saying to people, 'Just give me your money and maybe you'll see us later.' It isn't any wonder some people said 'no.' But we persevered and we did it," laughs Fox, adding that "only a farmer could ever understand how to run a business with no money."

At least one co-op encountered fierce pockets of resistance. "Some people were dead against us and tried

Ken Welsh, the chairman of the Chinook Gas Co-op, and his directors spent a great deal of time convincing people that the Co-op was in their best interests. Welsh (centre) is shown here with some of the Chinook directors in front of a plow.

## TWO CAN PLAY THAT GAME

*A customer once refused to allow the Rockyview Co-op to bring a second pipe across his land to supply gas to a neighbouring farm. Recalls one director: "We received a letter from his lawyer saying it was not in his client's 'best interests' to cooperate with us. We bided our time until later this same landowner needed another gas line himself. When we found out we would have to cross another farm to do it, we sent this fellow a copy of his own letter and told him, 'Sorry, but it wasn't in his neighbour's best interests.'" The uncooperative landowner suddenly had a change of heart and signed the original easement, thus enabling his neighbour to finally get gas.*

to form a propane co-op just to stop us," says one former director of the Buck Mountain Co-op. "A few coal users tried promoting coal, but they got shot down by other coal users who were tired of shovelling the stuff. Maybe we were pretty green when we started canvassing, but we got called crooks and liars and were almost run off with shotguns by our own neighbours. At one place I was trying to tell a couple all the good things about gas when suddenly the husband says, 'I think we should give the bloke $20 to get rid of him.'" It took Buck Mountain five years to sign up enough customers.

Opposition such as this was thankfully rare. Still, directors everywhere had to spend hours carefully outlining the Rural Gas Progam. "Edmo Peyre spent twenty hours a day, in the coffee shop or in people's homes, convincing them to participate," recalls Prairie River's Arnie Cowell. Peyre's persistance paid off. "About twelve people took contracts even though they had no intention of using gas. They just wanted to see the project go ahead," says Cowell.

### Taking an End Run around the Problems

Other directors took a rather casual, indirect approach to soliciting business. One of the directors of the Summerview Co-op in Pincher Creek will always remember the long evening spent signing his first customer. "People told me I would never be able to sign this guy. But we played a lot of crib and drank a gallon of coffee, and he signed. But boy was my bladder stretched. He didn't have an inside toilet." Ted Latimer of the Pembina River Co-op in Jarvie helped to calve a cow and

shared a hearty supper of leftover hash browns before popping the question to neighbour Jack Montgomery. "Jack said, 'well, now that you helped me with the cow, I don't dare not sign up,'" says Latimer.

Many co-ops had trouble convincing people to join. Minco Co-op had to install their system bit by bit, but they went ahead with construction. This photo shows a power mole drilling a hole under a road for the Minco Co-op.

Cardplaying, long chats, helping with chores—nothing seemed to work for the directors of the Minco Co-op in Innisfree. After a year of canvassing, Minco had signed up only 40 of 1100 potential customers and was ready to disband. "It looked like we'd never get the 66 per cent sign up required by the government," remembers former secretary/treasurer Victor Yaremcio. "Finally the government allowed us to proceed on an area-by-area basis. First we'd get 66 per cent sign-up in a small area, give them gas, then start in on the next area."

A number of co-ops made special arrangements with the government. For example, Jim Musgrove of Jenner could round up only ten fellow farmers for the Atlee Gas Co-op, incorporated in April 1974. "Neighbours were sceptical we could do it on such a small scale, but there was no other way to get gas," says Musgrove.

Similarly, the Benjamin Gas Co-op in the Rimbey area south-west of Edmonton had only thirty-four customers when it began in the summer of 1974. Both Atlee and Benjamin, the latter led by beekeeper Rudy Heyn, had been refused membership in nearby existing co-ops and so were given permission to proceed by the government. "Doug Brooks [head of the Rural Utilities Branch] thought we would be too small but decided to give us a chance," says Benjamin chairman and original director Tom Thomas. It would turn out to be a smart gamble as by 1989 both co-ops would be debt-free.

Stories of canvassing troubles may give the impression that nobody but the co-op directors wanted gas. But this wasn't the case. Some co-ops enjoyed a remarkably speedy sign-up. Incorporated within days of the program's announcement, the Crossroads Co-op in Innisfail had 1200 customers by July 1973 when it ceremonially plowed the first yard of pipe at Fred Radomske's farm near Huxley. Directors at Alder Flats had no trouble drumming up customers thanks to freezing weather the night of the organization meeting. "Half the propane tanks in the country had frozen up," recalls one director. "It was a great night to have a meeting because everybody sure wanted natural gas."

Benjamin Gas Co-op had only 34 customers, but the tiny co-op was successful. This flare-up ceremony was held March 14, 1976.

"With the advent of the Rural Gas Program we grew like topsy," says Beryl Brantner, manager of the Triple W Co-op. "Every time Herb Warner came down from Edmonton our area enlarged. From 1973 to the end of 1976 the time passed like a dream (or nightmare). Often there were two plows going, with dozens of others working on yards, tie-ins, road crossings, and testing. Children rode on tractors to help measure pipeline by counting a white mark on the tractor wheel."

In Cochrane, Cochrane Lake Co-op chairman Garnet Ovans was inundated with requests to expand his

## A REVEALING EXPERIENCE

*In the summer of 1976, Cochrane Lake Co-op director and cattle rancher Mickey McBain decided to put his adult son to work gathering pipeline stakes. Although reluctant at first, the junior McBain soon acquired a certain zest for the job. Recalls McBain: "We were out in an isolated area looking for stakes when we came across a woman sunbathing in the nude. Suddenly a child yelled out, 'Mommy, mommy. Men coming.' The woman grabbed her towel, jumped up and ran slam bang into my son. He was a keen worker from then on."*

franchise area. In Rosemary, one elderly couple was so eager to join the local co-op that they paid the $50 deposit with their "egg money"—a bag of coins. An elderly bachelor purchased his contract from the Battle River Co-op with old bills bearing the face of King George V.

## THE PROBLEMS OF SUCCESS

"The program exploded in size beyond what we had expected," recalls Herb Warner. "At so many meetings we told people to wait a year because there were six or eight co-ops ahead of them. But they would bang the table and say, 'We can't wait. We are going ahead now.' " Equally impatient was Farran, who worried the program would become mired in bureaucracy unless implemented quickly. Recalls the former minister: "I thought if I didn't get everybody all excited and worked up the program would wither on the vine. I told the civil servants to let the program run on a loose rein; we could tighten up later."

### Spiralling Costs

The huge demand quickly outstripped the supply of engineers and construction contractors. Of course, whenever demand exceeds supply, prices rise. Making matters worse was an influx of inexperienced engineers and contractors eager to make their fortunes from the spiralling demand for gas. Rookies to the gas business, they made costly mistakes resulting in innumerable lawsuits and serious headaches. Difficult terrain and the vast distances separating farms in many franchise areas also added heavily to installation costs. As a result of all this, the average cost of installing gas jumped to $3500 from $1700 per customer soon after the program's launch. Working around irrigation canals pushed up costs considerably for the Dinosaur Co-op, says former manager Sam Alberts. "Machinery got stuck, sometimes for two or three days, in the wet ground around irrigation ditches."

The special equipment and long hours required to tackle rugged country and human-made barriers boosted the construction price-tag for many co-ops. Crews used "hole-hogs," hydraulically powered boring machines shaped like giant bullets, to punch holes beneath roads, railways, and some canals. Two or three cats working in tandem were often needed to pull plows through shallow creeks and rivers. Crossing rivers with steel pipe was even more difficult.

The East Smoky Co-op spent four days laying steel pipe 70 yd. across the Little Smoky River east of Grande Prairie. Backhoes scooped out a trench in a 5-ft. deep

section of the river while crews attached concrete weights to the steel to prevent it from floating. The pipe was then attached to a dragline machine cable, pulled into place and buried. In all, East Smoky had four major river crossings.

Crews for the Chinook Co-op had to dynamite some outcroppings of rock. When the first charge proved insufficient, they detonated a second larger one that not only blasted the rock, but blew the dust off the top of a grain elevator a 1/4 mile away.

Construction in the Rocky Mountain Foothills and Red Deer River Valley was often precarious. Cats equipped with ripper blades capable of tearing through rock had to be winched down steeply sloping sandstone and shale foothills in the Cochrane Lake Co-op franchise area west of Calgary. "Cochrane Lake was one of the toughest co-ops I had to do," says contractor Glen Skocdopole. "Some hills were almost solid

Many co-ops had to struggle with difficult terrain and spiralling costs. These men are putting swamp weights on pipe laid across the Vermilion River.

## ADVENTURES IN PLOWING

*Soothing the occasional savage farmer was all in a day's work during construction. For example, manager Phil Lane of the Lac La Biche Co-op once had to persuade an infuriated landowner not to shoot the plow crew. "I got a call from my crew telling me to get out to the field quick. When I arrived a huge man was aiming a rifle at my men. I said, 'What do I have to do to calm things down a bit?' The man said, 'Ask me.' I said, 'Well, I'm asking you—what do I have to do?' We repeated this series of questions a few times until I finally realized he wanted me to ask for permission to cross his land. He'd already given us an easement, but nobody had mentioned we were coming. So I asked his okay, he put away the gun, and the plow started moving again."*

*No farmer staged as complete and surprising a turnaround as one encountered by former Dry Country Co-op chairman LaVerne Opheim. "We had his easement and everything was alright when I talked to him the day before plowing. But when the crew got to his land, he drove over on his tractor, waved a rifle and said, 'I'm gonna shoot you bastards if you go any further.' The crew fled, leaving the plow behind, while I called the RCMP to calm the man and escort our plow to the road. As soon as the RCMP officer left, the young man again threatened to shoot the crew if it tried to do a road crossing next to his property. So that night at about 10 p.m., the crew and I did the crossing, while an RCMP officer stood guard with flashlight and drawn pistol. Nobody knows why the fellow changed his mind."*

sandstone and shale, which was hard on equipment. The welding truck was never too far away." Agrees Cochrane Lake chairman Garnet Ovans: "We had it all out there—rocks, rivers, trees, hills. I remember the first time we had to plow down a steep, almost 90 degree slope. Our cat driver grabbed his lunch and quit. A couple of days later he agreed to go down the hill, but only if another cat held and winched his machine." Similarly, plows had to be winched down the sides of coulees in the Dry Country Co-op district in Oyen, near the Saskatchewan border. Additionally, say Dry Country directors, crews had to contend with rocks "as big as the kitchen table."

Huge boulders and sandstone bedrock slowed the building of the County of Smoky Lake gas system. In one area, says county Reeve Alec Makowichuk, crews had to blast open a path. "We made holes in the sandstone bedrock, then drove a 1/4 mile away, lit the fuse and went into our truck. When it blew, little pieces of rock flew through the air, some even denting the hood of our vehicle. The other guy with me wanted to hide under the truck."

Burrowing beneath a spiderweb of existing pipelines added 20 per cent to the cost of building the Evergreen Co-op system in the Drayton Valley area south-west of Edmonton. The most expensive part of the job in the first year of construction was locating some 466 foreign pipelines with government maps and a sensitive metal detector imported from West Germany, says co-op manager Leah Lysak. Foreign pipelines posed another difficulty; landowners accustomed to receiving big dollars for easements from oil companies were reluctant to give the co-op right-of-way for only $1.

Four NOVA pipelines were the biggest construction obstacles faced by the Atlee Co-op, recalls founder Jim Musgrove. "NOVA wouldn't let us bring backhoes on its right-of-way, so we had to dig trenches by hand. That was a lot of digging, I'll tell you. We almost lost our crew over it."

Crews installing the Iron Creek system near Sedgewick bulldozed through bush, moved boulders, and once had to winch a hopelessly mired cat from muskeg. Making matters worse was one farmer's odd request that plow crews crossing his land restore his muskeg to the precise condition in which they had found it. "He even wanted the weeds put back in the same place," recalls a co-op director.

The Northeast Co-op in the Bonnyville area was among those with virtually every terrain trouble imaginable—bush, rock, rivers, hard-packed soil, and dreaded muskeg.

Drainage ditches challenged the ingenuity of crews building the Ankerton system. Recalls one director: "We had to dig trenches 8 ft. below each ditch in case the farmer decided to deepen it in future. So we had to dig holes and lower in the trenching machines so they could reach far enough down."

Equipment wasn't always up to the challenge of weather and terrain. A contractor for the Battle River Co-op nearly lost his D9 cat when it fell through the ice on a creek. The machine remained semi-submerged for two days until a second cat could be hired to winch it out.

## THE TROUBLE WITH ENGINEERS

*Rosebud manager George Comstock laughs when he recalls the sales pitch of some engineering firms. "They told us, 'It's no problem at all. You hire us to set the whole system up for you. All you do is sit back and watch the money roll in.'" The gas business, as it turned out, wasn't that simple. As one of the directors of the East Peace Co-op in Donnelly once remarked: "We had to watch everything like a hawk, even though we didn't know what we were looking for."*

*Some engineers designed gas systems without first doing a proper land survey or discussing pipeline routes with the affected farmers. Recalls Don Hall, a director of the East Central Co-op in Hanna: "One engineer showed me a municipal map with the proposed pipelines on it. I noticed one line led to an old house that I knew had been abandoned by the original homesteader years ago. The engineer didn't believe me because his map showed an occupied farm there. Trouble was, the map was outdated." Directors at the Chinook Co-op say an engineer once accidentally plotted a pipeline through a cemetery.*

*According to several co-ops, other engineers hired incompetent surveyors to stake the course of pipelines for plowing crews. Directors at Foothills in Olds insist one of their surveyors was shortsighted and so continually strayed from agreed-upon routes.*

*Jim Musgrove of Atlee says one engineer hired "two old guys" to survey a line. "They had no surveying instruments and very few wooden stakes. They were costing us $200 a day and not doing very much." Contractor Glen Skocdopole says inexperienced surveyors were continually staking lines through swamp, sandstone, or steep, rocky hills. "They just didn't know where heavy equipment could go or what it could do." Some surveyors were downright sloppy, suggests Skocdopole. "One told me, 'See that cow over there? Head for it.' Of course, the cow wandered off across the field."*

Often, pipelines had to be laid across existing lines. This line (small one), owned by the Big Country Gas Co-op had to cross the large utility line. It was a delicate operation.

Unfortunately for gas co-ops, the energy industry's bonanza fuelled a construction boom, which drove the price of engineers, contractors and materials higher than ever over the next few years. Moreover, rising gas prices soon created public relations problems for co-op directors who had signed customers on the promise of cheap gas forever.

Yet another international development caused program costs to spiral even higher—a worldwide shortage of the resin used to make polyethylene (PE) plastic pipe. The problem surfaced in late 1973 when Alberta's five plastic pipe manufacturers—Building Products of Canada Ltd., Dom-X Plastics Ltd., Polytubes Ltd., Plastex Extruders Ltd., and Beta Plastics Ltd.—told Farran and Brooks they could no longer get PE resin from their usual suppliers, the CIL and Dupont chemical companies. For their part, the companies said a burgeoning global demand for plastic meant they could not meet the Alberta pipe-makers' suddenly increased demands.

"The program was threatened with a complete shutdown," recalls Roy Farran. "I said, 'Damn it, we have to get the resin from somewhere. We've sold these farmers all over the province on gas. The program can't be brought to a sudden halt.' We didn't want to go back to using PVC because it reputedly didn't last as long. So I began looking all over North America [for the PE resin]."

The program's inflationary woes were exacerbated in late 1973 when Arab oil producers, seeking to undermine US support for Israel, slashed production. The cartel's embargo tripled the price of non-Arab energy overnight. This was good news for Alberta's oil patch, which flourished for the rest of the decade as oil and gas prices alike climbed to unprecedented levels.

## PIPE TYPES

*Alberta's rural gas system consists of interconnecting steel, aluminum, and plastic pipelines. By far the most common type of rural gas pipe is made of polyethylene (PE). At the end of 1988, there were 51 000 miles of it in the system, compared to only 3300 miles of aluminum, and 1400 miles of steel. First used to carry gas in the U.S. in 1945, PE is cheaper and more flexible than steel and aluminum. Able to safely withstand internal pressures of up to 100 psi PE is ideal for transporting gas over relatively short distances of several miles. Early co-ops used another type of plastic called polyvinylchloride (PVC), which is more rigid and so more prone to breaking than PE. In the 1980s most co-ops replaced their PVC lines with PE ones.*

*Although much more expensive, steel and aluminum can withstand higher pressures than plastic and so are used to transport gas over long distances. Aluminum can safely handle up to 700 psi, steel double that amount. All three types of pipe come in varying sizes. The greater the volume of gas to be carried, the bigger the pipe. All pipe must be pressure tested to the satisfaction of government inspectors before being used.*

*In most co-ops, a high pressure foreign pipeline owned by NOVA or a major utility carries gas into the franchise area. RMO stations (Regulating, Metering, and Odourizing) built next to line taps regulate or reduce the pressure of gas flowing into the co-op's largely plastic lines. As their name suggests, RMO stations also measure the amount of gas going into the co-op system and they inject a sulphur-based compound called mercaptan into the gas to give it a rotten-egg odour. Smaller regulators and meters govern the flow of gas from the co-op line into the customer's home. Pipelines of different sizes and materials are connected to one another by t-shaped devices called, appropriately enough, tees.*

A shortage of plastic pipe threatened many co-ops. This line, stored in a farmer's yard, was owned by the Pembina River Co-op.

firms. By April 1974 Farran had secured 11.8 million lb. of PE resin from Dow and Dupont. Unfortunately, most of the pipe made from the Dow resin, dubbed 3306, would prove faulty and have to be replaced at a cost of nearly $35 million to the Alberta government. But more on that story in chapter 7. For the moment, at least, Farran had solved Alberta's pipe crisis.

Most of the pipeline made from 3306 resin proved to be faulty and had to be replaced. This man, working for the Lac La Biche District Gas Co-op, is inserting a probe into the pipe to locate a leak.

At Doug Brooks's suggestion, Farran telephoned the eastern-Canadian-based executives of CIL, Dow Chemical, Dupont, and Union Carbide.

Both Dupont and Dow agreed to produce the precious resin, but they lacked a vital ingredient—ethylene, itself a byproduct of natural gas. So Farran went to the producers of ethylene—Imperial and Esso in Sarnia, Ontario—and persuaded them to supply the chemical

The crisis was further alleviated in late 1974 when engineer Bruce Palmer and his contractor partner Tom Christie secured pipe supplies from several companies in Canada and the US, including the Phillips 66 Chemical Company in Bartlesville, Oklahoma. Says Christie:

"We phoned every pipe maker we knew in Europe and North America." In 1975, Phillips opened a twenty-employee branch plant in north-east Calgary. Business was so brisk the company soon hired thirteen more employees and moved into larger quarters in the city's south-east, where it remained until closing the plant in December 1984 because of dwindling demand from the Rural Gas Program.

## DEALING WITH DEBTS

Next Farran turned his attention to the inflation problem. By now the average cost of installing gas had climbed to nearly $4000 per customer and pressure was mounting on Farran to help the co-ops out. Unwilling to charge customers more than $1700 (the figure

outlined under the Rural Gas Program) for their gas contracts, co-ops were borrowing heavily to cover the unexpectedly high costs of construction. In April 1974, representatives from about fourteen southern Alberta co-ops met with Farmers' Advocate Helmut Entrup in Lethbridge to complain about their growing and, in many cases, crippling debt. Meanwhile in Edmonton, Social Credit MLA Ray Speaker warned Farran that farmers would soon start bolting from co-ops unless the government increased program grants.

Certainly many co-ops were strapped for cash. Cochrane Lake owed $250 000 to the Royal Bank during its first months of existence, says chairman Garnet Ovans. "Inflation had driven costs so high we could barely operate anymore," recalls Ben Hovelkamp, the chairman since 1976 of the North Peace Co-op in

Co-ops often had to operate with next to nothing, and offices were still being set up in basements or abondoned buildings. The Dry Country Co-op office pictured here was luxurious compared to what they used before.

## THE TROUBLE WITH CONTRACTORS

*As any co-op director knows, plastic gas pipe should be plowed at least 30 in. deep to avoid being snagged by cultivators or other farm machines. Unfortunately, this basic rule was frequently broken during the early years of the gas program, with costly consequences for some co-ops. Recalls one director from the East Central Co-op in Hanna: "Once a farmer decided to level the ground behind the plow with his cultivator. After several hundred feet he looked behind him and saw his cultivator had snagged the pipe and was dragging it out of the ground behind him." But shallow plowing was only one contractor sin. Others included plowing on forbidden ground and failing to repair damaged property.*

*Rosebud manager George Comstock remembers carefully arranging with a plow crew to circumvent a quarter section of standing grain at a customer's request. "The next time I drove past the property there was a black strip right across the middle of that beautiful wheat field. Was that customer ever angry with me." A number of co-op directors say plow crews frequently trekked across land without right-of-way. According to*

*directors at Natural Gas Co-op #52, one contractor ordered his crew to plow in a 'W' rather than straight line to increase footage. Contractors were, of course, paid by the foot.*

*Directors of the Rocky Co-op in Rocky Mountain House recall impressing upon one contractor the need to quickly repair damaged fences since he was working in cattle country. "Immediate attention on the fences. It was all down in writing, all signed. But within half an hour of construction starting we had calls coming in about cows and horses being out. We had to continually remind the contractors about the fences." Other directors say cat operators (who towed the plows) regularly ripped up front lawns, tore down clotheslines, and rumbled over gardens and cabbage patches.*

*"One contractor plowed through a customer's irrigation field," recalls a Bow River Co-op director. "That customer got so angry he came to see me and shoved a shotgun in my side. He was drunk. Luckily, the gun was not loaded, but for a minute, I could see headlines."*

Fairview. Agrees contractor Glen Skocdopole: "It was tough going in those early years. Some co-ops couldn't afford to pay us until a couple of years after the work was done." Directors at the South Flagstaff Co-op in Alliance held bingos to raise cash for engineering bills. Few co-ops could afford to rent office space; those that did generally had rough accommodation. For several years the Chinook Co-op in Milk River operated out of a cement shed behind the local lumber yard. "The floor sloped so bad, stuff kept sliding off the desk," recalls chairman George Russell. Other co-ops could afford decent office space, but no furniture. "It was something being a director in those days," chuckles Harvey Pellerin, chairman of the East Smoky Co-op in Crooked Creek. "All those bills floating in and nothing to pay them with."

In April and May of 1974, Farran announced several measures to alleviate the co-ops' financial burdens. First, he expanded the program to include non-heating uses of gas such as grain drying and irrigation pumping. This allowed co-ops to sell more contracts and generate bigger gas sales. For co-ops in sparsely populated parts of Alberta, this meant the difference between economic viability and bankruptcy. Second, Farran committed the government to covering the full cost of building

Sometimes, there was considerable damage done to private property during plowing. Here Ken Sydnes, director and board secretary of North Peace Gas Co-op, assesses the damage to a field.

high pressure steel and aluminum transmission lines, and to paying 50 per cent of the installation costs above the $3000 per farm connection.

The co-ops received yet more help when Farran unveiled Alberta's gas rebate plan on May 3, 1974.

Under the plan, designed to shield urban and rural residents alike from dramatically rising prices, Albertans paid only about 65 per cent of the Alberta border price for natural gas. Thus the fuel remained a bargain compared to propane, which was also becoming more expensive. Still, the end gas price to rural consumers, even with rebates, was nearly double the 47 cents per gigajoule (50 cents per mcf) earlier promised by co-op directors.

In any event, the additional government help allowed co-ops to concentrate on building their systems. From April 1974 until March 1975, nearly 8400 miles of plastic and 600 miles of steel pipe were installed under the program, bringing gas to another 9513 rural customers. In all, the government paid out $13.97 million in grants, enabling twenty-five co-ops to complete construction and another thirty-four to get underway. Obviously Farran's "loose rein" strategy was achieving impressive results.

Still, a number of co-ops continued to pile up debts and newspaper stories were beginning to appear in which co-op directors grumbled about inflation, material shortages, and delays in dealing with the government. In January 1975 the Lamco Co-op board of directors wrote Farran a letter threatening to resign en masse unless he helped them with their fiscal troubles. Among the first co-ops to begin construction under the program, Lamco had charged its members only $1350 per contract. Unfortunately, according to a memo written by John Mann, head of Rural Power and Gas Co-ops, "spiralling costs and an enlarged franchise area have catapulted their [Lamco's] construction costs from less than $3000 to today's average cost of $3800." Like so many other co-ops in this situation, Lamco had borrowed to make up the difference and now found itself strapped for cash. (Lamco later assessed its members an extra $600 each to pay for construction costs.)

## A Change in Leadership

By March 1975 it appeared as if the utility companies had been right when they warned the government back in 1972 that its Rural Gas Program would be trouble. But the government remained solidly committed to the program and, after winning the provincial election of March 26, 1975, appointed Dr. Allan Warrack to the helm at Telephones and Utilities. (Farran became solicitor general.) Now the man who had helped conceive

Dr. Allan Warrack became minister of Telephones and Utilities in 1975. He was responsible for the continued organization of Alberta's Rural Gas Program.

of the rural gas project would guide it through tough times to ultimate success. As Hugh Horner once remarked: "Farran got the program booted off by the seat of its pants. Warrack got it settled down and organized."

# CHAPTER 7

## The Gas Rush Continues

Laying pipe through muskeg and brush was often time-consuming and therefore more expensive. Accidents often happened in these situations. This backhoe overturned in the Embarass River while working on the Yellowhead Co-op gas pipeline.

Dr. Allan Warrack had been Minister of Utilities and Telephones for about two months when a farmer asked him if he was sorry the Rural Gas Program had ever started. "I'm not a bit discouraged," replied the enthusiastic university professor. But nobody would have blamed him if he had been. "Like any new program with thousands of people involved, lots of things went wrong," confided Warrack years later. "I'm an organizer. I can't stand disorder and I went through hell for the first year and a half. But by the last two thirds of my term things were quite positive. I think a lot of people now would say we brought order out of chaos."

Warrack began his Utilities tenure by meeting with "every MLA, every co-op, and every person that I could possibly meet with given the reality of a twenty-four-hour day." Among the groups he met with most often was the Federation of Alberta Gas Co-ops, which regaled Warrack with the by now familiar litany of complaints about engineers, contractors, high gas prices, faulty pipe, and administrative confusion. In the legislature, Socred MLA Ray Speaker pointed out that the costs of building the Little Bow Co-op (located in Barons, north of Lethbridge) in his riding had escalated by 40 per cent since the project's start. "And in the meantime we've been arguing about procedure, how does the application get in, who signs it, who doesn't, and technicalities like that," fumed Speaker. Undaunted, Warrack chirpily termed the grievances "happy problems" and set about solving them.

First Warrack asked the Association of Professional Engineers, Geologists and Geophysicists of Alberta (APEGGA) to investigate engineering complaints. Then, to help co-ops with runaway construction costs, Warrack brought in NOVA to build and operate major transmission lines. And he introduced special grants to cover the costs of building in difficult terrain or in areas with an unusually high number of obstacles like canals, highways, or railroads.

This pipe is weighted with concrete and laid across the Little Smokey River. The East Smoky Co-op faced many of the same problems as the Yellowhead Co-op.

It was Tom Christie of Palmer Engineering who in June 1975 negotiated the first special grant—$100 000 for the Yellowhead Co-op in Edson, an area rife with muskeg and brush. "I was known as 'Bad Tom' around the Utilities department," chuckles Christie. "I was always in there arguing for more money, telling the top brass they had to take into consideration the extra costs of laying pipe through muskeg, brush, and rivers as opposed to just prairie."

Framers of the Rural Gas Program certainly hadn't envisioned areas like the Yellowhead franchise when devising a grant formula. Nestled up against the Rocky Mountains, Yellowhead comprises 892 sq. miles of rock, hills, creeks, muskeg, bush, and timber. In addition to plowing pipe, crews had to clear hundreds of acres of brush and trees and dynamite their way through solid rock. Many people, including some government officials, doubted Yellowhead could be built. In a brief history written by the co-op, a director notes that by July 11, 1973, "we were ready to go—sounded real easy—we were all determined to make it happen. We knew what was ahead. Lots of bush, muskegs, rivers...We were told it couldn't be possible, which made it more of a challenge...

"We were ready to go and no money for brushing. The board of directors decided we [should] approach Tom Christie to see if he would be able to get an extra grant for brushing...also we had a lot of muskeg to go through. He sent a man out to check and when he returned and reported the situation, nobody would believe him. So Tom came himself and was amazed at the amount of brush and muskeg..."

## INSIDE THE DEPARTMENT

When not conquering the elements, co-ops were usually dealing with officials in Edmonton, a frustrating experience for public servant and farmer alike in the first few years of the program. "The days were horrendous," says Gordon Campbell, a Northwestern Utilities engineer loaned to the Utilities department for several months in 1976. "From 8 AM until 5 PM we met with co-ops, back to back, without even breaking for lunch. Sometimes whole co-op boards came in to talk about grants or designs."

To smooth relations between co-ops and the department, Warrack did three things: he recruited J.W. Dodds, the president of Alberta Government Telephones and, in Warrack's opinion, one of the best managers in Edmonton, to be his deputy minister; he assigned each co-op to a specific staff member who acted as the co-op's broker in dealing with other officials; and, he personally fielded directors' complaints. Says Warrack: "I took whatever calls I could."

Warrack's measures certainly helped. Additionally, Northwestern engineer Campbell, who became a

## DO-IT-YOURSELF CONSTRUCTION

*A number of co-ops tried to avoid contractor woes by forming their own construction companies. The first was the West Thorhild Co-op north of Edmonton in 1971. With tractors borrowed from local farmers and a custom-built pipe plow (designed by a welder friend of director Herb Holgate), co-op members—including some senior citizens—installed about 50 miles of pipe in less than a month. The members, each required to contribute forty hours of unpaid labour, were helped by engineer Bob Comfort and a couple of local heavy equipment operators. The farmers did such a good job they formed Thoralta Construction in 1972 and proceeded to install systems for other co-ops, including Coronado and Battle River.*

*In 1973, the Pembina River Co-op in Jarvie followed Thorhild's example and formed PemConstruction Ltd. With the help of Holgate's welder friend, the co-op remodelled an old telephone cable plow and, again with the assistance of engineer Comfort, installed their system. Recalls founding director Hardy Terhorst: "We had beautiful weather the first day of plowing, but by noon the next day it was snowing and twenty below." Pembina has laid every mile of its pipeline with its own equipment despite miles of bush and muskeg.*

*In May 1975, the Minco Co-op in Innisfree, impressed with Pembina's work, formed Minalta Construction. After some training at Pembina, the Minco directors hit the fields and, over the next two years, plowed in more than 600 miles of plastic and aluminum pipe. Co-op secretaries Joan Anderson amd Shirley Kulak ran parts from storehouse to field.*

*Not all co-op construction ventures succeeded. In June 1975, the Paintearth Co-op in Castor formed P.G.C. Co-op Services Limited to build the next phase of its system. According to the co-op's history, penned by chairman Herman Schwenk, "The board had had many problems with engineers and contractors in getting the first phase constructed. There remained several areas of dispute with both parties due to mistakes in construction which still had to be corrected before final settlement could be made. In analyzing the work to be done in 1975, it appeared the same problems would be encountered..."*

*Paintearth purchased or rented an assortment of equipment, hired a welder to build a plow, and assembled a couple of trailers for hauling equipment to the field. But directors soon found doing their own construction more trouble than it was worth and disbanded P.G.C. Co-op Services within a year, selling their homemade plow to the Lac La Biche Co-op. Wrote Schwenk: "Thus ended a venture that proved to have a most traumatic effect on the gas co-op of any development in its history."*

*In 1976, the Lac La Biche Co-op spent $100 000 on equipment, including the Paintearth plow, and formed Lacalta Construction. Directors dissolved the subsidiary in 1979 when equipment repair bills were hovering at about $28 000 a year. Says manager Phil Lane: "Our self-construction company was turning into a self-destruction one."*

This specially designed plow was used by Thoralta Construction to build the Battle River system.

permanent staff member in 1977, helped to streamline interactions between government and co-op. "He did a tremendous job helping to straighten out the program," recalls Tom Brown, now executive director of the Gas Utilities Branch. "He wasn't out front giving lots of speeches, but he had good ideas and worked hard behind the scenes during his nearly 10 years with the department." Some co-op directors had ways of their own for expediting department business. Once, stymied by delays, chairman Mervin Fox of the Rockyview Co-op in Crossfield, vowed to send three busloads of farmers to Edmonton to "explain" a grievance. Whenever a problem arose, serviceman Colin Storch of the Big Country Co-op in Morrin, liked to arrive at the department on a Friday morning and announce his intention to stay "all weekend if I have to" unless given satisfaction.

J.W. Dodds (centre) was appointed deputy minister by Warrack.

## MEETING THE GOVERNMENT

Although dealing with government was sometimes exasperating during the early years of the program, many co-op directors have pleasant memories about trips to Edmonton. Board members from the East Peace Co-op in Donnelly, south of Peace River, recall how their MLA, Al "Boomer" Adair, sometimes arranged for them to meet with several cabinet ministers for breakfast at 7 AM in the legislature cafeteria. Chairman

George Comstock of the Rosebud Co-op was once invited to Edmonton to have his picture taken receiving a $93 000 grant cheque from Roy Farran. When staff were unable to find the cheque, Farran's receptionist offered a $9 cheque of her own for the photograph, which eventually appeared in the newspaper. "Nobody could tell the difference," says Comstock, who later received the real thing.

Dry Country chairman Merv Meers recalls attending a meeting of the Federation of Alberta Gas Co-ops and government MLAs in Edmonton's Government House. At one point Meers asked for additional grants to cover the costs of serving his sprawling, nearly 4700 sq.mile franchise. "Hugh Horner asked me to tell everyone how far apart the people in my area were. I said, 'The people in this country are so far apart they have to keep their own tomcat.' Well, you could hear a pin drop. Then a lady MLA says in a loud whisper, 'What does he mean by that?' Horner jumped up and said, 'It's a joke. Laugh.' "

A cherished memory for Crossroads director Charles Moore is that of meeting Premier Peter Lougheed. He and two fellow directors were in Edmonton meeting with department officials when they decided to visit Lougheed and personally thank him for the Rural Gas Program:

*Of course, being hillbillies, we didn't know anything about protocol, or due course, or how to attempt these things. We thought we would just go to the Parliament buildings and do it. We made it to Lougheed's office and explained ourselves to his secretary who left for about five minutes. Then lo and behold, in he walks, saying, 'I hear you boys want to talk to me.' We were dumbfounded. Then Ed, who was supposed to do the talking, said, 'Charlie, will you tell Mr. Lougheed why we're here?' I didn't know*

The directors of the East Peace Co-op have many pleasant memories of their dealings with the government. They are pictured here with their MLAs, Al "Boomer" Adair, Marv Moore, and Larry Shaben, at the East Peace grand opening.

*what to say, but I thanked him for his program and said we really appreciated it. He was really pleased we'd taken the time to do it.*

Dealing with the Utilities Department became easier and more pleasant too as the program matured. Says Doug Brooks: "We provided co-op directors with key items to look for when dealing with contractors. We developed standard contracts, and we invited co-ops to come in and discuss problems with us. We tried to informally resolve disputes between co-ops and consultants." Moreover, officials like Brooks were often out in the field, attending annual meetings, talking to directors, attending zone meetings of the Federation of Alberta Gas Co-ops, and hobnobbing at opening ceremonies.

## WHAT ABOUT 50 CENT GAS?

Probably the toughest problem facing co-op directors was the one most beyond their control—the rising price of natural gas. Most directors had sold contracts during pre-OPEC days on the premise that gas would cost the consumer 47 cents per gigajoule (50 cents per mcf) and would rise in price by no more than 4 per cent a year over the foreseeable future. As it turned out, the foreseeable future was remarkably brief. By the time most co-ops had finished their systems and turned on the gas, rates were more than $1 per mcf and climbing. The government's gas rebate program helped keep rates down ($70 million in rebates were paid to natural gas distributors during the 1975-76 fiscal year). But the program was scheduled to end in 1976 and co-ops were worried the government might not renew it.

"We couldn't go to a wedding, or a funeral, or even walk down the street without somebody taking a strip off us about the gas rate," recalls North Peace chairman Ben Hovelkamp. "Our co-op lost credibility," says Ron Fox, manager of the Northeast Co-op near Bonnyville. "By the time we finished the first phase of construction, the gas price had risen considerably. Sign-ups dropped to almost nil and 10 per cent of our potential customers bought diesel-wood furnaces instead."

At least one co-op was sued for breach of contract. "Luckily the contract's fine print said directors could change the gas price whenever necessary," says former chairman Ken Welsh of the Chinook Co-op near Lethbridge. Customers of the Burnt Lake Co-op near Red Deer worried not only about price, but about future

supply. Recalls manager Cecil Flake: "The energy crunch came and rumours went around the country. People wanted to know why we were putting all these pipes in the ground when there wouldn't be enough gas left in Alberta to fill them."

The board of the North Peace Gas Co-op, above, were haunted by the rising cost of natural gas. Many of their customers blamed the directors for prices that were much higher than originally expected.

Despite the international forces at play, some customers blamed directors for increased prices. At several co-op annual meetings, members accused directors of fraud and demanded resignations. "It was almost like a lynch mob," recall directors of the Paintearth Co-op east of Red Deer. Other directors were openly called liars and avoided social functions. "Gas prices were a real public relations problem for years," says Nick Poohkay, a director of the Birch Hills Co-op north-east of Grande Prairie. Laughs Barb Boufford, manager of the Forty Mile Co-op near Medicine Hat: "Even today when I go to a dance and get out on the floor with some guy he'll ask, 'You guys got cheap gas yet?'" Adds I & J Co-op manager Mavis Stegen: "Believe it or not I still have a customer who asks me when he'll get 50 cent gas, and he was on the board!"

Rising gas prices were causing some public relations problems for the government as well. In early 1976, the Federation of Alberta Gas Co-ops released its annual brief urging the government to continue its price protection program. The brief also outlined ongoing co-op problems, thus sparking a wave of negative stories

Despite the problems in the initial stages, the government stood behind the Rural Gas Program. People like Dr. Allan Warrack, shown here meeting with Doug Brooks, worked very hard to make the program a success.

in the daily press. In a February 14, 1976, *Calgary Herald* story headlined "Gas Co-ops Pose 'Political Powderkeg,' " NDP leader Grant Notley warned that high gas prices were undermining rural gasification and urged the government to "immediately reassess the entire rural gas program."

For its part, the government remained more committed than ever to the Rural Gas Program. "There may have been problems with its implementation, but the program itself was sound," says Warrack, who introduced several measures in 1976 to help co-ops combat inflation and higher than expected gas prices. In February, he said the government would share a higher proportion of construction costs—75 per cent of per customer costs above $3750, up from 50 per cent. And in November, he announced, to everyone's great relief, a three-year extension of the gas rebate program.

## DIRECTOR DEVOTION

Increased financial support from the government certainly helped the co-ops to survive the inflation and shortages of the 1970s. But, ultimately, it was the self-sacrifice and dedication of the directors, their families, and other volunteers which brought the program through tribulation to triumph. Commenting on the program in 1989, Al "Boomer" Adair, who became Utilities minister in 1986, said: "It was the extra effort that made this program go. And I think that's what makes it unique and such a success story. Most people would have said, 'Oh forget it. Shut her down. Everything is going against us.' But nobody suggested quitting. Everybody just dug in their heels and worked their butts off."

For example, few directors received reimbursement

for the thousands of miles they clocked canvassing and obtaining easements. And few were paid for attending meetings, which were held weekly until 2 or 3 AM during peak construction. "You never even thought about getting remuneration in those days," recalls Eric Dick, the first chairman of the Rosemary Co-op east of Calgary. Agrees West Thorhild director Herb Holgate: "All these years the only ones who have been paid for their work were the eight men on the construction crew."

Sunshine director John Green says his co-op tried to reimburse directors but "the figures got so high and the job so poor that no one turned in a bill except those who made trips to Edmonton."

The following excerpt from the history of Paintearth Co-op, illustrates the degree of dedication required of directors:

*It is difficult to describe the effort and frustration and the sense of futility that was involved in being a director of the Paintearth Gas Co-op from the time it was organized till the third annual meeting in March of 1976. The board held 68 meetings plus a few special meetings from March 9, 1972 till March 25, 1975. Many of these meetings lasted till 2.00 or 3.00 in the morning. In addition to the meetings, many of the directors spent countless hours and miles of driving canvassing members for sign-ups and getting the various documents signed that were necessary. Many times, there was a meeting once a week. There were many times when it seemed that it would be impossible to get in control of the operation.*

Directors' spouses contributed untold hours to the cause as well. "Every director was really two directors because of the work his wife put in handling phones 90 per cent of the time, obtaining easements, and making lunches for construction crews," says Benjamin Co-op director Tom Thomas. "It was a community effort," says Jack Macklin, a founding director of the Foothills Co-op in Olds. "Our wives and kids signed people up, looked after the farm. The neighbours helped out when we needed a hand. Everybody helped." Adds another director: "If it wasn't for the volunteers, the co-ops wouldn't have succeeded."

Many chairmen worked full-time without pay during the early years of their co-ops. Former Ankerton chairman Ken Gerber reportedly worked day and night phoning neighbours, meeting with government officials, and dealing with the bank to get his co-op off

Gas co-ops were community efforts and they only survived because of thousands of hours of volunteer labour. The Foothills Co-op picnic is an example of some of the lighter moments members were able to share.

the ground. Helping him was a sizeable thirty-four-member board of directors. Mervin Fox, the first chairman of the Rockyview Co-op north of Calgary, spent ten unpaid hours a day overseeing construction and running the office. Fox was at least partially motivated by a sceptical utility representative. "He told me I couldn't build a gas system because I didn't know anything about it. I said, 'You've got one thing right—I don't know anything. But I will by the time we've finished.'"

"A hell of a lot of people spent a lot of time making sure construction was done properly and that no money was squandered," says Cochrane Lake director Frederick Kidd, the MLA for Banff-Cochrane from 1975 to 1979.

Foothills director and former manager John Nesom became so busy with co-op affairs he sold his hog farm. Laughs Nesom: "The ironic thing was I got involved with natural gas because I wanted it to heat my barns."

"Anything that had to be done in those days, we did," says Central Peace Co-op secretary and former manager Coreen Bilawchuk. "Once I had to unload a truck of tracer wire bales when the driver refused to do so because it wasn't his job. I was so mad, I determined to do it myself, even if I was wearing a sundress and high heels. So he pushed the 16-lb. spools, one by one, to the edge of the truck, and I lifted them and waddled away. It took three hours, but I was going to show him. I didn't walk right for a week after that."

Herb Wohlgemuth juggled the job of manager of East Smokey and the work on his farm. He is shown here in the Co-op's storeroom.

### AN EXAMPLE OF DEVOTION

*Running the biggest co-op in area in Alberta was often a round-the-clock job for Gordon Blanchard of the Forty Mile Co-op. A teacher and farmer, Blanchard was, along with Alex Onody, instrumental in bringing gas to the sprawling franchise around Medicine Hat. He ran the co-op for several years from his home in a room wallpapered with maps and cluttered with filing boxes of easements and contracts. Preoccupied with co-op affairs from dawn to dusk, Blanchard hired somebody to run his farm. A handyman to begin with, Blanchard took several courses and was soon out repairing lines any time of day or night in all types of weather. He managed the co-op until 1980 when he became first vice-president of Unifarm. "People like Blanchard deserve a lot of credit," says Onody. "They were key to building the rural gas system."*

costs were high and our other bills mounting feverishly. Some people were pushing to disband the co-op and Ted began talking about giving people their money back."

Selleck died suddenly in August 1975, during the peak of the co-op's problems. Shortly after the funeral, directors learned that Selleck, a bachelor, had willed part of his estate to the co-op to help it retire its debt. Although deeply moved, directors did not accept Selleck's gesture and the estate was left to his brother, Frank. For their part, directors were able to negotiate a more reasonable settlement with the engineer; within months of Selleck's death, the co-op was out of fiscal danger.

East Smoky director Herb Wohlgemuth was another who tackled the manager's job without pay, dividing his days between farm field and co-op office, which for the first year was in his father's house. Another newcomer to natural gas, Wohlgemuth studied gas fitting and pipe fusion at the Northern Alberta Institute of Technology (NAIT) in Edmonton so that he could repair regulators and pipes. Many managers and service-people have trained over the years at NAIT, the Petroleum Industry Training Service (PITS) in Edmonton, and at the Westerra Institute of Technology in Stony Plain. In addition, directors have attended seminars sponsored by the Federation of Alberta Gas Co-ops.

Fellow East Smoky director Frank Stevenson also took fusion courses and remembers being out in twenty below weather the week after Christmas of 1980 fusing pipe together.

Edward (Ted) Selleck, a founding director and the first manager of the Three Rivers Co-op in Whitecourt, devoted his life to the co-op. An out-going, tall, wiry jack-of-all trades, Selleck worked from 7 AM to 10 PM every day trying to solve the co-op's financial problems. "We were in bad shape," recalls Three Rivers director and real estate agent Claude Gould. "Our engineering

## KITCHEN TABLE OPERATIONS

To keep overhead costs to a minimum, most co-ops operated from members' homes. In fact, many still do. Beryl Brantner, the manager of the 700-member Triple W Co-op near Lethbridge, began running co-op affairs from her kitchen table—typically covered in papers and surrounded by coffee-drinking customers—in 1971. "When I first started there were only ten customers and plenty of room in the filing cabinet to duck the mending," says Brantner. "My husband, Lloyd, has put up with eating on the corner of the kitchen table around a calculator and papers, and has often relinquished the chesterfield to construction maps."

Bachelor Harry Christensen began operating the sixty-member Dalum Co-op in Drumheller from his home upon becoming co-op manager/secretary/treasurer in 1971. He set up the office in his bedroom, keeping co-op records in two small filing cabinets, and storing gas ledgers and receipt books in cardboard boxes under his bed.

Foothills' John Nesom ran the co-op from his basement together with wife, Muriel, who handled contracts and easements. (They were among several husband and wife co-op management teams.) Other non-farming directors handled co-op business from their regular offices, like Central Peace director and insurance agent Frank Spurgeon, and Birch Hills' director and village secretary James Rutherford.

## A RECORD CONSTRUCTION YEAR

For all the challenges confronting them, the gas co-ops made remarkable strides during the first year of War—

rack's tenure. By April 1976, another 11 612 rural customers had been served with gas, bringing the total to 25 379. Another 7725 miles of plastic and 685.2 miles of steel and aluminum lines were in the ground. In all, thirty-five co-ops had completed their systems, and another thirty-four were underway, the bulk of those half-finished.

In the legislature rural MLAs defended the program from Opposition critics by stressing the success and determination of co-ops in their ridings. Declared MLA J.E. Butler (PC, Hanna-Oyen) on March 11, 1976: "The concept of the co-op and this gasification is going to be successful. It's going to be successful because the men who are running it are the kinds of men they are. They have helped build the province, and they'll build these co-ops. And when they are built and completed, they will own a multi-million dollar gas distribution system. They'll be damned proud of what they did,

By April 1976, another 11 612 rural customers had been served with gas, bringing the total to 25 379. The construction of rural gas systems continued to boom throughout the early 1970s. A small trencher/backhoe putting in a service for the East Smoky Gas Co-op Ltd.

and they know it, and that's why they're staying with it."

MLA Bob Bogle (PC, Taber-Warner) was equally adamant in the program's defence:

*It has been suggested by some members of this Assembly that the public has been misled, that directors are fed up, and that promises were made and subsequently broken by the Alberta government. There are three natural gas co-ops in my constituency: first Chin Coulee, . . . Triple W, . . . and Chinook. About three weeks ago I had the privilege of attending two of the three annual gas co-op meetings. The feeling I received from the meetings was one of pride and satisfaction, pride in the local initiative, and satisfaction in the progress that has been made to date. Under the dynamic leadership of people like Roy Neilson and Beryl Brantner of Triple W, Ken Welsh and Tom Gilchrist of Chinook, and Alex Powell and Don and George Leahy of Chin Coulee, the co-ops are standing up for their rights and running their affairs in a most businesslike way. And, Mr. Speaker, they will succeed.*

This man is preparing to join a new reel of aluminum pipe by using the "high energy joining" method.

## GAS ON THE RESERVE

*"One aspect of the Rural Gas Program I have always been proud of is its inclusion of Indian bands and Metis settlements," remarked Roy Farran in a 1989 interview. By 1989, eleven Indian bands and one Metis settlement owned their own gas systems, while several other bands had obtained service from a major utility.*

*Among the Indian bands to benefit from the program was the Heart Lake Indian band north of Lac La Biche. According to manager Rick Stedman, Heart Lake built its system, which consists of 9 miles of pipe and twenty-eight services, in 1985. A band-owned construction company installed the system. Before gas, the Cree band heated with fuel oil. However, the costs of trucking oil into the remote community—accessible only by logging road—were prohibitive.*

*High fuel costs inspired the Dene Tha Tribal Administration to build its 118-service gas system in 1986. Additionally, says serviceman Barry Toker, the band council wanted to create some jobs and improve the quality of life on its several reserves west of High Level. "Gas has had quite an impact on the lives of people here. They were burning wood before. Now they are using gas stoves, clothes dryers, and hot water heaters," says Toker.*

*Moreover, the system employs two servicemen and one secretary, all band members. Employees—including two gasfitters—at the Goodfish Lake Gas Corporation in Goodfish, north-east of Edmonton, are also all band members.*

*In 1986, two Metis-owned companies installed the Paddle Prairie Co-op system in the 1000-member Metis settlement of the same name south of High Level. Also managed by Barry Toker, the co-op draws gas (through NOVA) from some of the 200 wells on settlement land. Says co-op chairman and founder Albert Wanuch: "I knew other communities had managed to get gas even though they were miles from a gas source. So I thought, 'Why not us?' " A former meter station operator for NOVA, Wanuch proudly notes that Toker is training a settlement member to become co-op manager.*

Albert Wanuch is a former meter station operator for NOVA and one of the Paddle Prairie Co-op's founding members. He was the first chairman of the co-op which brought gas to the 1000-member Metis settlement of Paddle Prairie.

## THE BUILDING CONTINUED

Certainly no directors had been more determined to succeed than those of the East Smoky Co-op in Crooked Creek east of Grande Prairie. Incorporated in December 1973, the co-op struggled for years to sign up members and negotiate grants. Penniless, with only a leaky, poorly insulated camp trailer for a home, the co-op persevered and finally, in the spring of 1976, was ready to build. "Then our engineer went bankrupt," says director Herb Wohlgemuth. Undaunted, the co-op found another engineer and was again ready to go that autumn. But unusually heavy rains turned the area into a mud bowl and slowed plow progress to a crawl. An early frost shut down construction until the following spring.

The East Smoky Co-op held the official opening ceremony four years after forming. Progress had been slowed by bad weather, financial problems and contractor problems. The Little Smoky River crossing (above) was an example of the adverse conditions the co-op faced.

Finally, in September 1977, more than four years after forming, the co-op held its official opening ceremony at a local school. As director Harvey Pellerin carried a flaming torch through the crowd of members, students, and MLAs, co-op chairman Arthur Dievert exhorted the children present to never take their utilities for granted. "They don't happen by themselves," said Dievert, who had learned that lesson the hard way.

In 1978 East Smoky took over the dormant Peace Portal Co-op in the Valleyview area. "We doubled our size by taking it on," says chairman Harvey Pellerin. "We never dreamed we'd get that big when we started."

## THE TROUBLE WITH 3306

As it turned out, East Smoky's late start was a disguised blessing. By the time it began building, the plastic pipe made from the Dow 3306 resin so painstakingly secured by Farran during the pipe shortage of early 1974 had been banned from the market. For reasons unknown, the 3306 pipe "leaked like a sieve," as several co-op directors put it, and had to be replaced, to the dismay of many customers. If the government had not stepped in to cover the pipe's replacement costs, co-ops which had used it to build most of their systems would likely have gone bankrupt.

Word of the 3306 problem surfaced in early 1976 when several co-ops reported massive leaks. The Bas-

sano Co-op south-east of Calgary claimed to have lost $23 000 worth of gas through holes in pipes. Directors at the Sunshine Co-op in Blackie, south of Calgary, were continually repairing leaks sniffed out by their gas-line patrol dogs. The Natural Gas Co-op #52 in Provost, south of Lloydminster, was losing 50 per cent of its gas to the air. All three co-ops, along with dozens of others experiencing leaks, contained pipes with large amounts of 3306. Sunshine had 385.8 miles of it; Co-op #52 had more than 600 miles. One Alder Flats director recalls vividly his discovery of a PE 3306 leak: "I could smell gas, then I could hear it, sort of roaring. So I started walking out in the fields. And you could see it, a hump in the plowed field like a cone in a volcano blowing the dirt up 2 or 3 ft. high."

In July 1976, the Energy Resources Conservation Board (ERCB) launched an investigation and held public hearings at which three of the more sorely afflicted co-ops—Bassano, Sunshine, and Deer Creek—gave evidence. In 1977, the ERCB called in plastics expert Frank Rice to examine the 3306 pipe. By March 1978, it had issued a directive calling for the replacement of all PE 3306 in service.

### A LEAKY TWIST OF FATE

*It was an unfortunate twist for the Iron Creek Co-op, but a lucky break for Chief Mountain. Iron Creek was awaiting a shipment of quality pipe from a California company, while Chief Mountain had just ordered a supply of 3306 from Beta Plastics in Edmonton. At the time, neither co-op knew of the 3306 problem. Hence it made perfect sense when somebody suggested the co-ops swap shipments rather than waste money trucking Edmonton pipe all the way to Chief Mountain at the US border, and California pipe all the way to Iron Creek in central Alberta. So the co-ops made the switch, a move for which Chief Mountain directors will be eternally grateful. For its part, Iron Creek began experiencing serious leaks within a month of the fateful trade.*

The ban saved co-ops like East Smoky from leaky turmoil, but it did nothing for the thirty-five co-ops with a collective total of about 2880 miles of bad pipe in the ground and more in storage. Already saddled with construction debts, they simply could not afford to replace the pipe. Thus the provincial government, determined not to see its program scuttled by such an unfortunate twist of fate, brought in a 3306 replacement program to cover the costs of installing new lines. For their part, eleven co-ops (and two county gas systems) launched a lawsuit in July 1977 against Dow Chemical and several by now bankrupt Alberta extruders. In 1984, the Alberta government launched a similar suit on behalf of itself, twenty-four more co-ops, the town of Manning, and ICG Utilities. The suits, and subsequent counter suits by Dow, were still ongoing during the writing of this book.

The Rural Gas Program also made it possible for counties to set up their own gas systems. This 1970 meeting of the County Council of Thorhild launched their gas program.

Pipe woes notwithstanding, the Rural Gas Program continued to post solid progress throughout the rest of the 1970s. By April 1979, co-ops and the utility companies were delivering gas to more than 50 000 rural customers. Inflation continued to be a problem, but more and more co-ops were working their way toward fiscal health as the government continued to step up support for the program. Indeed, several co-ops held debt-retirement ceremonies in 1979. Moreover, a 1978 government study of sixty-three member-owned co-ops found only twelve in financial distress. Speaking to the legislature in March 1978, MLA John Batiuk (PC, Vegreville) said farmers in Saskatchewan were

## COUNTY-OWNED SYSTEMS

*In 1974, County of Two Hills reeve John Dudar tried harder than anyone to start a gas co-op in his area, about 100 miles north-east of Edmonton. But farmers were simply unwilling to dole out $1700 apiece for gas service. Dudar refused to relinquish his dream. "When I was sixteen my father told me I would have problems and make mistakes, but to never give up. I remembered his words, went to council, and said, 'We need gas for our farms. We have to take over the building of a system.'"*

*Like co-ops, counties were eligible for Rural Gas Program grants. But unlike co-ops, counties were able to sign up members at a lower rate because they could, as municipal entities, take out debentures amortized over twenty-five years to cover the rest of the farmer's usual $1700 contribution. When Two Hills' farmers learned they could get gas for only $300 apiece, they readily signed contracts; by 1976 the county was ready to build. It hired an affiliate of Inter-City Gas Corporation (ICG) to design, inspect, and manage the project, which involved the installation of some 676 miles of plastic and aluminum pipe. And the county hired several local people to canvass and get easements. Says Dudar: "Three council members wanted to sell in 1982 because we were in trouble. But instead we hired a new manager, upped the service charge, increased the gas rate, and kept going. Today we are doing just fine."*

*Farmer Frank Wheat of Marwayne, north-west of Lloydminster, persuaded the County of Vermilion to get into the rural gas business in 1975 after he had failed to get the Vermilion River Gas Co-op off the ground. The county charged farmers $400 apiece for gas and financed the rest of its system through debentures, the gas rate, and gas program grants. Unlike Two Hills, Vermilion bought its own construction equipment and hired local workers to install gas lines. Says Wheat: "Our county philosophy was we would do a good job if we did our own job."*

*The County of Smoky Lake, north of Edmonton, and the nearby County of Thorhild also started their own gas utilities with help from the Rural Gas Program. Like many co-ops, the county-owned systems ran into inflation-induced fiscal problems in the early 1980s, but by 1989 had overcome them. However, one county system, Athabasca, did sell out in 1985 to ICG utilities.*

awed by the program's success. "He [the Saskatchewan farmer] still couldn't believe that there are over 40 000 farmers in Alberta with natural gas. He still goes—the old style with horses and wagon—to get trees from the bush [and] to haul coal."

By 1979, the Gas Program had reached more farms than anyone dreamed would be possible. Central Peace Co-op opened its system in an area which even Dr. Horner did not believe could be covered.

## TAKING ON THE NORTH COUNTRY

Still, the co-ops had much work ahead of them as they made the transition from the chaos of construction to the smooth, daily operation of their utilities. Meanwhile, in the north several co-ops were just getting ready to build their massive systems after years of delay caused by inadequate gas supplies and sparse populations.

Nowhere was the government's commitment to bringing gas to every farm more evident than in northern Alberta where several multi-million-dollar steel transmission lines had to be built to deliver gas to remote communities like La Crete (pop. 750), 300 miles north of Edmonton, and the town of Rainbow Lake (pop. 1146), in the top north-western corner of the province. Remarked Dr. Hugh Horner in 1989: "Not even I thought the Rural Gas Program would ever extend into the Peace Country."

# CHAPTER 8

# The Co-ops Come of Age

Lesser Slave Lake MLA Lawrence R. Shaben took over the Utilities department from Allan Warrack in 1979. He was faced with the tasks of making every co-op in Alberta financially stable, and extending the Rural Gas Program to northern Alberta.

When Lesser Slave Lake MLA Lawrence R. Shaben took over the Utilities department from Allan Warrack in 1979, two major challenges faced the Rural Gas Program: extending gas service to the northern-most reaches of Alberta; and, helping co-ops throughout the province achieve financial health.

Shaben's small-business background gave him considerable insight into the sorts of financial and managerial problems facing co-ops. Moreover, as a former town councillor for High Prairie, a town with its own gas system, he was familiar with natural gas. What's more, as an MLA since 1975 he had helped several co-ops in his riding to get grants or meetings with key officials. Thus Shaben was well suited to guiding the co-ops from the frenzied construction to the calmer operational phase.

By 1989, most co-ops had grown into viable, efficient small businesses with well-trained staff, equipment, service vehicles, modest new buildings, and money in reserve. With the bulk of construction behind them, co-op directors could now focus on improving safety and service and expanding their market to include industrial users and, in one case, a national park and American Customs border office.

## BRINGING GAS TO THE NORTH

Vast distances between homes, extensive swampland, and, in some areas, no natural gas, made rural gas service a seemingly impossible proposition for the top third

Central Peace was a northern co-op which started construction in 1977, against very tough odds. Despite a number of problems, the Co-op is a success. Pictured here are chairman George Shemanko, director Bob Scott, and secretary Coreen Bilawchuk.

of the province. Despite the obstacles, more than 70 per cent of the potential customers living in the massive Peace River country north of Edmonton had gas by 1989, with more coming on stream all the time.

As in central and southern Alberta, the persistence of directors and the unflagging financial commitment of the government lay behind the success.

After three years of solid canvassing, directors of the Central Peace Co-op in Spirit River were ready to start construction in the fall of 1977. "We were so excited and planned to put in 192 miles, but after only three weeks and 19.2 miles, the cat broke pulling the plow through frost. That ended the construction season," recalls founding director George Shemanko. But the prospect of cheap fuel for grain dryers motivated Shemanko and fellow directors to continue. Said Shemanko in 1989: "To us, the grain dryer is as important as a tractor or a combine. I would have lost a third of my crop over the last ten years if not for my grain

dryer." Central Peace turned on its first gas in 1978 and today has nearly 600 miles of pipe servicing 551 customers over more than 1600 sq. miles.

It [1980] was a madcap year, says Shemanko, a former auto supply store manager who chaired the co-op board during its peak construction phase. "One large rail shipment of pipe had spikes driven through the coils to attach them to their wooden pallets. That made a hole in the pipe every 40 ft. The construction crew walked out for a week over wages, and the engineer threatened to quit in the middle of the job. Then I couldn't find a contractor able to put in secondary yard lines. So we bought our own ditcher and I spent three weeks from first daylight to dusk putting in the lines myself with the help of two other directors."

The North Peace Co-op in Fairview launched its biggest construction year ever in 1979 after merging with the seven-year-old Manning Co-op about 42 miles to the north. With only about 100 members, the

## THE DUNNS: THE ONE-FAMILY UTILITY

*Surrounded by miles of nothing but forest, rancher George William Dunn was beyond the economic reach of utility company and gas co-op alike. But Dunn, who runs Red Angus cattle on 707 acres, 72 miles north-west of Edmonton, was determined to get gas. Thus he simply formed his own utility company and, in 1973, together with wife Edith and son-in-law Harry Stang, installed a system.*

*With the help of an engineer friend, Dunn designed a system, obtained requisite government approvals, bought some PE pipe, rented a trenching machine, and rigged his own contraption for carrying pipe coils. Then he and his family set to work clearing brush and digging trenches along the side of an old, abandoned trail running straight uphill from his ranch to an Alberta Gas Trunk Line lateral nearly a mile away. Unfortunately, they had to re-dig the trenches when monsoon-like rains filled them in before the pipe could be installed. Finally, after about three weeks, they were ready to lay the pipe, which AGTL hooked to its transmission line.*

*To lay pipe, Dunn mounted his homemade pipe carrier onto a wooden trailer, which he then hooked to an old tractor. While Edith drove the tractor down the winding trail, their son-in-law stood on the trailer and unrolled the pipe into the ditch. Recalls Edith: "The tractor had no brakes and I screamed all the way down." Afterwards, Dunn began shovelling in the trenches. Luckily, a couple of highway crew members who were hunting in their off-hours spotted him toiling and sent in a grader to do the job for him. "They told me nobody should have to work that hard," laughs Dunn.*

*By winter the $4500-system was complete and the Dunns were burning gas purchased through Gas Alberta. NOVA (formerly AGTL) periodically checks their meter and regulator, and the Three Rivers Co-op in nearby Whitecourt will send in a serviceperson should an emergency arise. "We are a private utility, so we could serve other customers if anybody ever moved into the area," says Dunn. But the land around his ranch is protected from development, so the chances of that ever happening are slim.*

George and Edith Dunn could not be serviced by any co-op or utility company, so they built their own system in 1973 with only the help of their son-in-law, Harry Stang.

Manning Co-op was a typical kitchen-table operation run by grain farmer Peter Dechant and his wife, Clara, both of whom received not a penny for their labours. "We hated to give up our little empire, but we were too small to be self-supporting," says Dechant, who was Manning's secretary/treasurer, serviceman, and chairman.

Unwilling to hire contractors as it had for its initial construction in the mid-1970s, North Peace borrowed $400 000 to buy its own equipment and hire a thirty-five-man crew. The following passage from North Peace's written history explains why the co-op opted for self-construction:

*The pipe was ploughed in shallow, there was poor workmanship and improper fittings on regulator stations, there were improper records kept, and there was pipe ploughed on land with no easements. The co-op members were completely walked over and this resulted in excessive damages, cost overruns and extremely poor public relations...the cost overruns broke the gas co-op.*

By the end of 1980 the co-op had connected another 288 members and installed another 289 miles of pipe, including a $3.4-million, 44-mile steel transmission line—financed by the province—from Fairview to Manning.

Although incorporated in 1972, the East Peace Co-op didn't start building until 1979 when it amalgamated with the nearby Smoky River Co-op. "In 1972 we had a system designed, pipe on order, and an engineer hired when we were denied permission by an oil company to use its wells," recalls original chairman Robin Hopkins. "We had to scrap our $7000 design." Stranded without a gas source, East Peace looked to Edmonton which agreed to build a $3.7 million steel transmission line through the heart of the franchise. While frustrating, the delay from 1972 to 1979 enabled directors to negotiate sufficient grants to become the first co-op able to build from scratch a system large enough to accommodate grain dryers.

By the end of 1980, East Peace had completed 85 per cent of its system, which covers 2505 sq.miles and serves more than 800 customers. As had North Peace, this co-op invested heavily in construction machinery and crews. Unfortunately for both co-ops, this would create serious financial problems down the road.

In 1979, the Alberta and federal governments jointly funded the construction of a 30-mile, $3-million transmission line into the town of High Level. The new pipeline enabled ICG Utilities to serve High Level. The next year the department extended the line to La Crete at a cost of $4.5 million. This allowed the Northern Lights Co-op, dormant since its incorporation in 1974, to finally build a distribution system for the nearby farming communities of La Crete and Fort Vermilion,

North Peace Co-op opted to install their own pipeline in the second stage of the project. Serious financial problems were created because of the heavy investment required for machinery and crews, but the construction was completed. This photo shows plowing in progress.

### THE MENNONITE CONTRIBUTION

*In the 1930s, the Depression spurred a number of Mennonites from Saskatchewan to move to the flat spaces and surprisingly temperate climate of Alberta's largely unsettled Peace Country. There they founded the tiny farming community of La Crete, now home to the Northern Lights Co-op.*

*Given their preference for isolation, La Crete residents were at first reluctant to join Northern Lights, which was originally headquartered in Fort Vermilion. Indeed, several residents tried to form their own co-op in 1980 but were persuaded by area MLA and future Utilities Minister Al Adair to run for membership on the Northern Lights board instead. They did, won eight of nine positions, and promptly moved co-op headquarters to La Crete. At first other co-op members worried about the new board's ability to fairly represent the entire franchise. They needn't have fretted. The board proceeded to build a safe and cost-effective system that in 1989 covered a sprawling 1760 sq. miles and served about 1400 customers, Mennonite and non-Mennonite alike.*

which until then had relied on spruce, birch, and poplar for heat. By 1989, the Northern Lights system covered 1760 sq.miles and served 1347 customers.

The province built and financed several more expensive steel transmission lines over the next few years. In 1981, it built an 18-mile, $1.1-million line carrying gas into the town of Rainbow Lake, about 72 miles west of High Level. And in 1982 it built a 34-mile, $2.7-million steel line along the southern shore of Lesser Slave Lake to bring gas into the Swan River Co-op, headquartered in Kinuso.

Incorporated in 1980, Swan River was founded by grain farmer Bill Karpa, who moved with his family from Poland to Alberta when he was eight years old. A longtime member of the Improvement District 17 council, Karpa viewed natural gas service as the key to attracting small industry to the Faust area. "At first we tried to join the Prairie River Co-op, but they had enough problems, and the Telephones and Utilities Department told us we had enough people to go it alone. I did get quite a bit of guidance from Edmo Peyre [original Prairie River chairman] though," recalls Karpa. "And government officials gave us good direction too. My hat is off to them."

The guidance obviously helped. Debt-free since 1986, the co-op has its own building, money in the bank, and in 1988 a net income of $95 000 on gas sales of about $245 000. "And we still haven't stopped expanding," says Karpa. Indeed, office administrator Jean Sheldon says the co-op does about thirty to forty in-fills a year.

## BREAKING THROUGH THE DEBT BARRIER

"Several co-ops were in tough financial shape when I took over the Utilities department," says Shaben. "But a phenomenal change occurred over the next few years. They tightened up management, cut staff, and reduced expenses. They improved so much, I began telling them to put away money in reserve accounts for future construction and repairs."

Indeed, only one gas co-op succumbed to bankruptcy during the gas program's entire history—the St. Paul Lakeland Co-op, in the town of the same name, northeast of Edmonton. In 1982, the co-op was put into receivership after chalking up nearly $3 million in construction cost overruns. When the government refused to bail out the co-op in 1983, it was put into receivership and subsequently sold to ICG Utilities.

The Cochrane Lake Gas Co-op was one of the successful co-ops. It was never in debt for an extended period of time. Chairman and manager, Garnet Ovans is pictured here beside the company van.

Says Shaben: "We had already put lots of money into St. Paul. Had I done a massive bail-out, other co-ops would have felt entitled to similar treatment. I

Arnie Cowell, pictured on his farm, is the chairman of the successful Prairie River Co-op. Like the Cochrane Lake Gas Co-op, Prairie River has a nearly debt-free history and a healthy reserve account.

think...St. Paul may have spurred other co-ops to clean up when they realized the government was not a bottomless money pit."

Of course, not all co-ops had money problems when Shaben took office. Except for a $250 000 loan (repaid within a few months) to finance construction in 1975, the Cochrane Lake Co-op had never been in debt. In 1988, it had an income of $300 000 and a reserve account of $400 000. "We didn't know anything about the gas business when we started. But we had lots of moxie and common sense," says chairman and manager Garnet Ovans. "Besides, being in the military prepares you to tackle anything," adds Ovans, a former test pilot and flight safety director for the Canadian airforce.

The Prairie River Co-op in High Prairie was another with a nearly debtless past and a healthy reserve account ($220 000) by 1988. Says chairman Arnie Cowell: "Our key to success was having a board that was tight with money. We worked out of a plywood shack that barely had room for a desk and a filing cabinet for years and generally only did what we could afford."

Co-ops with similarly bright fiscal histories abound in the province. Still, several co-ops in the early 1980s had nightmarish problems. Among the most troubled were East Peace and North Peace. Recalls East Peace manager Dale Dupuis: "This was a happening little place in 1979. We invested $350 000 in construction equipment and staff—at one point we had thirty-two employees, including three women in the office. But

we nearly went bankrupt. We were $1 million in debt from 1980 to 1983." North Peace, with its expensive new building and in-house construction crew, was equally troubled. High interest rates of more than 20 per cent made life even tougher for both co-ops.

After an intense two-hour meeting with government officials, North Peace decided to sell its equipment and deluxe building, and cut staff from more than forty to eight people. "The government had strongly suggested we take measures to cut our debt," says North Peace chairman Ben Hovelkamp. By 1985 North Peace was debt-free.

East Peace took similar measures in 1983. It trimmed staff down to three, sold its building, and raised its gas rate and monthly service charge to the highest levels in Alberta. Says Dupuis: "We took drastic steps to come to terms with the debt. By 1987 we were debt-free, with $350 000 in retained earnings."

Throughout the province, skilled managers—some hired from private industry, others brought up through the co-op director ranks—guided their co-ops from debt to prosperity. Saddled with a $250 000 debt in 1976, the Birch Hills Co-op near Grande Prairie hired retired general store operator Bill Lewis to turn things around. "He ran the co-op as if it were his own company," recalls former chairman Wallace Tansem. "We had $200 000 in the bank when Lewis left in the early 1980s." How did Lewis do it? "I paid the bills, attended to accounts receivables, and I didn't spend what we didn't have," he says. Throughout the province, co-op after co-op staged a similar turnaround.

## THE COLLECTOR

*As manager Ron Fox of the Northeast Co-op can attest, bill collecting is sometimes hazardous to one's health. Indeed, Fox was nearly run over by a pickup truck while attempting to settle an overdue account. "I was leaning on the hood of this fellow's truck, arguing pretty loudly about his bill. Suddenly, he put the truck in gear and took off. I barely managed to jump out of the way. Then he charged me with assault [he later dropped the charge]. I think he got upset when I told him he wasn't ripping off a big petroleum company, but his own friends and neighbours." In any event, says Fox, "the board teased me that our accounts receivables would really drop once customers found out I assaulted people who didn't pay on time."*

Penniless when it began, the Central Peace Co-op posted $500 000 in revenues in 1988 and in 1989 had the beginnings of a reserve fund. Several thousand dollars in debt in 1977, the Burnt Lake Co-op near Red Deer had more than $150 000 in investments in 1989. The Chin Coulee Co-op in Grassy Lake retired its debt several years ago when the board asked customers to pay an extra $683 apiece for their contracts. Similarly, the Lobstick Co-op in Evansburg paid off its debt by asking members to contribute another $325 apiece. To encourage members to pay up, director John Ohnysty told the following story at a co-op annual meeting: "One day a hunter out in the rain crawled into the hollow of a tree. The hollow shrunk and the hunter got stuck. Then he started to think of all the bad things he had done in life, including not paying his co-op $325. He began to feel so small, he walked out of the hollow."

Today, the Chin Coulee is a thriving co-op. The company van is pictured here in front of the office.

## PURSUING THE BIG CUSTOMER

Four central Alberta co-ops—South Flagstaff, Paintearth, Buck Mountain, and Chain Lakes—were managed, at various times, by Don Olesky. A former car dealer and oilfield foreman, Olesky nursed all of the co-ops from near-bankruptcy to fiscal health by streamlining operations and pursuing new customers. In 1983, he became the first co-op manager to outbid a major utility company for a large industrial service contract—the Union Carbide chemical plant in the Chain Lakes' franchise area north-east of Red Deer. (Under the Rural Gas Program, co-ops have the exclusive right to serve gas users

### THE HUTTERITES

*An unexpected side benefit of the Rural Gas Program was the growth of a close working relationship between co-op boards and the Hutterite colonies within their franchises. In fact, the tiny fifty-three-service Pekisko Co-op in High River was started and built by the MacMillan Hutterite Colony under the direction of Calgary engineer Bill Duffell in 1972.*

*The Triple W Co-op in Wrentham began life in 1971 with six farmers and four Hutterite colonies. Another five colonies joined the co-op the following year. "We've always had Hutterites on the board," says Triple W manager Beryl Brantner. "Actually, Jake Hofer did the lion's share of the work in forming the co-op and once agreed to pose for a directors' picture, the first time he ever allowed himself to be photographed."*

*The Chief Mountain, East Smoky, Chain Lakes, Forty Mile, Little Bow, Bassano, S.R.& B., Paintearth, and Livingstone co-ops also have from three to seven colonies in their areas. Hutterites have tended to be among the Rural Gas Program's biggest and most reliable users. For example, the five colonies in the Little Bow franchise north of Lethbridge consume 25 per cent of the gas sold by the co-op each year. Chief Mountain manager Gerald Beazer says the seven colonies in his co-op "are the main reason Chief Mountain has one of the highest average per customer consumption rates in Alberta."*

The Triple W Co-op services eleven Hutterite colonies, and members of the colonies take an active part in the Co-op. The board of directors is pictured here. This was the first time Jake Hofer (back row, far right) had been photographed.

Don Olesky rescued four co-ops from near-bankruptcy by streamlining operations and getting new customers.

of 10 000 gigajoules a year or less, but must compete with the utilities for bigger customers.)

"We were able to offer a better gas rate and cheaper installation costs," says Olesky. "That enabled us to go after Union Carbide, which uses 350 000 gigajoules a year. We're in the natural gas business just like Canadian Western or Northwestern Utilities. We run as good an operation. Having a big customer like Union Carbide has enabled us to lower our gas rate to rural users by 20 per cent."

By 1989, Chain Lakes, still under Olesky's management, had fifty commercial users burning a collective 980 000 gigajoules of gas a year, 80 per cent of the co-op's total annual gas consumption.

The Chief Mountain Co-op in Cardston was equally aggressive in its search for new customers. In 1981,

Large customers often make it possible for co-ops to lower their gas rates for rural customers. In 1985, the Chief Mountain Co-op provided gas to Waterton Lakes National Park. Pictured here is the opening ceremony for the Park's gas system.

manager Gerald Beazer met the Waterton Lakes National Park superintendent at a Rotary Club meeting. Says Beazer: "He was a Rotarian, I was a Rotarian. I said the park should have gas, and he took the idea to his superiors." Tired of digging out propane trucks in the dead of winter, the wardens readily agreed. Three years later, after a mountain of paperwork and discussion with federal brass, Chief Mountain started building the park's $550 000 system. Accompanied by a federal archaeologist who dug test holes for fossils and artifacts (all he found were buffalo bones), crews finished the job in 1985. With its 160 services, including twenty-four commercial users and a heated government swimming pool, Waterton generated about 20 per cent of the co-op's gas revenues in 1988.

A less lucrative but equally unique Chief Mountain customer is the American Customs office at the Port of Del Bonita in Montana. Located too far from American propane suppliers, the office asked Chief Mountain for service in 1982.

Despite assurances from the National Energy Board that streamlined procedures existed for approving this sort of thing, it took the co-op four long years to obtain requisite permits from a host of American and Canadian officials. Finally, in 1986, the co-op installed a plastic line across the border, becoming Alberta's only international gas co-op and the only one that must file a monthly gas export report with the Energy Resources Conservation Board (ERCB). In 1988, the border office

burned about 700 gigajoules, about four times an average household load. "It's not much," admits Beazer. "But we are in the business of selling gas, not turning away customers." Besides, the American government covered the $6000 cost of installing the line.

## PUTTING SAFETY FIRST

With major construction behind them and most potential customers burning gas, co-ops in the 1980s turned their attention to improving service and safety. Hundreds of co-op employees and directors took government-sponsored courses in everything from management to first aid. The Federation of Alberta Gas Co-ops set up training classes at the Westerra Institute, with government support. The classes were coordinated by federation director Bill Gray, who devoted hours to the cause.

"Directors must take the leadership in safety," says West Parkland director Al Olson. "They must keep staff members abreast of the safety manuals and ensure that safety, clothing, first aid, equipment, and training sessions, are used and kept current. Safety measures and proper instruction are vital to the well-being of the staff, system, and members."

"Alberta co-ops have an excellent safety record and have earned the respect of the major utility companies and government regulatory bodies," says federation head Henry Tomlinson.

Benjamin directors are certainly proud of their safety record. In fact, they recall only two major accidents,

---

**NO SURE THING**

*Half the Dinosaur Co-op was without gas for a week after a major explosion at NOVA's Princess plant near Brooks on February 26, 1980. Former co-op chairman Clint Hendrickson remembers the night well. "The fire lit up the surrounding fields like mid-day up to 6 miles away. The next day melted snow was still boiling in the ditches. The drapes melted to the window of a nearby trailer home. It could have been a catastrophe, but only two operators were at the plant that night. One got badly burned, the other ran away and rolled in the snow whenever he became too hot."*

*The incident taught Hendrickson, now vice-chairman, to take nothing for granted. "We thought we were sitting cozy and cute because we were getting our gas off this big pipeline which had never quit running, which had good gas—then one night Princess burned down and those nice lines didn't serve us a bit."*

---

**A RARE TRAGEDY**

*Ben Hovelkamp heard about the deaths on the radio. Three men laying pipe for the North Peace Gas Co-op were killed when their plow snagged a high pressure NOVA line and sparked a fiery explosion that could be seen for miles around. It happened on July 12, 1974. "It was a rainy day," recalls Hovelkamp, now co-op chairman. "The crew, which belonged to Spade Construction of Calgary, was nearly finished and eager to shut down for the weekend when it happened. The blast instantly killed the men walking behind the plow. The plow and cat drivers were injured but survived. The fellow on the cat was knocked out, but didn't fall off his machine. He woke up about a half mile down the field." As a result of this accident, contractors were required to hand expose all foreign pipelines before plowing.*

neither the fault of the co-op. In the first, fire from a coal oil stove burned down a house shortly before the gas was to be hooked up. In the second, a woman turned on her Cadillac headlights to read her gas meter. Her foot slipped on the accelerator, which sent the car smashing into the meter. The woman was unharmed in the resulting fire, but her vehicle and home were partly scorched.

Since 1987, the Chinook Co-op has devoted considerable time and effort to upgrading its system by rebuilding regulator stations, improving record keeping, and launching special maintenance projects each summer.

Allan Wallace, manager of the Ankerton Co-op, believes in maintaining and upgrading natural gas systems.

"We've really advanced in safety," says a director from the Crossroads Co-op. "I remember one night many years ago, a 2-in. line broke about a mile from the tap. It was blowing wild and the boys were out trying to repair it. They were working down in a hole and we had a skidoo sitting up on the bank with somebody revving its engines to keep its light on so we could see to fix the pipe. By today's standard, that was a bit risky."

## SERVICING THE SYSTEM

"Natural gas systems are like automobiles. They require continual upgrading and maintenance," says Al Wallace, the manager of the Ankerton Co-op in Bawlf. He

### ADVENTURES IN METER READING

*Once or twice a year co-op servicepeople head out in their trucks to read customers' gas meters, a job that can take up to four days in some larger franchises. For the most part without incident, meter reading does have its challenges.*

*Vicious dogs can make reading meters hazardous, says Peter Isaak, manager/serviceman of the Wintering Hills Co-op in Hussar. "Once I just missed getting bit by shoving my meter reading pad in a dog's mouth." Bob Hubl, the former kitchen-table manager of the Diamond Valley Co-op near Red Deer, has been bitten several times by German shepherds tied to gas meters, usually by owners who didn't want to be disconnected for unpaid bills. Wayne Grusie, one of three servicemen at the Birch Hills Co-op near Grande Prairie, doubles as the area's dog catcher. Says Grusie: "Most dogs don't fool with me."*

*Luckily for the servicepeople, customers read their own meters for most months and mail in the results. Although generally workable, this honour system can result in mistakes. Merv Meers, chairman of the Dry Country Co-op remembers receiving an "exorbitant" reading from one customer. "I sent the serviceman out to check it. The lady took him to the power pole, showed him the meter and said, 'There you are. Read it yourself.' The serviceman politely pointed out it was the power meter and then showed her where her gas meter was."*

*A few customers have tried to cheat. One co-op manager reports becoming suspicious after one of his customers won an award for having the most fuel-efficient home in Alberta. "The reason it was so efficient was that he was cheating on his readings."*

should know. In 1979, Ankerton purchased the gas systems of the villages of Rosalind, Heisler, and Strome from the Superior Gas Distribution Company and spent $600 000 upgrading them. When that job finished, Wallace thought things might slow down. "But I've given up on that idea," he laughs. "It is always busy here. Last summer we had three trenchers going steady doing yardwork for customers hooking up new barns or houses to the system. Right now we have a list of jobs as long as my arm."

Simply putting pipe in the ground is not the end of a co-op's work, agrees Tomlinson. "Among the things needing attention is cathodic protection of all metal lines." As an example, he points to the West Parkland Co-op, which has a main pipeline paralleling a Trans-Alta transmission line. According to West Parkland

Co-op service people work day and night to maintain gas service to their customers. Bob Wigton, pictured above, is the field operations manager for Cochrane Lake Gas Co-op.

founding director Ken Porter, voltages from the Trans-Alta facilities have had an electrifying effect on the pipe line. "At one point you could run a drill or power a lightbulb with the voltages off the line. We have to ground the system."

Providing service at any time of day or night—often in sub-zero weather—is among the most challenging aspects of running a co-op. Over the years co-op servicepeople—on call twenty-four hours a day, often for nominal monthly fees in the smaller co-ops—logged long hours repairing pipes, meters, and regulators, and reading meters.

The quality of service equals that of the major utilities, say several co-op directors. Indeed, a few co-ops returned to doing their own servicing after contracting the work out to a utility for a few years. A few smaller co-ops like the fifty-three-member Pekisko Co-op have decided to allow a neighbouring, well-equipped co-op to do all the service work.

Burnt Lake manager Cecil Flake was once called at 7 AM on a thirty below morning about a drop in gas pressure. "About 260 customers were without gas. I called NOVA, which operated the regulating (RMO) station. The company had the pressure back up within twenty minutes. Then we started a massive re-lighting effort. I got to give credit to the community. Pretty well

## FREEZE-OFFS

*During cold weather consumers burn more gas, which lowers the pressure in the gas line. A drop in pressure chills the gas, which can cause any moisture in the pipe to freeze and plug the regulator. When this happens servicepeople must trudge outside, inject methanol into the line to thaw it, and relight the furnace pilot lights of affected customers. Thankfully, this problem is rare. Still, nearly every co-op has its "freeze-off" story to tell.*

*The Bassano Co-op was once plagued by freeze-offs, according to chairman Walter Nasse. Initially his co-op was supplied by several Pan-Canadian wells. In the winter of 1976-77 the wells began petering out, resulting in a severe drop in pressure. Moreover, the gas contained lots of water and Pan Canadian's dehydrating equipment wasn't working properly. Says Nasse: "The wet gas was so bad, half the board of directors was running around trying to thaw people out. That winter we had freeze-ups twice a night. Once I went to the Cluny Hutterite colony to thaw the line. As soon as I returned to my yard, my wife told me to go back—the colony had froze up again. Thankfully, in 1978, we hooked up to a NOVA trunk line and we've had few problems since."*

*Former Battle River chairman Colin Storch once became so annoyed with a clogged regulator that he beat it with a pipe wrench. When that failed to solve the problem, he injected a full 40 gallons of alcohol into the line "to blow the water out of it."*

*Milt Ryan, former chairman of the Sunshine Co-op recalls spending one blizzarding, thirty-five-below New Year's Eve frantically trying to restore the flow of gas to seven of fourteen farms served by the same line. "We pumped some methanol into the line and got the gas flowing to the seven houses, but then the other seven ran out of gas." After repeated injections resulted in the same curious effect, Ryan called Canadian Western, which dispatched its own servicepeople from the surrounding communities of Nanton, Okotoks, Strathmore, and Lethbridge to temporarily connect the afflicted homes to propane tanks. (Gas furnaces are easily converted to propane use.) A few days later when the weather had warmed, Sunshine servicemen, still puzzled by the incident, opened up the line. Inside was a perfectly preserved mouse corpse. Says Ryan: "The pressure of the gas had caused it to slide back and forth along the line, alternately blocking gas to each set of farms."*

Many co-ops took advantage of their improved situations to build permanent offices. East Central Gas Co-op now operates out of a new building.

everybody who knew how to re-light a pilot went down the road to help a neighbour who didn't. By noon, everybody's gas was back on."

To improve service, most co-ops upgraded their facilities during the 1980s. Although many small co-ops

### A SERVICE TALE FROM COCHRANE LAKE

*Cochrane Lake Co-op chairman Garnet Ovans recalls the time lightning blasted a hole into some pipe buried just inside the fence of a particularly difficult landowner. "I told the boys to dig out the line and to carefully cut out the damaged section to take to the ERCB. They took out the piece and rested it on the ground when the landowner, a woman, came dashing over, grabbed the pipe and disappeared. When we told this to an ERCB official, he huffed and puffed, demanded to know where this lady lived, and went to see her. He never got the pipe back either."*

remained as kitchen-table operations, many more built clean, spacious, yet modest headquarters. Others installed computers. For example, the Bow River Co-op put its bookkeeping system on computer and now does its own billings. "We can bill irrigation customers only twice a year instead of monthly," says manager Howard Olson. "That way farmers can irrigate all summer and not pay us till January. It's an extra service we provide. If we can make the books balance with this type of billing, why not?" Most purchased equipment for doing yardwork, repairs, and annual in-fills. Many hired three or four employees, generally a manager, secretary, and one or two servicepeople. Most of the pre-act (that is, incorporated before the Rural Gas Act) co-ops took advantage of government grants to replace their original systems with PE pipe. Central Peace secretary Coreen Bilawchuk worried that customers would be upset when the co-op moved from a rented office into its own, new $150 000 building in 1986. "But instead people were proud of us. They said we finally looked like we were here to stay instead of like some fly-by-night operation."

## TRUDEAU'S TAX

Although unquestionably an era of success for Alberta's co-ops, the 1980s held their problems too. In 1980, the Liberal government of Pierre Trudeau imposed an excise tax on natural gas as part of its National Energy Program (NEP). As a result, co-ops were forced to increase their gas rates by nearly 77 cents a gigajoule over a two-year period. For directors who had weathered noisy criticism over gas prices during the inflationary 1970s, the tax was a deflating blow. In a 1981 report on the Foothills Co-op north of Calgary, a director lamented that, "the dream we had of a reasonably priced fuel for an already troubled agricultural community seems to be fading away with each new Energy Policy Agreement."

Other problems facing the co-ops included the annex-

In 1980, Trudeau's Liberal government imposed an excise tax on natural gas and Co-ops were forced to increase their gas rates. Prime Minister Trudeau is pictured here with Peter Lougheed in November, 1977.

ation of franchise area by expanding cities and towns, and the loss of irrigation customers to electrically-powered pumps. But the co-ops were not alone in overcoming these challenges. Throughout the 1980s, and indeed the 1970s, the Federation of Alberta Gas Co-ops continually lobbied behind the scenes for larger grants, price protection, and compensation for losses due to annexation. No history of the rural gas movement would be complete without a closer look at the work of the federation over the last two decades.

# CHAPTER 9

# The Federation of Alberta Gas Co-ops

In this photo, Federation members are boarding a plane in Texas after completing a tour of Phillips Co. pipe-making plants. Members often paid their own travel expenses because the budget was so small.

As mentioned in chapter 3, the Federation of Alberta Gas Co-ops was instigated in 1964 by engineer Jack Fears and directors from the Gem, Tirol, Meota, and S.R.&B. co-ops. Its membership and profile remained low, however, until after the introduction of the Rural Gas Program when federation directors met in November 1973 at the Olds Agricultural College to plot their organization's future. With gas co-ops springing up all over the province, the federation realized it was now more important than ever to have an organization to represent the interests of rural gas distributors. The federation urged new co-ops to join and it recruited more board members, who would turn out to be devoted and effective lobbyists for the rural gas movement. Commented Cochrane Lake manager Garnet Ovans in 1989: "I think the federation has been the strongest political lobby in rural Alberta."

Farmers' Advocate and former federation chairman Helmut Entrup took charge of the 1973 meeting at Olds College and prodded several capable co-op chairmen into joining the board, which was expanding from five to nine members. Among the new directors were Ste. Anne founder Henry Tomlinson, Forty Mile chairman Alex Onody, George Comstock from Rosebud, Fernand Belzil of St. Paul, and Crossroads chairman John Moran. Paintearth chairman George Ekman became federation chairman.

Remembers Tomlinson: "Helmut tapped me on the shoulder and said, 'Come on, get on the board.' I didn't want to because it would take too much time, but he assured me there would only be three meetings a year."

But soon the federation directors were meeting twice a month for two days at a time in Edmonton to discuss the myriad problems besetting rural co-ops. In 1974 directors had to pay their own travel and accommodation expenses because the federation's annual budget was, at $925, too small to reimburse them until much later. (In late 1974, the government gave the federation a one-time grant of about $50 000 to help it get established.) The federation itself had no real home, with Chairman Ekman running its affairs from the Paintearth office in Castor. Still, the federation wasted no time in lobbying the provincial government for program changes.

## A FORCE TO BE RECKONED WITH

"The ink was hardly dry on the Rural Gas Act when we were looking for more money to cover special circumstances like muskeg, timber, and bush," remembers Tomlinson, who became federation chairman in 1975. "The federation was continually behind the scenes, with government officials negotiating for higher grants. Some co-ops thought we weren't doing anything because we weren't out on the front steps of the legislature publicly demanding things. But we thought it was more effective to negotiate across boardroom tables."

In 1975, Federation directors repeatedly met with Utilities head Doug Brooks to air concerns. Among other things, the federation worried that major utility companies would take over co-ops once co-ops became successful. In a March 1975 letter to Allan Warrack, the minister, George Ekman wrote that directors feared that "we as farmers and co-op officials are being used only to do the ground work, get co-ops going on paying basis only to lose the whole thing to the Utility Companies or a complete civil service take-over." In addition to Doug Brooks, the federation met with Ministers Farran, Warrack, Shaben, Bogle, and Adair, and with deputy ministers J.W. Dodds, R.G. Steele, and Vance McNichol. Sometimes the federation met with the entire Conservative caucus at Government House in Edmonton.

In 1976, a meeting with Federation Board, co-op

The federation helped to provide many training programs for co-op staff. This class had just completed a co-op manager's course in Edmonton.

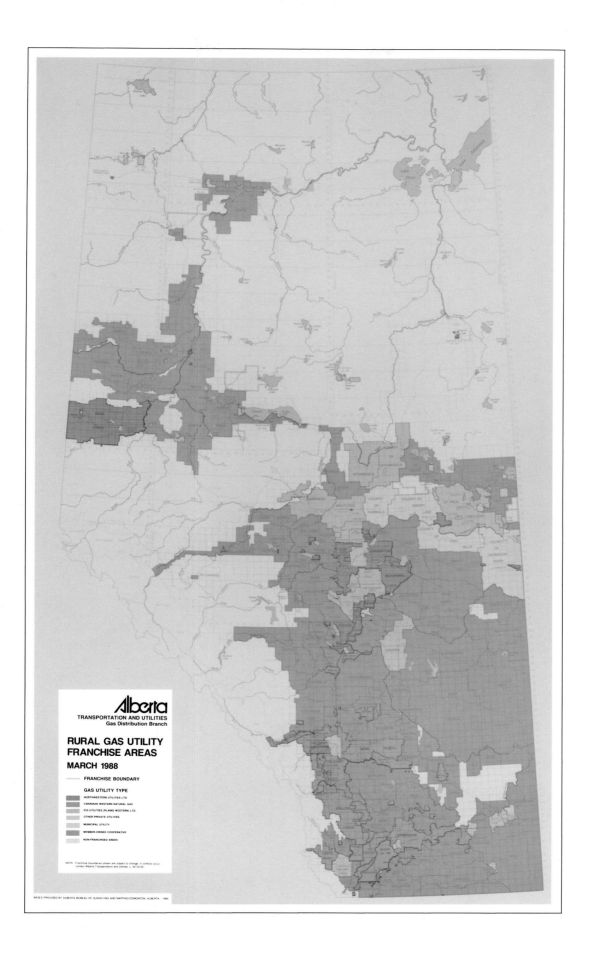

**Alberta**

TRANSPORTATION AND UTILITIES
Gas Distribution Branch

## RURAL GAS UTILITY
## FRANCHISE AREAS

### MARCH 1988

——— FRANCHISE BOUNDARY

#### GAS UTILITY TYPE

NORTHWESTERN UTILITIES LTD.

CANADIAN WESTERN NATURAL GAS

ICG UTILITIES (PLAINS WESTERN) LTD.

OTHER PRIVATE UTILITIES

MUNICIPAL UTILITY

MEMBER-OWNED COOPERATIVE

NON-FRANCHISED AREAS

NOTE: Franchise boundaries shown are subject to change. If conflicts occur
contact Alberta Transportation and Utilities — 427-0125.

BASES PROVIDED BY ALBERTA BUREAU OF SURVEYING AND MAPPING EDMONTON ALBERTA  1984

board members, and government caucus members, which at times grew intense, resulted in the government setting up a Rural Utilities Caucus committee under chairmanship of Neil Webber. This committee dealt with a myriad of problems and was a turning point in the program.

The federation's strategy of quiet consultation worked. Over the years it successfully pressed for several key changes. In 1975, the government dropped a plan to have utility companies build, own, and operate transmission lines after the federation "lobbied the hell" out of the idea. Moreover, the federation pressed for more grants, which led in 1978 to the government's introduction of Gas Transportation Grants to help co-ops with more difficult construction. In 1979, it urged the government to fully fund the replacement of faulty 3306 pipe. And it lobbied harder than any other organization for an extension of the government's natural gas rebate plan in 1975, 1978, and 1981. The federation even ran ads in big city newspapers urging people to write their MLAs. "I was amazed by how many people didn't know the rebates existed," says Tomlinson.

## WORKING FOR CO-OPS

In addition to lobbying government, the federation advised co-ops on how to handle problems with suppliers and contractors. Over the years it helped to provide training programs for co-op staff. It instituted regular zone meetings, which were attended by government officials, to voice complaints and new ideas. And, perhaps most important of all, in 1974, the federation obtained a common insurance policy for its members. "It was expensive for co-ops to get insurance on their own because companies didn't understand what they were being asked to insure," says Tomlinson. "Individual co-ops were paying as much in premiums in 1973 as they do today for twenty times the coverage. A combination of large numbers and good safety practices has enabled us to obtain insurance at a reasonable cost."

In 1974, the federation board engaged the services of M.K. Power, an insurance consultant, to design an insurance policy for the co-ops and municipal systems. All federation members still use this policy. Mike Power remains as insurance consultant. The insurance package is handled by Hal Roulston of Reed Stenhouse Ltd.

In June 1975, George Ekman resigned from the federation for personal reasons, leaving Henry Tomlinson in charge. Alex Onody became vice-chairman, and George Comstock secretary/treasurer. Comstock ran the federation office from a lean-to addition to his house. His wife, Jewel, handled phones and paperwork, while George juggled farming, Rosebud co-op affairs, and federation business. The Comstocks grew even busier in 1977 when they took over administration of a benefits and pension plan for co-op employees. And in 1980, they began processing applications for the federal government's Canada Oil Substitution Program (COSP), which offered a $800 grant to homeowners who switched to natural gas from oil. In 1986, the federation set up headquarters in Edmonton.

George Comstock became secretary/treasurer for the federation in 1975. He is pictured here with his wife, Jewel, who helped him run the federation office from their home.

Other federation directors were equally busy visiting co-ops throughout the province. In 1975, in the middle of a postal strike, Tomlinson organized the federation's first trade show. "I had to phone fifty or sixty companies to invite them." About forty companies showed up to display their products at the federation's 1975 annual convention at Edmonton's Westin Hotel. The show has since become a regular convention feature.

## TACKLING OTTAWA

In 1977, the federation supported Unifarm in tackling Revenue Canada. In 1974, Revenue Canada's Calgary office told Charles Brantner, the brother-in-law of Triple W manager Beryl, that he could claim his $1700 contract price as a business expense, a fact quickly passed on by the Brantners to every co-op in the province. Unfortunately, Ottawa disagreed with Calgary's interpretation of the tax law, and disallowed the claim. The federation and Unifarm decided to make Charles's a test case and filed an appeal on his behalf with the tax review board, which ruled in Brantner's favour.

In 1981, the federation battled Ottawa again, this time over its National Energy Program, which included a tax on natural gas that started at 28 cents per mcf and which was to rise to $4 per mcf. Gas bills rose virtually overnight. The federation argued the tax hurt low income earners and farmers who used natural gas in their operations. Moreover, it was discouraging people from using gas and hurting the manufacturing industry, which used natural gas as a feedstock in many products. The federation wrote a brief to this effect,

mailed it to every MP and, in January 1981, sent 18 delegates to Ottawa to bang on MPs' doors.

Before flying to Ottawa, the delegates met in a hotel near the Calgary airport to plan strategy. Upon arrival in the capital later that day, they split into four groups, each with a team captain, and fanned out through the parliament buildings. To their dismay they discovered that advance copies of their brief had gone largely unread; some had been shredded. Undaunted they photocopied more, in French and English, using the office of Conservative MP Gordon Taylor (Alberta - Bow River) as a base of operations.

Meanwhile, Tomlinson's team, which included Len Gabert, Cecil Flake, and George Moroz, went to visit Liberal MP Ian Watson, chairman of the Standing House Committee on Energy, and the only MP whom the Federation had pre-arranged to meet. On the way into Watson's office, Tomlinson asked a secretary if she had noticed an increase in her gas bill lately. Her reply: "Yes, Lougheed is really putting it to us." Says Tomlinson: "She had no idea this tax existed. But then neither did any MP east of Alberta."

Delegation member Henry Dick of the Bow River Co-op was astounded by the federal politicians'

In 1981, the Federation of Alberta Gas Co-ops sent 18 delegates to Ottawa to lobby against the tax on natural gas included in the National Energy Program. The delegates eventually met with Conservative leader, Joe Clark.

ignorance. Recalled Dick in 1989: "Some of those guys were dumb, so dumb. It's hard to believe they were elected MPs. I remember the energy critic for the NDP saying, 'What have you got against dinging the big oil companies?' I said to him, 'Man, you're not dinging the big oil companies, you're dinging all the small consumers all the way down the line. The oil companies will just pass the extra costs on.'"

A key passage of the federation brief dealt with this misconception on the part of many MPs: "In imposing the tax, the revenue department was probably under the impression it was taxing rich multi-national oil companies or the gas distribution companies. This is not the case. Every penny will ultimately come out of the pockets of the individual who may or may not be in a financial position to pay his share."

After listening to the federation's concerns and hearing of Tomlinson's difficulty obtaining a meeting with Roland Priddle, then deputy minister of Mines and Minerals, Watson picked up the telephone. Recalls Tomlinson: "While we were sitting there, he called Priddle and said, 'What the hell is going on over there? These people have come 2000 miles to talk to you, they should have the courtesy of a reply.'" When Tomlinson returned to his hotel room that night, the light was flashing on his phone. Roland Priddle had called. "I called him and we agreed to meet the next day at 9 AM in my room."

All eighteen delegation members were awaiting Priddle when he arrived promptly the next day. Says Tomlinson: "He perched on the dresser and listened while we explained our position. We listed all the products which used natural gas as a feedstock and when we had finished I said, 'And if what we've said gives you a headache, go take an aspirin, because that's made from natural gas too.'"

After the meeting, the group returned to the parliament buildings and visited nearly every MP's office. Alberta MPs Taylor and Gordon Towers (Red Deer) raised the matter of the federation's tax protest in the House of Commons. The federation held a press conference, lunched with a *Toronto Star* reporter, met with Conservative leader Joe Clark, and talked with representatives of the Liberal and NDP caucuses. Says Tomlinson: "We spent the first ten minutes with the Liberals trying to convince them we hadn't been sent by Premier Lougheed or a major oil company. We were here on our own nickel representing consumers."

The federation didn't persuade the Trudeau govern-

## CHAIRMAN TOMLINSON

*The evolution of hog farmer Henry Tomlinson into one of the most effective lobbyists in the province began on April 19, 1972, in the Onoway Community Hall. The local chapter of Unifarm had called a meeting for that night to discuss gas service. But the chapter leader, having had some teeth pulled earlier that day, was in no mood to speak and so invited Tomlinson to chair the proceedings. By evening's end, he found himself elected chairman of the Ste. Anne Gas Co-op. In 1973, he landed a directorship with the Federation of Alberta Gas Co-ops and within two years he became its chairman, a post he's held ever since.*

*Born in 1934, Tomlinson grew up on his parents' mixed grain farm in Onoway, about 30 miles west of Edmonton. Like so many other rural Albertans his age, Tomlinson's chores as a youth included shovelling coal into the basement furnace and cleaning out the ashes every day. In 1967, Tomlinson took over the family farm, managing to run it over the next sixteen years despite his heavy involvement in the Ste. Anne Co-op and the Federation. "I had to take many hours out from combining to settle problems," remembers Tomlinson. "Sometimes my wife, Janet, would do the seeding." Finally, in 1983, Tomlinson sold his farm to work full-time on federation business.*

*In taking on the federation chairmanship, Tomlinson was following a long line of rural gas pioneers. S.R.& B. Co-op founder Art Larson was the federation's first chairman in 1964. Tirol director and future Farmers' Advocate Helmut Entrup took the helm briefly in the late 1960s, followed by Gem Co-op director Ernie Walde, who held the job until 1973, when George Ekman, the chairman of the Paintearth Co-op, assumed the post for two years.*

*The normally chatty Tomlinson grows quiet and shrugs when asked why he has devoted so much of his life to the rural gas movement. But perhaps his sentiments are best captured in the words of friend and fellow gas crusader Helmut Entrup: "We weren't happy being the forgotten country bumpkin. We wanted to stand on our own two feet and be treated equal to the people in the cities."*

ment to revoke its tax, but they did generate public awareness about natural gas and certainly helped to persuade the Conservatives of the unfairness of the excise tax. As well they convinced many MPs that if they wanted consumers to switch from oil to gas, they

Henry Tomlinson (far right) became chairman of the Federation in 1975, and he still held the position in 1989. He is shown here in 1986 at the grand opening of the Evergreen Co-op. Also shown (left to right) are councillor Henry Rondeau, County of Parkland, local M.L.A. Shirley Cripps, and assistant deputy minister Doug Brooks.

should not peg the price of gas at 85 per cent of oil because it would be too expensive. The price of gas was later pegged at 65 per cent. And they impressed Liberal MP Watson, who in April 1981 invited the federation back to make a formal presentation to the Standing Committee on Energy.

Then in 1983, Henry Tomlinson, George Comstock, Alex Onody, and Garnet Ovans again visited Ottawa, this time to present a brief on behalf of the fertilizer industry, which was hurt by the excise tax and wanted it removed.

## NEW CHALLENGES

As the co-ops entered the 1980s, they were confronted by a new challenge—urban sprawl. "The growth of small towns poses a special threat to the future of the

co-ops," said a story in the February 18, 1981, edition of the *Calgary Herald*. Indeed, more and more towns were beginning to annex rural areas that were franchised to gas co-ops. Upon annexation, the utility company serving a town would point out to the town council that an agreement existed which gave the company the exclusive right to serve all areas within the town boundaries—including the annexed areas.

Naturally, the co-ops opposed this view based on the simple but logical principle that "we were here first!" However, there did not appear to be any clear legislative authority to support the co-ops' position. In the meantime, bewildered town councils were being told that they lacked the full authority to make a decision on the matter.

Faced with these facts, the Federation lobbied the government to clarify its legislation and to give the co-ops some rights—including the right to reasonable compensation for lost franchise territory. In 1983, the government amended the Municipal Government Act to grant town councils the full authority to decide which utility should serve the annexed area. In addition, the amendment laid out some clear guidelines for compensation. From then on, everyone knew the rules for serving newly annexed areas.

The Federation of Alberta Gas Co-ops grew throughout the 1990s. Henry Tomlinson is pictured here addressing the 1985 federation convention.

However, since the amendments were not retroactive, the position on many previous annexations was still vague and undecided. Fortunately, in 1985, a test case involving the Rocky Gas Co-op surfaced before the Public Utilities Board. The Board's decision on the matter was hailed as a victory for the co-ops, and resulted in the co-op receiving a substantially greater amount of compensation than it had previously been offered by the utility company.

A second case before the Board in 1985 tested the value of the government's 1983 amendment to its law. In that case, the town of Edson was granted approval by the Board to enter into a franchise agreement with the Yellowhead Gas Co-op. This precedent-setting ruling served as a model for future decisions affecting annexations of lands franchised to co-ops although, by 1988, only three other co-ops—Three Hills, East Central, and Big Country—had entered into special franchise agreements to serve annexed areas.

The federation helped pay the legal costs for both test cases. Additionally, it lobbied Edson town council on Yellowhead's behalf. "I knew the mayor owned the local IGA store," says Tomlinson. "So I told council big companies shouldn't get everything. 'We don't need a Safeway in every town.' That caught the mayor's ear."

Yet another challenge confronted co-ops in southern Alberta in 1984, when the Utilities department introduced a low interest loan program to help farmers install electrically powered irrigation—Three Phase Power—systems. Although not intended to do so, the program prompted many gas irrigators to switch to more convenient electricity. "We lost up to 150 customers and 100 000 gigajoules because of the three phase power program," says original Bow River Co-op director Henry Dick. To combat this new competition, the federation joined with the major utilities in the formation of the Alberta Natural Gas Distributors Association (ANGDA).

Utilities Minister, Bob Bogle, listened to ANGDA's concerns about the three phase power program.

As its first task, the committee lobbied Utilities Minister Bob Bogle about the problem. A former high school teacher and guidance counsellor, Bogle had been a strong proponent of rural gas co-ops ever since his election to the legislature in 1975 as the MLA for Taber-Warner. Thus he was quite receptive to the committee and in 1985 agreed to limit grants to farmers setting up new irrigation systems.

Additionally, the ANGDA set up the Joint Utility Irrigation Committee (JUIC) to promote the economic advantages of gas-powered irrigation with booklets, folders, newspaper supplements, a television program, trade fair displays, and seminars.

Among the selling points was a cost comparison showing that farmers could save several hundred dollars a year by using gas rather than electricity to power irrigation pumps.

## BEATING THE ODDS

In general, the federation did two things to ensure the success of the Rural Gas Program, says Ernie Walter, the federation's lawyer since the mid-70s. "It provided the vision, and, this may sound corny, but it provided the inspiration for co-ops. There were many trying times in the early years of the program when it seemed the system would never get on its feet and everybody lost faith except for Henry and the directors of the federation. They were the glue that held this whole thing together."

Over the years Walter, a senior partner with the Edmonton-based law firm Brownlee Fryett, has handled a variety of issues for the federation and gas co-ops involving everything from annexations to easements to engineering contracts. In many ways, the pairing of Walter and the federation was a natural. Born

ANGDA set up the Joint Utility Irrigation Committee (JUIC) to promote the economic advantages of gas-powered irrigation. This table was set up at the federation convention.

Pictured here in 1986 is the Federation of Alberta Gas Co-ops board of directors meeting with the Minister of Transportation and Utilities Al "Boomer" Adair and Deputy Minister Vance MacNichol (lower left).

in Paradise Valley, south-west of Lloydminster, Walter's own rural roots ran deep. Moreover, his firm—founded by former Alberta premier John Edward Brownlee—had been acting for rural municipalities since the 1930s. Shortly after the introduction of the Rural Gas Program, the firm had helped several counties establish their own gas systems. Thus Walter and Tomlinson had plenty to talk about when the two met at the federation's annual convention in 1974. Recalls Walter: "Henry said, 'I like your style young fella, I think we can work together.' " Walter happens to be Tomlinson's age.

"In the early days we were running from one fire to another," says Walter. "Since then the federation has matured and developed a credibility with government and the major utilities. In working with Tomlinson and the other directors I have learned that

Ernie Walter was the Federation's legal counsel since the mid-1970s. He is pictured here in 1986.

Utilities Minister Bob Bogle has long been a strong supporter of the rural gas co-ops. Here he addresses the Federation annual meeting.

people with a clear vision of what they want to do can overcome great odds and accomplish amazing things."

As the 1980s rolled to a close and the Rural Gas Program's objectives were largely achieved, some wondered if the federation might become less active. But, as the federation's 1988 brief to the Alberta government proudly notes, "Such is not the case! In order to stay competitive in the gas distribution industry, we are becoming more knowledgeable and proficient in our skills in many areas such as employee training, safety and customer service." With 113 gas distributor-members representing more than 68 000 customers, the federation will no doubt continue to play a leading role as Alberta's gas co-ops face the challenges of tomorrow.

Pictured here is Laverne Owen, secretary at the Prairie River Co-op.

# EPILOGUE

## *Those Crazy Little Co-ops*

In 1977 Tom Brown came to work for the Alberta Rural Gas Program after a stint of several years with the British Gas Corporation, the world's largest gas utility. "I'd assumed I would be dealing with utility companies. When I found out about all these little farmer-owned co-ops, I thought the idea was crazy," says Brown. Of course, today Brown, now executive director of the Gas Utilities Branch, is among the co-ops' greatest admirers. "I am a convert."

The achievement of "all those little farmer-owned co-ops" is truly remarkable and unique. There are no gas cooperatives anywhere else in the world, and certainly no rural gas distribution system as extensive, safe, and cost-effective as Alberta's. Since 1973, the Rural Gas Program has resulted in fuel savings of about $1.2 billion to rural residents and industry, well above the $600 million capital cost of the program. As of 1989, the average rural customer was saving $800 per year on fuel by using natural gas instead of propane. At current energy prices, the total annual fuel saving to rural Alberta amounts to roughly $100 million, an important cost reduction in an increasingly competitive farm marketplace.

Says Henry Tomlinson: "The real, lasting value of the investment in the Rural Gas Program is the amount of money saved in heating and farm costs. Natural gas is delivered to the user ready to use, clean, environmentally acceptable, efficient, and safe. The comfort and convenience may be taken for granted by city dwellers, but the older rural generation who remember coal,

Natural gas is invaluable to Alberta agriculture. This grain dryer fuelled by natural gas can make a farmer competitive in today's demanding market.

George Ekman chaired the Federation of Alberta Co-ops during its formative years, from 1973 to 1975.

wood, and cow chips can truly appreciate natural gas."

The program has resulted in other economic benefits. The co-ops have generated local employment by hiring staff and purchasing services and supplies from community businesses. Attempts to diversify the Alberta economy have been made easier thanks to reliable rural gas service, an important amenity to industry. In dollar terms, the Rural Gas Program has been a success. In human terms, the program is proud testament to the will, determination, and ingenuity of rural Albertans.

In a sense, Brown's initial impression was probably right. It was rather crazy to think all those little farmer-owned co-ops could build one of the most extensive pipeline systems in the world. Chances are a program like this wouldn't have worked anywhere else. But the men and women who built and operated the co-ops were, in many cases, the sons and daughters of immi-

The dry areas of Alberta have been able to increase their productivity with natural gas irrigation pumps.

grant homesteaders—second generation pioneers. In short, they were made of stern stuff and they'd been further steeled by growing up during the Depression. Burnt Lake Co-op manager Cecil Flake has no doubt that the lessons of the Dirty Thirties were a significant factor in the program's success. "Most people in the Rural Gas Program grew up through the Depression," he observes. "During that time everybody worked hard and pitched in. It was a good education."

Now that they've conquered all manner of adversity, most co-op directors are a little awed by their accomplishment. "It was a far-fetched dream," says Evergreen Co-op manager Leah Lysak. "We couldn't know then how it would turn out. But we have done it. We have done something for ourselves that many said couldn't be done and we have made a mark on our community."

Simply turning on the gas for the first time was enough to amaze Eric Dick of the Rosemary Co-op.

"It was a bit like turning on electric lights for the first time. We finally saw the result of all our leg work. I was kind of surprised it actually worked."

With the awe comes genuine appreciation for the benefits of natural gas. "The most important effect has been the availability of efficient, convenient, clean fuel to heat shops, hog and poultry barns," says Kneehill Co-op manager Terence Toews. The next most important effect? "No more getting up at 5 AM to stoke the furnace as my father did." Former East Central Co-op director Don Hall agrees. "The Rural Gas Program meant a lot to us because we'd been hauling that coal for thirty-four years."

But for Henry Dick of the Bow River Co-op, the program's greatest benefits were human ones. The program forged lifelong friendships in a way that only shared adversity and triumph can.

"Not once has anybody ever gotten angry and gone

Ken Gerber, pictured here with his wife, Edith, was the first chairman of Ankerton Gas Co-op. This co-op has grown from 26 members in 1968 to nearly 1600 in 1989.

home mad. Not once in all those years. It really says something for people in the community. The co-operation among everyone to better our way of life was just out of this world." Laughs a director from the Crossroads Co-op: "We probably all went into this thing thinking we'd be done in six months to a year. It took a little longer than we thought, but it sure has been a lot of fun."

To Lac La Biche manager Phil Lane, the most striking aspect of the last fifteen years has been the dedication of co-op directors. "When I was reading the minutes from 1972 to date, one of the things that amazed me was not so much the fact that they put in so many miles of pipe or hooked up so many customers, but that these directors were able to hang together, maintain the dream, and never give up."

# *Alberta Natural Gas Co-ops*

## ALDER FLATS

- Headquartered in Alder Flats.
- Total area: 129.05 sq. miles
- Total services: 184
- Total pipe installed: 79.54 miles

**Directors Past and Present:** Morris Dunn, Norman Moore, D. Parker, Gordon Foss, R. Wennerstrom, R.F. Hare, R. Parker, O. Knight, Alex Damyluk, Dale Sargent, Ray Tompkins, Gerald Seely, Ted McLean, Norman Fontaine, Louis Thrower, Joren Kofed, Dale Nestegard, Victor Forchuck, Harvey Miller, O.J. Schauerte, Ted Maciborsky, Gordon Shanks, Doug Patton, Jim Hammond, John Chung, John Darroch, Orville Knight, Dalton Parker, J.L. Seely, Bob Chapchack.

**Manager:** Leigh Miller.

Directors of this co-op designed their own distribution system with the help of an engineer from the local sour gas plant. Along with pipeline expertise, the plant has supplied the co-op with cheap gas (52 cents per gigajoule/55 cents per mcf) since 1971. When this supply contract expires in 1991, directors, who have never held an opening ceremony, say they may hold a "crying" one instead.

Directors still talk about one farmer at their organizational meeting who shared a dangerously desperate method for thawing his propane tank. " 'It had frozen one time too many,' he told us. So he put some lawn mower gas into a whisky bottle, stuffed a rag into it, lit it, and threw it at the tank."

## ANKERTON

- Headquartered in Bawlf.
- Total area: 850.57 sq. miles
- Total services: 1594
- Total pipe: 775.18 miles

**Directors Past and Present:** James Helmig, Ken Gerber, John Davis, Morris Leiren, Lil Bohmer, Charles Archibald, Wilf Aspenes, Eric Beddoes, Norman Berg, Laurie Blades, Edward Blatz, Norm Burkhart, Henry Ehlert, Bert Friend, Lloyd Hagen, George Hetzner, Paul Kletzel, Walter Komarnisky, Frank Lemke, William Lindsay, Ole Lovrod, Charles McDonald, Milton Nielson, Robert Olsen, Gordon Peacock, Bernard Rostaing, Ken Schneider, William Stern, Gary Stordahl, Gordon Teske, Robert Wilcox, Allan Kerr, Robert Lee, Stuart MacGregor, James Mohler, Donald Uglem, Leonard Hoffman, Karol Ilnicki, Jerome Kalawsky, Calvin Sitler, Russel Nielson, Jerome Beuerlein.

**Manager:** Al Wallace.

This co-op grew from only twenty-six members in 1968 to nearly 1600 in 1989, thanks partly to its merger with the proposed Melrose Co-op of Bawlf in 1973 and its purchase in 1979 of a privately owned utility—Superior Gas Distribution. Selling contracts has never been hard for Ankerton, which was serving 97 per cent of its potential customers by 1989.

On November 7, 1975, Ankerton invited suppliers, consultants, contractors, government officials, and, of course, members, to an "official opening" banquet. According to the local *Booster* newspaper, which covered the event, Utilities Minister Allan Warrack commended the co-op for doing what "they said couldn't be done, making this a truly significant event in the development of rural Alberta." Also on hand was Farmers' Advocate Helmut Entrup who praised Ankerton for "realizing a dream."

## ATLEE

- Headquartered in Jenner.
- Total area: 252.9 sq. miles
- Total services: 34
- Total pipe: 57.94 miles

**Directors Past and Present:** Stan Krause, Jim Musgrove, Lawson McBurnie, Alec McLachlan, Dave White, Simon Schonhofer, Ernie Aebly, Eric Musgrove.

**Manager:** Stan Krause.

Nearly 2.8 miles separate each of the customers in this tiny sixteen-member co-op, giving Atlee one of the highest pipe-per-capita ratios in the rural gas system.

Original director Jim Musgrove likes to tell the story of a trick played on the co-op's consultants: "The government wanted several copies of everything, which was getting to our contractor. So we had somebody make a rubber stamp of Mickey Mouse looking aghast at a pile of papers, and we stamped this mouse on all our paperwork. Everybody laughed except our engineer who had to bring the papers to officials in Edmonton."

# BASSANO

- Headquartered in Bassano.
- Total area: 431.72 sq. miles
- Total services: 185
- Total pipe: 203.73 miles

**Directors Past and Present:** David R. Hall, Peter Steinbach, K. Matoba, Roy Clark, Harvey Fuller, Walter Christensen, Abe Reimer, Wayne Arrison, Arnold Armstrong, Don Fraser, Walter Nasse, Martin Hofer, Fred Saunders, Robert Lassiter, Angus Clyne, Barry Bell, Don Bartman, Allan Konshuh, Peter Paetkau, Wesley Rowen, Robert Beringer, Jim Reimer.

**Manager:** Walter Nasse.

With two major highways, three railroads, ten canals, three creeks, and a bridge to cross, this co-op had to borrow lots of money to cover the unexpectedly high cost of construction. When it finally paid off its loan in March 1979, the co-op held a mortgage burning, with director Roy Clark holding the ashtray and fellow director Harvey Fuller lighting the match. A utility company has offered to purchase the system since, but manager/chairman Walter Nasse says, "the board told me to put those offers in file thirteen."

In 1989 the co-op moved into its own new building, a major improvement over its previous homes which had included a spare room in a member's house, space in an old curling rink, and a portion of the original town office.

# BATTLE RIVER

- Headquartered in Ferintosh.
- Total area: 405.78 sq. miles
- Total services: 819
- Total pipe: 352.2 miles

**Directors Past and Present:** Chauncey Flint, Alex Drummond, Merv Giem, Leroy Snider, Ted Eikerman, Ernest Lindholm, Keith Braim, Ken Wold, Fritz Enarson, Don Graff, Glen Bussard, Frank Jackson, Joel Schiele, Robert Keller, Dan Astner, Blake Norman, Norman Berglund, Reg Fuller, Terry Gabert, Melvin Sonnenberg, Larry Steves, Ray Megli, Mel Guderjan, Barbara Lede, Albin Anderson, Ian Bastin, Hans Brockhoff.

**Managers:** Don MacMillan, (June Giem, Darrell Skjavland).

After buying itself out from Anchor Pipelines in 1974, this co-op held an official opening at the farm of MLA Gordon Stromberg (PC, Camrose). While setting up the standpipe for the traditional flaring, somebody accidentally plowed through Stromberg's septic tank. Luckily, the resultant stench was cleared up before Stromberg and then-Utilities minister Roy Farran flew in from Edmonton for the ceremony. "Afterwards we cracked open a bottle of Irish malt whiskey for Farran," says founding director Merv Giem.

Giem was one of the few co-op people forewarned that natural gas would skyrocket in price. "We did get some timely advice from one of our original gas suppliers. He told us gas was going to go up about ten times in price. We laughed at him. Within two years he was right."

## BENJAMIN

- Headquartered in Rimbey.
- Total area: 214.87 sq. miles
- Total services: 207
- Total pipeline: 154.8 miles

**Directors Past and Present:** Bruce Christianson, Tom Thomas, Rudy Heyn, Bob Sears, Sid Hopper, Chuck Simpson, Fred Harrison, Eddie Grumbach, Greg Beddoes, Art Frayn, Ivan Houston, Jack Hansen, Melvin Dolman.

**Manager:** Anko Buwalda.

Directors formed Benjamin after being refused membership in the Gull Lake, Deer Creek, Rocky, and Diamond Valley co-ops. When they could get only a 37 per cent sign-up, directors approached Utilities assistant deputy minister Doug Brooks for permission to start anyway. Brooks said, "Okay, we'll give you a chance." Plowing began in September 1975 and was complete one month later.

One crew insisted on plowing through a swamp despite a director's fervent protests. Sure enough, the plow cat sank nearly 7 ft. into the muck, becoming mired for the next thirteen hours until another cat could winch it out. "That taught them to pay attention to farmers," laughs one director.

## BIG COUNTRY

- Headquartered in Morrin.
- Total area: 629.86 sq. miles
- Total services: 456
- Total pipe: 333.6 miles

**Directors Past and Present:** Howard Persinger, Colin Storch, Gordon Adams, Don Adams, Doug Stanger, Jack McKay, Rick Sharpe, Norman Chambers, Mel McNaughton, Gordon Dodd, Doug Grenville, Murray Johnson, Walter Stoneman, Larry Meyer, Fred Shadlock, Michael Rowe, Leonard Vandale, Albert Moe, George Michie, Tom Kempling, Jack Helmer, Jim Wilson, Stan Schedel, Charlie Laisnez, Larry McKee, Gerald Foesier, Dennis Walker, Jim Gaschnitz, Tony Hermus, Joe Gaschnitz, Gerry Kopjar, Gordon Watson.

**Managers:** Colin Storch, Jerry Kostrup.

In the mid-1980s, this co-op nearly lost its biggest customer, the Tyrrell Museum of Paleontology, to annexation by the city of Drumheller. But the Federation of Alberta Gas Co-ops helped the directors win the right to continue serving the museum, making Big Country the second of only three co-ops to retain an annexed portion of a franchise area. (Yellowhead and Three Hills are the other two.)

Original chairman Colin Storch will never forget one trip into Edmonton to pick up a grant cheque. His driver, Percy Sibbald, hit the side of a bus at a busy intersection. "We sat there for an hour waiting for police and transit inspectors to arrive. Traffic was completely stopped. People had to get off the bus and walk. Finally they moved us out of the way into a service station."

# ALBERTA RURAL GAS PROGRAM
## PROGRAM CAPITAL COSTS VERSUS FUEL
## COST SAVINGS TO CONSUMERS

## Total Program Summary

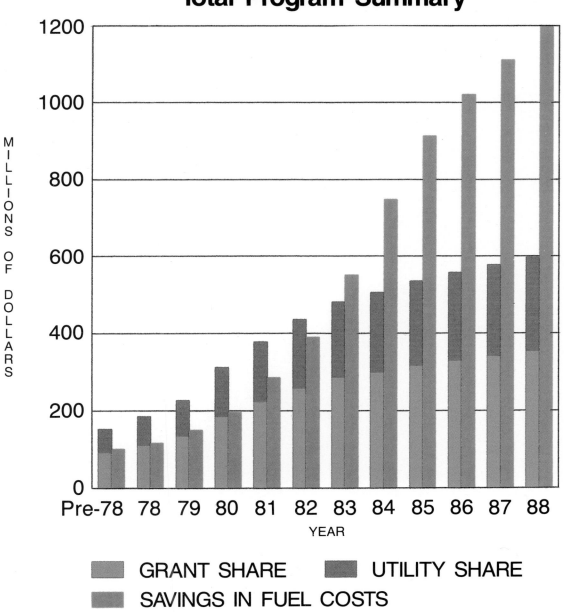

## BIRCH HILLS

- Headquartered in Wanham.
- Total area: 920.06 sq. miles
- Total services: 698
- Total pipe: 434.56 miles

**Directors Past and Present:** Wallace Tansem, Carl Nagel, Dennis Sather, Nick Poohkay, Gunder Sveinunggaard, Frank Lambright, Ben Boettcher, Matthew Wozniak, Mike Nikolaychuk, Clarence Webber, Alex Bice, George Sohramm, Klass Sipma, Edmund Pawluski, Rudolph Knitel, Bernhard Schuett, John Stanich, Albert Wells, Ken Hansen, Rosaire Chenard, Allan Scott, Robert Chaput.

**Managers:** Jim Rutherford, Bill Lewis, Ray Willoughby, Doug Dueck, Wayne Grusie.

After many trips to Edmonton, directors persuaded the government in 1974 to provide grants covering the extra costs of building a system big enough for grain dryers. Original chairman Wallace Tansem recalls the deciding meeting: "Our MLA Grant Notley arranged a meeting for us with Dr. Hugh Horner and several other officials in April 1974. Horner spread a map of our area on the floor of his office, and got down on his hands and knees to figure out how we could later loop our lines to accommodate dryers. It became apparent it would be much easier to just build a big enough system right away. We got our grants in June." Adds Tansem: "The prospect of a better way to dry their grain along with a cost saving proved to be the incentive for many to sign up for gas."

## BOW RIVER

- Headquartered in Vauxhall.
- Total area: 1438.80 sq. miles
- Total services: 1106
- Total pipe: 812.32 miles

**Directors Past and Present:** Henry Dick, Gerald Vanden Dungen, George Friesen, Ken Whitmore, Albert Glas, Ray Wakelin, Dale Reynolds, Selmer Peterson, Pete Stokes, Donald Beagle, Darrel Maronda, Dale Dunn, Bob Stevenson, Doug Walker, Henry Hagen, Bryan Sproule, Glen Tolton, Jake Unruh, Leroy Howg, Joe Lindstedt, Eric Pedersen, Harry Wolosuk, Eric McKay, Jerry Lukey, Ron Wright, Tom Emelson, John Mitchell, Harvey Severtson, Gil Pakarno, Mel Williamson, Roy Hammergrin.

**Managers:** Howard Olson, Richard Thorne.

Construction crews had to ford more than 300 canals, ranging from 4.9 ft. to 198 ft. in width. Despite its high installation costs, Bow River was debt-free and paying dividends to members by 1985.

On June 16, 1976, Little Bow MLA Ray Speaker became the first irrigation farmer in the co-op to get gas. "He must have had pull," laugh directors. Today, 65 to 70 per cent of this co-op's gas goes to irrigation each year, giving it one of the highest per customer volumes in the province. Says one director: "One of the biggest boons to the district has been having natural gas for pumping."

## BUCK LAKE

- Headquartered in Buck Lake.
- Total area: 58.51 sq. miles
- Total services: 146
- Total pipe: 49.3 miles

**Directors Past and Present:** Vic Miller, Don Siegel, John Adams, Fred Drader, A.J. Berezansky, George McLeod, Stanley Krysta, H. Letourneau, Cliff Begg, Bob Stewart, Louie Banack, Peter Murry, J. Bartman.

**Managers:** Don Seigel, John Bartman.

At 24 cents a gigajoule, this co-op's gas rate is among the lowest anywhere in Canada.

## BUCK MOUNTAIN

- Headquartered in Warburg.
- Total area: 1062.20 sq. miles
- Total services: 1193
- Total pipe: 745.39 miles

**Directors Past and Present:** Norman Bittner, Harvey Greenhough, Adolf Besler, Don Day, Harvey Sharp, George Ambrose, Victor Leonhardt, G.J. Beatty, H.R. McNaughton, Wayne Shirvell, Henry Nixon, Allan Sims, Steve Nemeth, John Szepesy, Robert M. McCulloch, Thomas A. Impey, Lyle W. Sargeant, Gordon Davidson, Francis Lachance, Lavern Gillespie, Paul Bokowski, Jack Aldrich, Morris Hoffman, Gerry Davidson, Fred Bijou, Harold Blize, Bernard Johnson, B. Galloway, Frank Laczo, Tom Cliff, John Langley, Max Lemermeyer, Allan Hughes, Bob Fudger, Allen Fenneman, Tony Czirfusz, Aaron Brown, Joe Taschuk, Hubert Leeder, Ray Holmgren, Stan Tomaszeski, Walter Nachuk, Lawrence Fisher, Donald Vath, William Klatt, Dennis Martin.

**Managers:** Don Olesky, Bill Stacey, Ivan Johnson.

After spending an entire day carefully shovelling a trench beneath several foreign pipelines, a tired crew called it quits for the night. When it returned the next day it discovered, to its horror, that a farmer had filled the dirt back in with a front-end loader.

Directors of this co-op have heard nearly every possible excuse from late-paying customers. Among the most inventive: "My wife left me with three kids and I have a cold"; "Our granddaughter ate the gas bill"; and, "There was a week missing off my calendar." Luckily the majority of customers, including many dairy farmers with large barns to heat, pay on time and have enabled Buck Mountain to whittle down its debt to a manageable level.

# BURNT LAKE

- Headquartered in Spruceview.
- Total area: 343.1 sq. miles
- Total services: 608
- Total pipeline: 343.56 miles

**Directors Past and Present:** Fred Johannson, Gordon Stickland, Earl Fitch, John A. Swainson, Earl Grimson, A.C. McGhan, Tom Hagerman, William Schruder, Walter Hanna, Gordon Conn, Wes Stewart, Bill Sloan, Gordon Bosley, Cecil Flake, Bernie Bystrom, Lyle Olesen, Alex Wolf, Barbra Chaput, Rubin Jobs, Robert Jensen, Bill Lewis, Gordon Johnson, Dennis Moore, Dietrich Ammeter, Chester Peterson, Robert Brownlee, Paul Craig, John Lindman, Emil Hehr, Hans Lehrman, Frank Sigurdson.

**Manager:** Cecil Flake.

This co-op had two phases. The first, started by farmer Earl Grimson in 1969, had fifty-three farms. Then in 1973 Bernie Bystrom, a farmer who had been unable to obtain gas service from a nearby plant, and acreage-owning teacher Barb Chaput teamed up to start phase two. They called a sign-up meeting at Spruce View Hall in the hamlet of the same name, about 25 miles west of Red Deer. About 200 people showed up, including one man who refused to finance his contract with a lien note against his farm. Recalls one director: "He hammered on the table and said, 'If you don't take cash, I don't want it.' We didn't have arrangements for taking cash, but in the end he took the contract, we took the cash."

Manager Cecil Flake remembers one potential woman customer demanding to know "how much does a gigolo cost?" Flake knew she meant "gigajoule", but couldn't resist replying, "Depends how good he is."

# CENTRAL PEACE

- Headquartered in Spirit River.
- Total area: 1639.54 sq. miles
- Total services: 551
- Total pipe: 562.17 miles

**Directors Past and Present:** William Chalus, Armand Dion, Stanley Ash, Robert Scott, Gordon Derksen, Rod Graham, Ozzie Salzsauler, Ted Smythe, Andy Clarke, Stewart Plantings, Don Williams, Gerry Smyth, Larry Holthe, Jack Lowe, Hugh Young, Art Krefting, George Shemanko, Frank Spurgeon, J. Isaac, John Zan, H. Fitzsimmons, Myland Mitchell, R.S. Hagerman, Harold Wiebe, Allan Fletcher, Peter Anderson, Alex Graham, Wm. Zahara, John Sekulic Jr., William Woronuk, Lloyd Buck, Ray Weisenburger, Harry DeBoer, Peter Kroll, Tex Fimrite, Armand Cyr, Marcel Berghs, Len Morrison, Dennis Decheif, Ralph Jarvis, John Baxter, Willis Fitzsimmons, Gordon Howell.

**Managers:** Tom Hickmore, Coreen Bilawchuk, Terry Livingston.

About 200 people turned out to this co-op's formation meeting, organized by Municipal District fieldman Bob Scott. A handful of detractors declared, "You'll never make it. Let the government do it all." But most people were too eager to get gas to pay them any attention.

Secretary and former manager Coreen Bilawchuk will never forget her job interview with co-op directors in 1977. "I walked in and saw all these boxes on the floor jammed full of receipts, contracts, and other papers. Then I looked at these four guys staring at me and I said, 'What do I have to do?' They said, 'We don't know.' We agreed to a three-month trial period."

Former chairman George Shemanko and Bilawchuk still recall the thrill of receiving a $1 million grant cheque in 1985. "I'd never seen or held a cheque that big," laughs Bilawchuk. Adds Shemanko: "That was beautiful, even if we did have to write out $1-million worth of cheques to creditors the same week."

## CHAIN LAKES

- Headquartered in Tees.
- Total area: 805.95 sq. miles
- Total services: 1137
- Total pipe: 757.47 miles

**Directors Past and Present:** Frank Pewtress, Ken Morton, Ken Knight, Ben Linklater, William Neis, Alphonse DeLeeuw, Robert Walin, Vernon Dick, Bob Walls, Harvey Sim, Ronald Barclay, Graham Reed, Jake Waldner, Fred Mueller, Ludwena Walton, Charles Stone, Marie Knight, Glen Weins, Philip Lake, Jim Murdock, Gordon Whitehouse, Allan Cole, Larry Walton, Wilfrid Toth, Allan Baird, James Grose, Murray Griffiths.

**Managers:** Carl Bakke, Leroy Graham, Don Olesky.

This co-op held its early meetings in the local Church of God. "Maybe that's why things turned out so good," laughs one director. Indeed, Chain Lakes began to post earnings in the early 1980s and in 1989 had a reserve account of more than $100 000.

With some fifty-five commercial users, this co-op is acquainted with a wide range of gas uses. Still, directors were puzzled when one long-haired group of "hippies" began heating a small shed made of poles and spruce boughs. Recalls one director: "Turns out they were growing marijuana in there."

## CHIEF MOUNTAIN

- Headquartered in Cardston.
- Total area: 1306.16 sq. miles
- Total services: 906
- Total pipe: 576.73 miles

**Directors Past and Present:** Harry Beazer, Ralph Salt, Morris Palmer, Fred Rice, Harold Leavitt, Veryle Leavitt, Blaine Leavitt, Howard Synder, George Linder, Lawrence Cahoon, Curtiss Pilling, Leon Bator, Chris Jensen, John Bevers, Gerald Bennett, Pete Higgins, Harold Farries, K.N. Stewart, John Weing, Fred Strate, Lynn Sommerfeldt, Calvin Olsen, Calvin Wellman, Robert Wocknitz, Dick Richards.

**Managers:** Harry Beazer, Gerald Beazer.

Managed by Gerald Beazer, this is the only international gas co-op (it serves an American Customs border office), and the only one to serve a national park—Waterton.

Meeting environmental requirements made installing Waterton's system a challenge, says Beazer. But others working in the area faced even greater restrictions. "A bridge contractor was working in the park next to us," recalls Beazer. "Park authorities wouldn't allow him to drive his equipment on the river bank. Was he upset with us when he saw we were allowed to plow right through the river with a big backhoe and dragline."

Chief Mountain is also one of a handful of co-ops partly built by Algas Engineering, a NOVA subsidiary set up during the peak years of the Rural Gas Program to design and oversee co-op construction. Other Algas co-ops included Iron Creek, Rocky, and Evergreen.

## CHIN COULEE

- Headquartered in Grassy Lake.
- Total area: 908.97 sq. miles
- Total services: 521
- Total pipe: 494.92 miles

**Directors Past and Present:** Alex Powell, Ed Hendricks, Alden Fletcher, Ray Hart, Allen Fletcher, Don Leahy, Ted Allen, Clarence Jesperson, Herb Kuehn, Frank Fletcher, Bob Powell, Jack Knibbs, Peter Hooge, Fergus Russell, Forrest Christensen, Charles Foote, Brian Foote, Jim Gow, Merle Nelson, Frank Brewin, George Leahy, Al Machacek, J. Collins, R.K. Bailie, Lorne Syversen, J. Milder, Claude Stevens.

**Manager:** Jim Brown.

In 1983, the co-op took several measures to get out of debt: it took over the customers of a privately-owned utility operated by Canadian Western, and charged members an extra $683 apiece. By 1989 it was debt-free.

Irrigation was and remains a major load for the co-op. Says manager Jim Brown: "Natural gas keeps those irrigation systems purring right along." As well, the co-op sells gas to oil companies for their battery sites.

Directors resigning from Chin Coulee must find a replacement before they go, an effective method of bringing new blood onto the board. "We try to rotate three new directors onto the board every year," says a director.

## CHINOOK

- Headquartered in Milk River.
- Total area: 1373.13 sq. miles
- Total services: 359
- Total pipe: 473.38 miles

**Directors Past and Present:** Ken Welsh, Harold Anderson, Gordon Thompson, Stan McCulloch, Tom Bianchi, Jim Blackmer, Joe Dies, Harold Hierath, George Russell, Steve Balog, Hovey Reese, Dick Losey, Ralph Dixson, John Obbagy, Tom Gilchrist, Ralph Lee, Raymond Taylor, George Henline, Ken Reese, Gordon Peterson, Ron Hierath.

**Manager:** Scott Russell.

During its formative years, this co-op stored all pipe and equipment at the home of its first secretary/treasurer Harold Anderson.

Not all members fully appreciated the benefits of gas, according to one director. "I told a farmer 'Now your boy can work in a nice warm shop all winter.' The farmer said, 'Hell, he never works in the summer.'"

Directors will always remember one young construction crew member so dedicated to his job he refused to take time off for a honeymoon. Instead, his new bride rode beside him on his cat.

## COCHRANE LAKE

- Headquartered in Cochrane.
- Total area: 736.57 sq. miles
- Total services: 1083
- Total pipe: 542.07 miles

**Directors Past and Present:** Bert Powlesland, Garnet Ovans, Jon Hutchinson, Fred Kidd, Mike Thompson, Don Edge, John Pawson, Vair Reid, Don Tannas, Ralph Olson, Gary Kjersem, Les Beddoes, Jud Pickup, Grant Bird, Mel Farquharson, Wilf Britton, Don Stewart, Bob Turner, Malcolm McBain, Graham Barnard, Buck Miller, Ken Lloyd.

**Manager:** Garnet Ovans.

To generate member interest, directors invite new customers into the office for a briefing on the Rural Gas Program and how the co-op operates. Says chairman/manager Garnet Ovans: "We find it cuts down on questions later. And people are really surprised to learn how much of Alberta is served by gas co-ops."

Ovans and fellow board member Jon Hutchinson remember well the many hours spent unloading reels of plastic pipe from boxcars. "They had beautiful big inflated plastic bags in there packed around the pipe," says Ovans. The bags did a good job of protecting the pipe, but they could be hazardous, recalls Hutchinson. "We would stick a knife in the bags to deflate them. Every now and then one would explode rather violently and blow your hat and glasses off. Those bags went 'boom' when they blew."

## CORONADO

- Headquartered in Gibbons.
- Total area: 59.92 sq. miles
- Total services: 528
- Total pipe: 81.88 miles

**Directors Past and Present:** Gerry Dykstra, Andy Kapicki, Don Lasell, Don Hood, Morley Kuzyk, Harold Briggs, Terry Tourigney, John St. Nicholass, Bob Sinclair, Orest Melnychuk, Bill Cochrane, Jim McMeckan, Metro Zapesocki, Mike Rozak, Loren Jacobson, Dick Zeigler, Julius Madsen, John Lukawesky, Bert McNeil, Andy Panchyshyn, Ken Wacowich, Lorne Hallett, Andrew Woywitka, Bert Hall.

**Managed by Board.**

This co-op's organizational meeting was held in February 1972 when the temperature was forty-two below and people were in the mood to talk about cheaper heating fuels. Indeed, people were so eager to get gas, they couldn't wait for the start of the Rural Gas Program and installed their system that year without any government assistance.

In June 1989, this co-op amalgamated with North Edmonton. The union made sense. Both were small organizations with offices only 1/2 mile apart. A new twelve-member board was elected (six from each co-op) and Laverne Murray made unofficial manager.

## CROSSROADS

- Headquartered in Innisfail.
- Total area: 1583.13 sq. miles
- Total services: 1810
- Total pipe: 1264.9 miles

**Directors Past and Present:** John Moran, Kenneth Hoppins, Alex Gorr, John A. Christie, George H. Kinsey, Charles R. Moore, Leon Layden, Angus W. Park, Dan Ray, Allen Painter, Edward Kober, Charles Siltala, Art Meding, Murray Jensen, Gordon Layden, Richard Biggs, Bill Stevenett, Bill Johnston, Ike Wiebe, Claude Trenholm, Kent Knudsen, Raymond Layden, Ken Burns, Austin Fisher, Don Cote, Mel Richards, Terry McKay, Art Vincent, Dennis Scott, Arnold Jensen, Ken McLaren, Phillip Gongaware.

**Manager:** Reg Olson.

The first co-op to begin construction under the Rural Gas Program, its directors had to re-do 2000 easements because of a clerical mistake made on the first round.

Director Bill Stevenett likes to tell the story of one rather eccentric gas holdout. "We were about to plow in line at a farm run by two brothers when their sister—my old Sunday school teacher—came running out of the house waving a pitchfork at us. One of her brothers chased her back into the house with a lawnmower. A few minutes later she poked her head out and yelled, 'Bill Stevenett, you're the cause of all this trouble.' I didn't think she had remembered me." But old ties don't necessarily bind. Says Stevenett: "To this day, that woman is still burning coal."

## DALUM

- Headquartered in Drumheller.
- Total area: 148.75 sq. miles
- Total services: 59
- Total pipe: 54.33 miles

**Directors Past and Present:** Ray Snyder, Svend Andersen, Niels Mortensen, Harry Christensen, Norman Christensen, John Holmen, Edmund Vogstad, Reid Jorgensen, Leo Jensen, Svend Dahl, Olav Palleson.

**Manager:** Harry Christensen.

Named for an agricultural school in Denmark, this co-op has only fifty customers. Still, says manager Harry Christensen, "you need to travel 100 miles to get to them all." Luckily, most customers pay their bills by mail. "The rest either drop in to pay me at my home or I go to their place to collect, visit, and drink coffee," says Christensen, who is proudly conscientious about his billing duties. "I had a hip replacement last March and figured I would have to delay sending bills out till the end of April. But I got home from hospital by the end of March and had the bills in the mail by the regular time. No delay at all."

## DEER CREEK

- Headquartered in Bentley.
- Total area: 593.91 sq. miles
- Total services: 307
- Total pipe: 259.12 miles

**Directors Past and Present:** Keith Bresse, Don Hoar, Calvin Turner, Bill Unland, Ron McDowell, Carl Christiansen, Ernie Santee, Robert Nielson, Dan Wilson, Jerry Miller, Frank Cissell, Merle Cissell, Darrell Doran, Frank Lind, George Irwin, Larry Fipke, Wayne Carr, Bruce Boyes, Bruce Tona, Roy Sargent, Gerry Hoar, Mike Hatala, Les Fenwick, Ron Sperber, Harry Ekkel, Dale Hoar, Larry Vetsch, George Braithwaite, Sandy Bennett, Robert Braithwaite, Royce Frank, Arnold Hemsing, John VanAnkum.

**Managers:** George Irwin, Joanne Wigmore.

Original manager George Irwin did everything he could to salvage this system, built entirely of PE 3306 pipe. But even reducing the gas pressure to a lowly 15 psi failed to stop the endless springing of leaks. Finally, the co-op had to replace every inch of plastic. Recalls one director: "It created some bad feelings and made it hard to sell more contracts. It nearly caused the downfall of the co-op." It didn't help matters when a plow crew lost its way in the woods and laid miles of unneeded pipe. But directors, being bred of hardy pioneer stock, refused to quit. Thanks to their dedication, Deer Creek survived and now shares a manager—Joanne Wigmore—and computer with the nearby Gull Lake Co-op.

## DIAMOND VALLEY

- Headquartered in Eckville.
- Total area: 329.75 sq. miles
- Total services: 825
- Total pipe: 346.62 miles

**Directors Past and Present:** W.T. Burns, R.H. Lewis, Bruce Hagerman, Jack Sheppard, Dave Pearson, Vern R. Nielsen, Charles Skocdopole, R.A. Staniforth, Geo. Braithwaite, Jim Savage, Don Hansen, Wilbur Kubik, A.W. Bretelsen, A.M. Hoven, R.A. Hubl, August Kasper, Glen Skocdopole, Les Hake, Les Finkbeiner, Al Turner, Arelin Von Hollen, Mel Knopp, Clarence Moos, Bill Palm, Gerry Gustavson, Dick Jennings, Harold Caton, Lloyd Johnson, Roger Knopp, Ron Kult, Al Gaetz, Alf Jones, Gordon Bowen, Roy Mattson, Claude Caton.

**Managers:** Bob Hubl, Rod Daniel, Mark Melhoff, Debbie French.

Bob Hubl, Charlie Skocdopole, and W.T. Burns first talked about gas while sitting in the local Co-op store coffee shop. Recalls Hubl: "By this time Charlie's company was doing construction for other co-ops. I'd been thinking about gas to myself since 1960. The oil patch was booming and I couldn't see any reason why we couldn't run lines to our homes."

Strange things can turn up in the search for leaks, attests field manager Lloyd Stevens. Called out at 2 AM to check a gas leak in a house, Stevens was making his way through a crawlspace, flashlight in hand, when he came upon a ball of fur. "It was a dead cat. When I told the owner he shrugged and said, 'We wondered whatever happened to that one.'"

## DINOSAUR

- Headquartered in Brooks.
- Total area: 457.56 sq. miles
- Total services: 427
- Total pipe: 231.31 miles

**Directors Past and Present:** Sam Alberts, Len Rowe, David Houseman, Don Alberts, Monte Mortenson, Don Berg, Jim Neely, Les Conners, Clinton Henrickson, Tom Musgrove, Charles Charlton, Cody Morris, John Slomp, R.L. Edwards, Lavern Rose, Tony Rommens, Joe Valarian, Del Giles, Manny Schmitke, Don McIntyre, Max Elsbett, Shawn Campbell, Dough Waugh, Walter Duncan.

**Managers:** Sam Alberts, Monica Huculak.

Every single customer uses gas for irrigation. Says original director Len Rowe: "Irrigation is the heart of this system. We fought hard to convince government officials to grant us enough money to build a system big enough to accommodate irrigation."

To improve efficiency, the co-op bought a computer four years ago. "It now takes two hours to do billings compared to a week by hand," says Rowe.

## DRY COUNTRY CO-OP

- Headquartered in Oyen.
- Total area: 4618.67 sq. miles
- Total services: 1110
- Total pipe: 1124.09 miles

**Directors Past and Present:** Stan Gillespie, Bob Bamber, Bert McFadyen, Murray Huston, Bruce Morrisett, Burt Jorgenson, Roy Jaques, Perry Thurston, Starkey Chudleigh, Jack Butler, Tom Machell, Mervin Meers, Richard Anderson, John Kloberdanz, Donald Adams, Rudy Brockmann, Norman Evens, Ed Hogan, Don Martin, Syd McCurdy, Len Rinker, Joe Thornton, LaVerne Opheim, Harold Steinley, Pete Wiens, Chester Nielson, A. Suchotzky, Verne Caskoy, Olaf Skjenna, John Levick, Harry Chiliak, Ted Baier, Alex Makronoff, Milton Symes, B. Holmes, Don Chiliak, H. Schmidt, Melvin Bingeman, Glen Shantz, Lorne Patterson, Don McCurdy.

**Managers:** Del MacLean, Ray Girletz.

As the name suggests, rainfall is scarce in this co-op's area. Nevertheless, it rained steadily for fourteen days straight during construction, making it nearly impossible to cross a major road. Remembers manager and rodeo cowboy Ray Girletz: "The rain kept filling up the hole we had dug for the pipe."

As one can imagine, installing a system in an area larger than the province of Prince Edward Island is expensive. "You're looking at 15 cents per foot of pipe. That's a lot of dollars," observes a director. "Without special Gas Transportation Grants you may as well have forgotten the whole program. We had to borrow $400 000 as it was. We would have had to borrow nearly three times that without grants and carry the debt into the gas price. That would have resulted in fuel costs higher than propane."

# EAST CENTRAL

- Headquartered in Hanna.
- Total area: 3900.82 sq. miles
- Total services: 851
- Total pipe: 1193.23 miles

**Directors Past and Present:** Albert Storch, Leon Gall, Lloyd Hutton, Jim Peacock, Harry Gordon, Lou Lohrman, S.J. Slorstad, John Kaempf, Norman Van Dam, Ken Burgemeister, Don Hall, George Aaserud, Delbert Gillespie, Lewis Heyler, Art Bergman, Bill Smyth, Tom Scott, John Davies, Morris Solberg, Roger Pearson, Nelson Annas, Ted Allen.

**Managers:** Al Taylor, Carol Pelchat.

Originally this co-op was to take in what is now Dry Country's franchise area. When directors and the Utilities department realized this would be too unwieldy, the area was split in half and re-incorporated as two co-ops.

Directors found most landowners quite willing to pay $25 for an engineering feasibility study. However, one farmer, wielding a knife and hatchet, chased a director from his property. Apparently, he wasn't interested in gas.

# EAST PEACE

- Headquartered in Donnelly.
- Total area: 1557.07 sq. miles
- Total services: 815
- Total pipe: 627.43 miles

**Directors Past and Present:** Robin Hopkins, Gilles Bouchard, Ray L'Hirondelle, Steve Glodek, Evans Lavoie, Mike Gach, Bob Timmermans, Ron Schofield, Vern Milligen, Paul Belzile, Pete Naturkach, George Griffith, Alan Whiting, Alex Bekewich, Nels Armstrong, Gerard Forget, Raymond Alm, Walter Gacek, Steve Petluk, Rene Garant, Armand Cloutier, Andre Albanati, Henri Paul Blanchette, Réal Bessette, Ray Cunningham, Julien Berube, Norman Doucette, René Nolette, Jean Langelier, Germain Bastien, Donald Lesh, Richard Dion, John Krall, Gabe Turcotte, Norman Langelier.

**Managers:** Len Haley, Dale Dupuis.

One farmer accidentally ripped into the co-op's high pressure aluminum line while digging a trench for an unrelated purpose. Says manager Dale Dupuis: "He twisted up about 300 m [990 ft.] of the line, picked up part of it and said, 'What's this?' Luckily nothing ignited the gas before the co-op could fix it."

Manager Dupuis was tempted to quit during his first month on the job. "I was working for the Alberta Wheat Pool when I met then-East Peace manager Len Haley at an agricultural fair. He invited me to work for the co-op as a landman [East Peace had to negotiate 1200 easements] for $1600 a month. When my first paycheque was for only $800 I questioned Len, who said, 'You'll get your $1600 a month. It might take three years, but you'll get it.' For some reason, I stayed anyway."

## EAST SMOKY

- Headquartered in Crooked Creek.
- Total area: 1825.61 sq. miles
- Total services: 783
- Total pipe: 672.93 miles

**Directors Past and Present:** Maurice Moore, John Wohlgemuth, William Wohlgemuth, Philip Isaac, Arthur Dievert, James Pushor, Willard Logan, Harvey Pellerin, Gerald Gunby, Monroe Loewen, Ed Huber, William Reimer, Carl Schartner, Art Macklin, Bob Balisky, Herb Wohlgemuth, Allan Dievert, Richard Ratzlaff, Frank Stevenson, Corney Petker, Paul Tschetter, Chris Weiss, Peter Warkentin, Art Baron, Peter Paetkau, Aurey Carter, Norman Klassen, Erhard Dallmann, Don Gourlay, Harry Merrifield, John Bandzul, Scott Jensen, Terry Peterson, Tony Peterson.

**Managers:** Herb Wohlgemuth, Vic Plamondon, Bill Kiernan, Dan Wilson.

Directors have adopted the following poem as their unofficial philosophy:

*When things go wrong, as they sometimes will,*
*When the road you're trudging seems all up hill,*
*When the funds are low and the debts are high,*
*And you want to smile but you have to sigh,*
*When care is pressing you down a bit—*
*Rest if you must, but don't you quit.*

***"Don't Quit"*** —Author unknown

But directors weren't always so game. Indeed, the co-op nearly disbanded in 1975 because of stalled negotiations over grants. Recalls former chairman Arthur Dievert: "We were so frustrated we wanted to turn the whole thing over to the local Improvement District." But the I.D. wasn't interested, so Dievert and the board instead rolled up their collective sleeves and built a system that in 1988 generated net earnings of $108 482. Laughs current chairman Harvey Pellerin: "We decided to grab the bull by the horns and go for it."

## EVERGREEN

- Headquartered in Drayton Valley.
- Total area: 495.53 sq. miles
- Total services: 711
- Total pipe: 286.28 miles

**Directors Past and Present:** Ralph Goertz, Dave Jouan, Verna Hines, Art Smith, Jack Tyler, Albert Martin, George Moroz, Manuel Schultz, Gerald Pohing, Joe Jouan, Dave Banks, Joe Dubeau, John Prociuk, Wesley Davidson, Hugh Kapteyn, Robert Whaley, Cathy Polsfut, Andy Leteta, Ben Harrison, Walter Evenson, Mary Ann Evenson, Arne Bystrom, Herb Zander, Leah Lysak, Bill Urchyshyn, Jim Selin, Fred Hunley, Albin Osredkar, Wade Trimble, Bill Boos, Richard Krawchuk, Gerry Toews, Don Boorse, Raymond Broadbent, Don Baumann, John Reid, Ann Neumeyer.

**Manager:** Leah Lysak.

Manager Leah Lysak was among the first women managers in the rural gas system. "I've done it all—staked lines, gotten easements, inspected pipelines, hung and read meters, and balanced the books. I would recommend the job to any woman," she says.

Born on a farm three miles from her current home, Lysak was a bank teller and later an unemployment insurance claims officer before becoming co-op manager. Through the Federation of Alberta Gas Co-ops, she took courses in management, administration, pressure and measurement, and pipeline inspection. She has her fusion and high energy joining tickets, and four children aged 21 to 30 who have known how to set regulators since they were 10 years old.

## FOOTHILLS

- Headquartered in Olds.
- Total area: 957.07 sq. miles
- Total services: 1374
- Total pipe: 833.77 miles

**Directors Past and Present:** Jack MacKlin, Dieter Feuerhelm, Chris Randers, Nels Eskesen, Ken Rose, Eric Rose, Bob McRae, Clair Fisher, John Nesom, Ben Heuven, Stan Spicer, Fred Notley, Ken Turnbull, Steve Pankow, R.L. (Dick) Wiens, Hugh Thompson, Alvin Scheer, Jean Conrad, Dick Grant, Dave Groom, Ted Kostenuke, Ron Sande, Wayne Whitehair, Boyd Petersen, Jim Pearson, Norm Morasch, Dennis Roemelle, Vern Petersen, John Pochapsky, Doug King, John Haynes, Gordon Luft, Wilbur Black, Vera Edwards, Gordon Johnson, Mike Wild, Len Hartzler, Muriel Nesom, Darwyn Findlay, Joe Vietenhiemer, Casey Greebe, Albert Sailer, David Shields.

**Managers:** John Nesom, Nick Van Waes, George Schweiger, Larry Grandahl, Don MacMillan.

This co-op provides an excellent example of the dedication of directors throughout the rural gas system. After hearing that sparks from a major fire were blowing toward the co-op office in the centre of Olds, secretary Muriel Nesom and several directors headed straight for town. They ducked police road blocks by sneaking down back alleys, made it to the office, snatched all the co-op records, and drove back out of town. Luckily, the flames never did reach the co-op building.

On another occasion, when the co-op had run out of pipe, directors jumped into their trucks and headed to Calgary to pick up more. "Those were great times in a lot of ways," says one director. "They sure brought a lot of people together."

## FORTY MILE

- Headquartered in Whitla.
- Total area: 4778.76 sq. miles
- Total services: 868
- Total pipe: 1111.41 miles

**Directors Past and Present:** Alex Onody, Gordon Blanchard, Frank Romeiki, Albert Mack, John Wutzki, Ron Davis, Peter Biemans, Joe Van Ooyen, Tom Noga, Brian Shatz, Ron Geldreich, Vern Simonton, Perry Olechowski, George Schile, Henry Haugan, Paul Gogolinski, Jack Kolody, Richard Sauer, Herman Reuber, Elmer Schlenker, Willie Will, Vern Schultz, Len Nelsen, Pete Armstrong, Ernest Mudie, Norm Schneider, Mel Klaiber, Norman Bauer, Larry Roeder, Gary Meidinger, Vic Ley, Brian Hubka, Abe Dyck. From amalgamated Bowell Co-op: Les Gunderson, Len Olson, Pat Gunderson, L.B. Pancoast, George Lapp, Mark Schaeffer, Nels Bartoli, Mike Wittevrongel, Hubert Zieman, Elmer Rothfus.

**Managers:** Gordon Blanchard, Del MacLean, Barbara Boufford.

Crews had to lay nearly 60 miles of pipe to bring gas to only six customers. But such vast distances between farms are common in this franchise, which is the largest in the province.

Interestingly, this co-op began life in much smaller form. Recalls original chairman Alex Onody: "We'd mapped out an area for about eighty customers, but Edmonton urged us to take on more of the country, and so we did." Of course, this meant obtaining several thousand easements, which proved an especially tough job for one director. Explains Onody: "He was a member of a surface rights board and had been telling farmers not to give oil companies blanket easements. Then he had to go back and persuade the same farmers to give blanket easements to the co-op."

# GEM

- Headquartered in Gem.
- Total area: 314.11 sq. miles
- Total services: 128
- Total pipe: 75.52 miles

**Directors Past and Present:** Jake Doerksen, Milton Ryan, John Van Bergen, Lawrence Scheibner, David Klassen, Robert Wallace, George Paetkau, Ernie Walde, Joe Milne, Neil Wallace, Henry Walde, R.L. Scheibner, H.M. Wiebe.

**Manager:** George Paetkau.

Directors hired local farmer Phil Andrus to install pipe because he had an old Ford tractor with a trencher attached. Recalls former serviceman Roy Pritchard: "Phil liked to talk to that machine like it was a dog or something. He'd say, 'Smarten up or I'll smack you.' He'd pound on it with his hammer, hop back on, and sure enough, it would run better."

Not everybody believed this early co-op would succeed. One of the original ten members even refused to take out a contract until six years ago.

# GULL LAKE

- Headquartered in Bentley.
- Total area: 156.04 sq. miles
- Total services: 688
- Total pipe: 152.76 miles

**Directors Past and Present:** Lawrence Henderson, August Kasper, R.W. Sargeant, Walter McNary, August Liivam, Don Hoar, Martin Koleyak, Frank Rice, William Jaffray, Albert Kamps, C. Planck, D. Hueppelsheuser, E. Ten Hove, Al Ingles, Ken Fargey, Ken Wigmore, Fred Ladwig, Lyle Kilpatrick, Lorne Greaves, Jim Nelson, John Buit, Alfred Skjonsberg, David Carlyle, Larry Moore, George Hancock, Merlyn Wilson, Roy Duncan, Jack Hagerman, Jack Siebenga, Glen Nelson, Ted Micheals, Ralph Drost, Phil Hunt, Darrel Symington, Keith Brittain, Max Moore, Ray Neimula, Fred Lenz, Don Freeman, Ray Park, John Predy, Harry Craig, Harvey Haarstad, Klaas Brouwer, Archie Carlyle.

**Manager:** Joanne Wigmore.

In 1973 members contributed an extra $250 apiece to buy their co-op from the bankrupt Anchor Pipelines. Today, the co-op is managed by Joanne Wigmore, who has had some interesting meter reading experiences in her time.

In one home, the gas meter was in the customer's bedroom. Recalls Wigmore: "I literally had to crawl across the bed to read the meter. I'd rap on the door before going in, but still, I always expected to find a body in there. I never did. But I never found the bed made either."

# I & J

- Headquartered in Jenner.
- Total area: 215.07 sq. miles
- Total services: 92
- Total pipe: 73.07 miles

**Directors Past and Present:** Walter Olson, Paul Nygaard, George Lewandoski, John Ignatius, Ken Olson, Albert Ritz, Ed Aebly, Melvin Johnson, Delmoure Stennes, Murray Knutson, Don Osadczuk, Ben Stegen, Lloyd Nygaard, Tom Osadczuk, Martin Hofer, Warren Bergdahl, Vic Stadnicki, Alec Hudec, George Juss, Jack Osadczuk, Andrew Burnat.

**Manager:** Mavis Stegen.

Originally there were plans to form two co-ops in this area, one in Jenner, and a second in Iddesleigh, about 6 miles to the west. But when so many farmers between the two hamlets wanted gas, the founders decided to amalgamate. Hence the name—"I" (Iddesleigh) and "J" (Jenner).

Distances between customers are so vast farmers joke that area jack-rabbits need to pack lunches.

Manager Mavis Stegen says one construction problem led to soured relations between the co-op and one member. "The crew had accidentally plowed through the drainage field for this farmer's septic tank. The co-op repaired the damage, but the man was so mad he refused to hook up to his riser for more than ten years."

# IRON CREEK

- Headquartered in Sedgewick.
- Total area: 1588.39 sq. miles
- Total services: 795
- Total pipe: 846.37 miles

**Directors Past and Present:** Henry Lien, Tom Mattinson, Keith Currie, Harry Christian, Rusty McLean, Allan Darling, Joe Makar, Jerry Mark, Erling Nilson, Bill Lawson, Paul Mazure, Rick Davidson, Dave Wylie, Leo Slavic, Oswald Koehli, Ron Bergseth, Albert Child, Don Hays, Bert Hill, John Burden, Harold Hauser, Gordon Hoines, Sterling Moller.

**Managed by Board.**

Founding director Tom Mattinson can't recall then-Opposition leader Peter Lougheed's pledge to gasify rural Alberta, although he does remember shaking Lougheed's hand during the 1971 election campaign. Still, says Mattinson, "the Rural Gas Program was the impetus for the co-op. No grants, no co-op. That simple."

Director Albert Child and his wife Sheila enjoyed meeting the many drivers who trucked in pipe to be stored in their backyard. Recalls Mrs. Child: "Sometimes they arrived during the night, slept in their cabs, then had breakfast with us. Often they brought their wives along too."

## KNEEHILL

- Headquartered in Linden.
- Total area: 197.97 sq. miles
- Total services: 253
- Total pipeline: 196.6 miles

**Directors Past and Present:** Milton Toews, Peter Baerg, Cornie Wiebe, Lyle Haining, David Dick, C.C. Toews, Ray Ratzlaff, Edger Penner, George Wickersham, Harvey Schindel, Vern Meek, Bob Elliott, John Koot, Samuel Megli, Robert Boake, Abe Thiessen, Morris Jackson, Ray Scaffer, Harvey Thiessen, Horst Wiebe, Gladwin Toews, Allan Megli, Kalman Bobely, Clifford Pool, Dale Fox, Otto Bertsch, Lewis Esau, Lloyd Ratzlaff, John Empey, John Reid, Frank Barkman, Henry Dick.

**Managers:** Robert Theissen, Terrance Toews.

Farmers in this area were especially receptive to the gas co-op idea, says director C.C. Toews. "We had such good experience with co-ops in the past—we had a co-op cheese factory, a mutual telephone company, a cooperative health unit, a rural electric association, and a co-op store. We were used to working together."

Continues Toews: "We got power in 1944 and celebrated with a "burning the lantern" ceremony. Then in the 1960s, the Gem people were so satisfied with their gas system, and we were so tired of using coal, that I presented the idea of a gas co-op to the board of the Kneehill Farmers Telephone Mutual."

## LAC LA BICHE

- Headquartered in Lac La Biche.
- Total area: 1021.53 sq. miles
- Total services: 947
- Total pipe: 394.8 miles

**Directors Past and Present:** John Lachowich, Ron Sampietro, Paul Rizzoli, Mike Torresan, Harvey Yoder, Ed Nowicki, Lucien Bourassa, Bert Arthurs, John Menard, Alex Connelly, Glen Meyer, Fern Ulliac, Marilyn Auriat, Les Bates, Edgar Belanger, Peter Beniuk, John Clark, Louis Damphouse, Lloyd Deutscher, Rienhart Eckburg, Albert Happner, Calvin Kumpula, Morris Lamoreux, George Michetti, Steve Onciul, Terry Peden, Albin Plamondon, Don Polowich, Gordon Rayment, Bernie Romaniuk, Eugene Routhier, Jerry Sykes, John Tesolin, Lawrence Turgeon, Paul Wowk.

**Managers:** John Clark, Terry Peden, Vic Plamondon, Bernie Romaniuk, Mike Torresan, Phil Lane.

Local beavers have acquired a taste for plastic pipe and frequently gnaw at gaslines buried in the creek beds. Directors once found 8 ft. lengths of pipe, left over from construction, built into several beaver dams.

Manager Phil Lane has fielded some unusual complaints in his day. Among them was one from a farmer's wife who insisted a trencher had run over her fruit trees. Says Lane: "I went to her place and walked along the trench looking for fruit trees, but couldn't find any. Finally the woman had to point them out—they were only 2 in. tall. Still, she sent us a bill of $45 per tree."

# LAMCO

- Headquartered in Lamont.
- Total area: 1389.52 sq. miles
- Total services: 1345
- Total pipeline: 1034.91 miles

**Directors Past and Present:** Kent Harrold, Mike Kapicki, Nick Seniuk, William Diduck, Ben Rosnau, George Kuzyk, Peter Palischuk, Leonard Siracky, John Kawyuk, Elgin Ziegler, Charlie Dayton, Ron Goeglein, Ernie Klymchuk, Jim Snipe, John Homeniuk, Albert Grinde, Hans Mayer, Pete Gabert, Les Paull, Albert Hennig, Art McLellan, William Herchek, Keith Thorne, Mike Schiller, Doug Maschmeyer, Dan Giebelhaus, Bert Frey, Clarence Klammer, Mike Cherniawski, Andy Woitas, Jim Tymchak, Orest Kuly, August Knysh, Albert Geiger, Andy Jonker, Jim Mundy, William Gray, Ken Motiuk, Ernest Riley, Ray Sampert, Glen Hennig, Fred Pewarchuk, Garnett Frey, William Stack, Jim Ostapowich.

**Manager:** Don Schultz.

There was still no gas in the lines on the day of this co-op's opening flare-up ceremony. But with Premier Peter Lougheed scheduled to fly out by helicopter to light the flare, directors weren't about to cancel. Instead, they hooked a propane tank up to the flare standpipe. It worked liked a charm and nobody, including the premier, ever knew the difference.

Among Lamco's claims to fame is mole-trouble. At last count, the little creatures had chewed at least 141 holes in Lamco line. "It's our territory," sighs one director. "You drop an alfalfa seed and on the third day there's a mole."

# LITTLE BOW CO-OP

- Headquartered in Barons.
- Total area: 797.17 sq. miles
- Total services: 381
- Total pipeline: 428.78 miles

**Directors Past and Present:** Clarence Travis, Leslie Krasman, Plenny Anderson, Glen Anderson, Alan Fraser, Rudolph Hubka, Harold Cutforth, Henry Konynenbelt, Raymond Schuler, Allen Mueller, Glen Fath, Klaas Poelman, Lloyd Anderson, Loyal Turner, Case Sinnema, Axel Sundquist, B. Nauta, P. Curle, E. Hemmaway, A. Odegard, F. Hall, G. Hobbs.

**Manager:** Sheldon Albrecht.

Pipe shortages delayed initial construction at this co-op for eighteen months, while inflation drove the price per contract from $3000 to more than $5000. At one point things looked so bleak, directors considered folding the venture. But the Utilities department unveiled its Gas Transportation Grant in time to save the co-op. By 1989, Little Bow was debt-free, with a sizeable reserve account.

One former co-op secretary will never forget her first board meeting. Tensions were high and the profanity plentiful as the co-op's engineer and contractor came to verbal blows. "It was just one swear word after another. I can't handle that and I said, 'I would appreciate it if in my presence you did not use my Lord's name in vain.' I wasn't officially hired yet, but I thought, 'I'll just say it, and if I don't get hired, I don't get hired.' " She got hired.

# LIVINGSTONE

- Headquartered in Cowley.
- Total area: 182.78 sq. miles
- Total services: 61
- Total pipe: 56.71 miles

**Directors Past and Present:** Dave Glen, Bernard Smith, Pat Dwyer, Frank Fisher, John Sekella, Michael Elton, Dale Dennis, Hilton Pharis, Ernst Lank, Walter Wolbert, Jim Lank, Vern Dennis, Steve Sapeta, Brian Cochlan, T. Smith, Jack Dezall, Ray Shaw, Kevin Lewis.

**Manager:** John Sekella.

Bell and Fenske designed the system for this splendidly scenic co-op nestled against the Rocky Mountains. Crews began plowing in 1971 and often needed dynamite to blast open trenches for the pipe.

Today, Livingstone is plagued by "pocket gophers" or moles, which have punctured about 100 ft. of gasline and nibbled the coating off 125 ft. of tracer wire. They appear to prefer orange to black gas pipe, although how these colour-blind creatures can discern the difference, especially in the dark, is anybody's guess.

# LOBSTICK

- Headquartered in Evansburg.
- Total area: 912.14 sq. miles
- Total services: 627
- Total pipe: 434.02 miles

**Directors Past and Present:** John Ohnysty, Frank Geinger, A.E. Nelson, Alex Beniuk, George Williams, William Brenenstuhl, Emil Ponipal, Abe Winifield, Earl Masterson, Cora Wilson, Frank Dickson, Fred Willett, Judy Sichkaryk, Fred Fausak, Ben Zerb, Mike Mazeppa, Mike Hotra, Ewald Kwirant, Lee Davis, Lloyd Lerohl, Elon Johnson, Dale Majer, Bill Saxer, George Webster.

**Managers:** Bob Wilde, Andy Nelson, Gary Howe, Judy Rurka.

A rough, brush- and muskeg-filled country, the Lobstick franchise area challenged the ingenuity of construction crews, who worked through fall into late winter, burning straw to unfreeze the ground. The co-op had to pay winter rates for plowing and dole out extra cash to rent a ripper cat for slicing through rocky soil. Expenses mounted even higher when a D7 Cat became mired in muskeg for three days.

As most people in the rural gas movement know, it often cost money to be a director. In this case, each board member contributed $100 toward a downpayment for their co-op building.

## MEOTA

- Headquartered in Priddis.
- Total area: 60.45 sq. miles
- Total services: 323
- Total pipe: 82.98 miles

**Directors Past and Present:** Robert Chalmers, Stan Jones, Herb Bond, James Griffith, Hugh Powell, Fred Rishaug, Elwyn Evans, John Schaal, Cedric Hopper, Leo Ohlhauser, John Patterson, John Ogilvie, Don Eagleton, Herb Padwick, Gwen Blatz, Rod Stewart, Joan Duerholt, Ray Glasrud, Tom Adams, Albert Thorssen, Alan Carscallen, Doug Elves, Jim Francis, Jim Grose, Don Hossack, John Hyatt, Bill Jackson, Kyle Johnson, George Johnston, Al Kemp, Bob Lailey, Connie Lakie, Jim Lineham, Ross Marshall, Beverly Miller, Eunice Park, Lyle Pretty, Ned Price, Bob Renner, Jim Ross, Jim Scott, Shannon Seaman, Yosh Shima, David Smith, Jack Steen, Bob Ward, Don Woodside.

**Managers:** Tom Adams, Jim Lineham, Rod Stewart.

Canadian Western has often offered to purchase this gas co-op, the very first to be owned and operated by its members. Says director Tom Adams: "At one annual meeting a few years ago a utility man said we'd get better service by selling. Somebody stood up and said, 'We've never been out of gas yet. How much better service can you get?'"

Meota remains very much a kitchen table operation. Co-founder Adams is still serviceman, on-call twenty-four hours a day, while his wife Jesse handles billings and daughter Gwen the secretarial duties. They work from their homes, while co-op manager Rod Stewart runs things from his office, and bookkeeper Sharon Williams computes figures in the back of her store.

## MINCO

- Headquartered in Innisfree.
- Total area: 1339.98 sq. miles
- Total services: 850
- Total pipe: 765.06 miles

**Directors Past and Present:** Elgin Ziegler, George Austin, Wayne Tuck, Ed Baxandall, Steve Rigelhof, John Sawiak, Rex Cunningham, Victor Yaremcio, Robert Fowler, Daniel Lefsrud, Peter Tarapacki, Donald McDonald, Hugh Sangster, Pat Cotter, Bernie Eyben, Robert Rustad, William Soloway, Norman Wascherol, Tony Baker, Bob Bown, Roland Buchanan, Mike Ewashko, Edwin Klein, Al Lechelt, Andy Mazurek, Jake Petroskey, John Stewart, Leonard Grabas, Borden Kaminski, Dale Weder, Robert Tod, Lloyd Tovell, Robert Farkash, Jack Earle, Sharon Bury, Hennig Haverslew, Ed Calder, Ed Sokolski.

**Manager:** Steven Nott.

In 1972 Victor Yaremcio and a friend met Helmut Entrup at a Unifarm natural gas display. At Entrup's urging, they formed a co-op, with Yaremcio becoming secretary/treasurer and his wife, Mabel, converting their children's bedroom into a co-op office. For their part, the little Yaremcios slept in the basement until the co-op moved into a "real" office in 1974.

Director Peter Tarapacki was watching a backhoe operator fill in a deep trench when he noticed a pair of horse ears poking through the dirt. After re-excavating the ditch, he found the rest of the still-breathing, albeit shaken, animal attached. Apparently, the nearly blind nag had tumbled into the open trench the night before. Its owner, insisting the animal had been a "top-notch racehorse" before the fall, demanded and received $160 in compensation from the co-op.

# NATURAL GAS CO-OP #52

- Headquartered in Provost.
- Total area: 1695.70 sq. miles
- Total services: 600
- Total pipe: 776.08 miles

**Directors Past and Present:** Percy Motley, Phil Hochhausen, Lorne Maull, Ambrose Broemeling, John Kozlinski, Ray Ganser, Bill Hawken, Lloyd Smith, Cliff Paulgaard, Robert Murray, Art Woyen, Paul Mazure, Ed Southoff, Ernie Hope, Rod Todd, Jacques Lefebvre, Gordon Carson, Lloyd Cuthbert, Lief Pederson, Jim Kennedy, Gunnar Pederson, Louis Delange, Bernie Flaade, John Bobryk, Orville Broemeling, Alfred Symington, Alex Ference, Phil Hansen, Gordon Cheram, Gillman "Fritz" Crone, Ron Lindsay, Ralph Maull, Roy Fraser, Robert Beatty, Harold Taylor, Keith Boomhower, Robert Johnson, Andrew Rehman, Lawrence Frank, Armand Gerard, Roland Larouche, Cameron Dallyn, Melvin Haldenby, William Beatty, Brian Stempfle, Carl Manske.

**Managers:** Keith MacLean, Brenda Schectel, Daire Ceh, Paula Motley.

It was local farmer Ernie Hope who moved that Unifarm sponsor a co-op formation meeting. Although enthusiastic, those who attended were prevented by community rivalries from agreeing upon an appropriate name. Hence the selection of the unusual but neutral moniker of number fifty-two.

This co-op had to replace 500 miles of faulty PE 3306. Once during re-plow, an angry farmer marched into the co-op office with an armload of muddy, wooden stakes and flung them onto the secretary's desk. He didn't want any co-op pipeline crossing his land. As it turned out, the stakes had been planted by an oil company's seismograph crew which was, understandably, distressed by the mysterious disappearance of its handiwork.

# NORTH EAST

- Headquartered in Bonnyville.
- Total area: 1335.77 sq. miles
- Total services: 1043
- Total pipe: 569.57 miles

**Directors Past and Present:** William Swiderski, Mike Slevinsky, Rodger Williams, Ed Reddecliff, Ted Ganske, William Keen, Les Mitchell, John Zaboschuk, Tom Poulin, Ruby Keen, George Elchuk, Mike Mytrash, Romeo Lefebvre, Dave Godfrey, Walter Penner, Harry Furman, Paul Ulfsten, Paul Bourget.

**Manager:** Ron Fox.

Unable to sell gas as cheaply as the nearby Bonnyville Gas Company, supplier to the town of Bonnyville since 1949, directors asked the utility to build and operate a system for them. The company refused, which stalemated the co-op until 1976 when local rancher Ron Fox became its secretary/treasurer. As the utility officer for the Municipal District of Bonnyville and former rural gas engineer for the province, Fox was able to guide the co-op through construction into operation. "It's been so much fun," commented Fox as manager in 1989. "I often tell directors I should pay them for letting me work here."

As an example of the fun, Fox tells the story of a contractor who once offered a case of whisky to a crew member if he could dump the project engineer overboard during a river crossing. The thirsty crew member readily hopped into a boat with the unsuspecting engineer, rowed to the middle of the river, and, while the engineer checked the depth of pipe, began violently rocking the tiny vessel. "What are you doing?" hollered the engineer, who stubbornly clung to his seat. Recalls Fox: "The crew member was shaking so hard—he wanted that whisky so bad—he damn near fell out of the boat instead."

## NORTH EDMONTON

- Headquartered in Gibbons.
- Total area: 88.12 sq. miles
- Total services: 292
- Total pipe: 112.71 miles

**Directors Past and Present:** Keith Everitt, Ray Rigney, Bruce Bocock, John Shaw Jr., Mike Serink, Reg E. Austin, Don Bevington, John Kampjes, Peter Puchalik, Peter Visscher, Wilfred Shaw, Fred Van Ingen, Bert Hall, Leon Leclerc, James Klassen, Carmon Taylor, Earl Briggs, Clarence Minchau, Walter Wolansky, Henry Hofs, Art Davis, Peter Goutbeck, Larry Schneider, Russ Wessenger, Bernard Blum.

**Managed by Board.**

As a Hallowe'en prank one year, a few construction crew members spraypainted a farmer's pigs red, yellow, green, and blue. When the farmer failed to complain or even mention the incident, then-manager Roy Pritchard asked him if he knew who had decorated his animals. "He did but he wasn't going to give anybody the satisfaction of getting upset. Besides, he figured a little paint wouldn't hurt a hog."

Original director Mike Serink recalls the time Mother Nature intervened to solve an easement problem. "One gentleman, who I will call Mr. X, refused to allow us right-of-way to his place, which was in a vital location. However, nature took our side as Mr. X soon became the late Mr. X and his heirs quickly gave us our easement."

This Co-op has now been amalgamated with Coronado.

## NORTH PEACE

- Headquartered in Fairview.
- Total area: 4057.13 sq. miles
- Total services: 1893
- Total pipe: 1569.31 miles

**Directors Past and Present:** Ben Warren, Ed Pimm, George McKenzie, Larry Schur, Walter Doll, Gordon Allan, Albert Pimm, Carl Przybylski, Ben Hovelkamp, Leo Dechant, Ken Sydnes, Jess Alexander, Peter Polukoshko, Rudy Brauer, Ron Heck, Robert Biggs, Emil Penno, Al Hammerschmidt, Bernard Fedorowicz, Helmut Dewitz, Ed Lueken, Harley McIntyre, Frank McPhail, Elmer Odette, Jim Rasmussen, Lee Rasmussen, Jim Morrison, Ernie Bass, Fred Reaume, Victor Wadsworth, Tom Neary, Gerald Rasberry, Don Hart, Willie Russnak, Peter Dechant, Dennis Fraser, Herm Kastendieck, Bryan Nilsson, Burnice Bamping, Doug Burlock, Allan Bettensen, Jim Sharkey, Irwin McAllister.

**Managers:** Larry Nelson, Harold Watson, Stan Paul.

Co-op founder Ben Warren originally intended to sell propane, but readily switched fuels when the Rural Gas Program came in. Says director Leo Dechant: "We were familiar with the advantages of gas. Northwestern Utilities served the town of Fairview and several farmers had managed to hook onto Northwestern's pipeline."

The biggest North Peace customer is the Town of Manning, which annually accounts for about 25 per cent of the co-op's total gas consumption. Although supplied by the co-op, the town handles its own gas distribution and operations which, says North Peace chairman Ben Hovelkamp, makes it an ideal customer.

## NORTHERN LIGHTS

- Headquartered in La Crete.
- Total area: 1760.35 sq. miles
- Total services: 1347
- Total pipe: 600.89 miles

**Directors Past and Present:** William Fedeyko, David Elias, Fred Deklien, Eugene Dextrase, Walter Kowal, Denise Eek, Henry Schlamp, Ted Lanti, Edward Martens, William Neufeld, Corny Driedger, Ernest Dyck, Dave Neufeld, Isaac Driedger, Peter Friesen, Henry Boehling, David Peters, Joe Foster, Edwin Ward, Peter Chomiak, Jake L. Peters, Al Wilson, Russel Paul, Hal Thiessen, Harold Crieghton, David C. Peters, Dave Klaasen, Dale Robertson, Ben K. Goertzen, Reg McLean, Brian Walker, Gordon Reid, G.A. Toews, Isaac O. Fehr, Joe Janzen, Bob Van Hook, Marten Wieler, Ben Wiebe, John Neufeld, Gordon Peters, Abe Schmidt.

**Managers:** Isaac Peters, Jack Eccles.

Members of this most northerly co-op pay no more for gas than do Edmontonians, a remarkable feat considering the large distances and tough terrain separating customers. Says manager Jack Eccles: "We've done well at keeping expenses down. We're a bunch of cheapskates."

This co-op is also proud of its distinctive logo. Designed by a former staff member, it depicts an Eskimo driving his sled and dog team beneath the aurora borealis.

## ORKNEY

- Headquartered in Carbon.
- Total area: 153.04 sq. miles
- Total services: 93
- Total pipe: 95.95 miles

**Directors Past and Present:** Mort McGhee, Harold Mueller, Frank Davidson, Andy Nakaska, Des Carney, Ken Ferguson, Harry Stanger, Ray Cannings, Don Appleyard, Harry Church, Richard Johnston, Tim Kubinec, Greg Frolik, Ed Nakaska, Elmer Currie, Lloyd Bender, Ted Kubinec, Jim Bishop, Jr., Brian Sowerby, Ted Stahl, Jim Rock, George Rock, Harold King, Gordon Bell, Allen Huxley, Keith Halstead, Grant McIntosh, Finley Code, Gilbert Giesbrecht, Len Andrew, Ted Andrew.

**Managed by Board.**

A customer once built a dam over top of a co-op gas line and stocked the resultant reservoir with fish. When he found the fish floating belly-up a few days later he threatened to sue the co-op for killing them. Worried directors phoned the local Fish and Game warden who not only absolved the co-op of blame, but fined the customer for stocking fish without a licence.

Directors still shiver when they recall the freeze-off of January 1973. "It was cold, blizzarding. Everybody's gas went off. We had to take four-wheel drives and skidoos to get to the regulator station. The first regulator had froze off, and the relief one had clogged and so didn't kick in. We removed the regulators and brought them to my farm shop where we cleaned and thawed them by my coal stove. It was 1 AM before we got them back on and phoned everybody to re-light their furnaces," says one director. Adds chairman Ken Ferguson: "I spent two thirds of the night wandering from my house to the school, the church, and back again re-lighting the furnaces. The pilots would light, act normal, then go out again as soon as I left. Some air must have gotten into the line."

## PADDLE PRAIRIE

- Headquartered in Paddle Prairie.
- Total area: 673.96 sq. miles
- Total services: 129
- Total pipe: 64.08 miles

**Directors Past and Present:** Albert Wanuch, L.M. Villeneuve, Gregory Calliou, Dwayne Calliou, Reta Nooskey, Elmer Ghostkeeper, Tina St. Germain, Helen Christian, G. Christian.

**Manager:** Barry Toker.

This is the only Metis settlement in Canada to build, own, and operate its own gas distribution system. Says chairman Albert Wanuch: "I thought it would be cheaper if we built it ourselves. I'm proud we did rather than relying on outsiders to do it."

Wanuch's past experience as a compressor and meter station operator for NOVA certainly came in handy.

## PAINTEARTH

- Headquartered in Castor.
- Total area: 2375.8 sq. miles
- Total services: 1062
- Total pipe: 1096.98 miles

**Directors Past and Present:** George Ekman, Walter Pickles, Bill Richardson, Ken Schultz, Len Schofer, Ken Penosky, Herb Heir, Bill Green, John James, Jim Schaffner, Len Gabert, George Smith, Walter Hudson, Cliff Downey, Ken Godberson, Charles Freeman, John Forrest, George Kerl, Allan McArthur, Don Yates, Herman Schwenk, George Watson.

**Managers:** George Ekman, Don Olesky, Allan Dietz.

This co-op's first chairman, George Ekman, helped to promote the Rural Gas Program throughout the province as chairman of the Federation of Alberta Gas Co-ops from 1973 to 1975. According to current chairman Herman Schwenk, "there was no one person that had put as much time and effort into organizing and developing" the Paintearth Co-op as Ekman, quite an amazing accomplishment considering his heavy federation duties.

One staff member devotes nearly all of his time to checking for gas line leaks. The reason? Says manager Allen Dietz: "Moles are tunnelling along the pipe, nesting on it, and chewing it in certain spots. There's nothing we can do except diligently walk the line."

# PEKISKO

- Headquartered in High River.
- Total area: 113.55 sq. miles
- Total services: 53
- Total pipeline: 68.89 miles

**Directors Past and Present:** Ralph Nelson, Roy Davis, Arnold Davis, Roy McLean, Tom Fiest, John Wipf, Jim Rockefellow, "Swede" Nelson, John Fitzherbert, Jim Hughes, Derek Runciman, Charlene King.

## Managed by Sunshine Gas Co-op.

When its engineer went bankrupt in 1976, this tiny co-op hired CU Engineering, a subsidiary of Canadian Western, to do its servicing. When Canadian Western disbanded CU in 1982, it offered to buy out Pekisko for $1800 a contract. It was a good price, but members too highly prized their autonomy and instead hired the nearby Sunshine Co-op to service their system. The arrangement has worked well for both parties ever since.

Among Pekisko's customers is the D Ranch, originally part of the EP ranch owned by Edward Prince of Wales in the 1920s.

# PEMBINA RIVER

- Headquartered in Jarvie.
- Total area: 1013.06 sq. miles
- Total services: 810
- Total pipe: 460.75 miles

**Directors Past and Present:** Ted Latimer, Noel Elgert, John Kochan, Stan Mendryk, Len Fox, Walter Manchester, Steve Rozak, James Rockwell, Hardy Terhorst, Jack Trickett, Peter Hansen, Max Zeise, Gordon Thomas, Jack Montgomery, Peter Walter, Louis Primeau, Don Baxandall, Victor Polak, Ed Taber, Geo Grabher, Ed Pearce, Don Petryshen, Louis Schreiner, Jim Armstrong, Frank Petryshyn, Lorne Johnston, Gordon Smith, Alvin Tugwell, John Tymkow, Ivan Watson, Tony Dirks, Harold Hood, Brock Alleman, Sam Yaremko.

**Managers:** Hardy Terhorst, Janet Theriault.

Area farmers first talked of forming a co-op in 1969. But it took a pep talk by co-op advocate Helmut Entrup in 1971 to convince them to proceed. "Helmut told us we couldn't afford to be without gas," recall directors.

However, directors faced a major hurdle—the franchise had no gas source. But the Utilities department rescued them by purchasing an unused oil line running through the area and upgrading it to enable NOVA to bring gas through it. Today, Pembina has its own building, money in the bank, and a reputation for good service.

## PRAIRIE RIVER

- Headquartered in High Prairie.
- Total area: 1277.16 sq. miles
- Total services: 882
- Total pipe: 515.35 miles

**Directors Past and Present:** Edmo Peyre, George Haldorson, Fred Chemerinski, Mike Redlak, Vern Cox, Wes Colton, Joe Zahacy, Lloyd Willsey, Arthur Smith, Steve Starko, George Gordon, Tony Charrois, Gloria Charrois, Willis Wilson, Clayton Bates, Lloyd Dewinter, Arnold Cowell, Darrell Edwards, Roger Houle, John Maxfield.

**Manager:** Larry Grandahl. Now managed by Board.

The manager's job at this co-op has always been shared among the secretary, serviceman, and board chairman. It's obviously a winning combination, for this co-op is debt-free, has a $220 000 reserve account, and an influx of about thirty to forty new customers a year.

However, chairman Arnie Cowell wouldn't mind larger turnouts to annual meetings. "One saving grace is that our employees are co-op members, so it boosts attendance," he laughs. "We'd like some new directors, but it's hard to find younger farmers able to make all the meetings, especially in winter when so many of them are trucking, logging, or out cat skinning. As for their wives, most of them are busy working off-farm."

## ROCKY

- Headquartered in Rocky Mountain House.
- Total area: 1671.03 sq. miles
- Total services: 1213
- Total pipe: 629.46 miles

**Directors Past and Present:** Veral Sims, Ben Simmerlink, R.W. Hallock, Charles Altwater, Arnold Magnus, Ross Godkin, Ron O'Connor, Sent Kloaster, Emery Demas, Chuck McArthur, John Harder, Bruce Graham, Charlie Smith, George Lee, Dennis Ladd, Sam Nelson, Carl Ringness, Wilf Benum, Clarence Klatt, Doris Long, Rupert Murphy, Norman Caukill, Hugh Halladay, Gary Devlieger, Leonard Godkin, Doug Bancroft, Ken Hankinson, Reg Kyncle, Murray Phillips, Tommy Thompson.

**Manager:** Rupert Murphy.

Thanks to this co-op's protests, the Alberta government amended its Municipal Government Act in 1983 to provide co-ops with some protection against annexation by growing towns. Today co-ops must be either allowed to continue serving customers in annexed areas or given compensation for lost revenues.

The co-op now serves an Indian reserve, greenhouses, oil recycling plants, a dry kiln plant, and fish and chicken hatcheries.

## ROCKYVIEW

- Headquartered in Crossfield.
- Total area: 777.74 sq. miles
- Total services: 864
- Total pipe: 641.07 miles

**Directors Past and Present:** Mervin Fox, Melvin Heinzlmeir, Eldon Stafford, R.V. Clayton, Dan McKinnon, Harold Randall, Alastair Groundwater, Don Miller, Harold Knight, Joe Bosch, John Geier, Martin Geier, Ned Williams, Allan Frazer, Ralph Wegener, Vic Koosey, Herman Roedler, B. Cissell, Joe Gallelli, Les Kent, Peter Mason, Leighton Perry, Arnold Jones, Fred Lyczewski, Harvey Baumann, Dave Swanson, Art Vanderwiel, Murray Hurt, Ken Sackett, Peter Harty, Bob Stuart, Gerry Hagel, Wes Henricks, Bob Dickie.

**Manager:** Ed Murray.

Monies Mushroom farm is among the largest customers of this co-op, which serves a mix of farms, ranches, and acreages up to the boundaries of the City of Calgary.

Directors once spent three days trying to find a pipeline which, according to an oil company map, had been built several years before. Unable to locate it, they called in company executives who, after a brief investigation, recalled they'd never actually gotten around to building that line after all. Meanwhile, recall directors, the "field was dug up so bad it looked like World War One out there."

## ROSEBUD

- Headquartered in Rockyford.
- Total area: 712.73 sq. miles
- Total services: 461
- Total pipe: 433.75 miles

**Directors Past and Present:** Duane Heberling, John Cammaert, Merle Marshman, Ernest Walker, Ray Moen, Ed Eskeland, Robert Georgsen, Bill Noy, George Comstock, C.G. "Buck" Braunberger, Jewel Comstock, Quentin Bertsch, Fred Knight, Niels Bach.

**Managers:** John Cammaert, George Comstock.

Assigned to bill collections, director Robert Georgsen soon developed firm but gentle persuasive powers. Once confronted by a lawyer who was always ninety days in arrears, Georgsen calmly asked him if he had his "axe and saw ready." When asked why, Georgsen replied, "Because next week you're going to be burning wood." Georgsen had his cheque that day.

Director John Cammaert remembers collecting a $200 gas bill from one woman. "She pulled out a wad of one dollar bills and began to count 1 . . . 2 . . . 3 . . . I said, 'Whoa, lady. Can't you just write me a cheque?'" Luckily, the woman could and did, thus saving Cammaert much valuable time.

## ROSEMARY

- Headquartered in Rosemary.
- Total area: 159.45 sq. miles
- Total services: 167
- Total pipe: 103.33 miles

**Directors Past and Present:** Eric Dick, Henry Braul, Walter Neufeld, Rudy Peltzer, John Janzen, Lammert Lyzenga, Vern Dyck, Jake Eckert, Pete Springer, Elmer Kropf, Corny Klassen, Henry Dyck, Carl Vern, Peter Dyck Jr., Alfred Peltzer, John Retzlaff.

**Managers:** Mark Watson, Henry Braul, John Retzlaff.

Founding chairman Eric Dick first inquired about getting natural gas in 1963. Although the Social Credit government of the day discouraged the idea as too expensive, Dick continued to discuss it among his friends and by 1970 had rounded up enough farmers to finance a small system. "Financing was tough because so many farmers had been hailed out the previous summer and had little cash," says Dick. "At first all we cared about was heating our homes, but now we use gas to irrigate and heat farm buildings."

## S.R. & B.

- Headquartered in Scandia.
- Total area: 126.19 sq. miles
- Total services: 343
- Total pipe: 162.6 miles

**Directors Past and Present:** Art Larson, C. Schmidt, E. Hofman, K. Anderson, G. Swenson, C. Reeves, T. Palko, Allen Nielsen, Doug Jacobson, Joe Piper, Joe Chomistek, Lawrence Johnson, Allan Sandau, Bernhard Schulz, Rodney Davidson, Casey Verschoor, George Timko, G. Hofmann, L. Swenson, G. Bierens, A. Ohama.

**Manager:** Sheldon Cox.

Named for the surrounding communities of Scandia, Rainier, and Bow City, this co-op was founded by Art Larson, first president of the Federation of Alberta Gas Co-ops.

One of the few serious accidents in the rural gas system occurred here in the spring of 1986. Three maintenance crew members were badly burned when a spark of static electricity ignited the gas in a leaking pipe.

## SOUTH FLAGSTAFF

- Headquartered in Alliance.
- Total area: 785.47 sq. miles
- Total services: 585
- Total pipe: 465.76 miles

**Directors Past and Present:** Peter Spady, Glenn Lunty, Fred Kuefler, Ernie Steadman, Don McMahon, Norman Martz, Andy Cameron, Jack Bateman, Walter Frederick, Hetty Cameron, Bob Forster, Doug Halberg, Dave Galletly, Robert Keichinger, Smith McLennan, Roger Jones, Ed Galm, Ken Hillman, Garth Lunty, David Grovet, Eric Christensen.

**Managers:** Don Olesky, Allan Dietz, Kelly Spady.

As with so many co-ops, members of the local chapter of Unifarm were instrumental in getting things started. Says founding chairman Peter Spady: "Without Unifarm there would be no South Flagstaff Co-op."

As of 1989, this was the only gas co-op with a female chairman—Hetty Cameron. And it was also one of the few co-ops which had to pay a landowner more than $1 for an easement. Recalls Spady: "He insisted on being paid $300. The contractor was getting close to his land and we couldn't reroute, so we paid him. But if he ever wants gas, we're going to get the money back."

## STE. ANNE

- Headquartered in Onoway.
- Total area: 878.87 sq. miles
- Total services: 4925
- Total pipe: 1253.68 miles

**Directors Past and Present:** Henry Tomlinson, B. Dixon, L. Nordlund, G. Carlin, J. Scott, D. Chauncey, D. Simpson, A. Kloeck, G. Miller, H. Brent, B. Dubovsky, E. Felske, S. Kettle, O. Javorsky, E. Hansen, J. O'Brien, C. Brand, F. Cooper, E. Standeven, C. Veltman, E. Struve, D. Thompson, B. Melenka, B. Piepgrass, John Sternberg, Frank Schymizek, Dick Craddock, Carl Christman, Ross Adams, Phil Jungworth, Ted Liss, Bill Golby, Dave MacIntosh, Dan McKeeman, Vic Albrecht, Fred Wheatley, Mark Free, Marg Bradbury, Russ Werenka, Bob Lynes, Roy Johnston, Bob Bell, Darlene Hart, Ed Brent, Jim Davis, Colin Zapotoski, Ernie LeMessurier, Al McEachern, Bruce Horner, Jim Heron, George Turk, Nels Peterson, Dick Huber, Phil Casavant, Bill Buchta, K. Pederson, M. Breitkreuz, B. Johnson, C. Parker, P. Chemago, J. Bencharsky, G. Andrews Jr., L. Javorsky, R. Pritchard, F. Johnson, Doug Brooks, Ed Klinke, Murray Tanchuk, Anne Hayes-Berard.

**Managers:** Roy Pritchard, Henry Tomlinson, Frank Florkewich, Dave Scheideman.

The hole-hog story is a favourite among directors of this co-op, the prototype for the Rural Gas Program. Crews were attempting to lay pipe beneath Highway 16 when they lost their hole-hog, a bullet-shaped, hydraulically operated device, about 4 in. in diameter, used to bore holes under roads. As they frantically dug to find it, a passing motorist stopped her car and demanded to know why they were digging so close to the highway. Upon learning of their loss she sniffed, "Surely no instrument is worth wrecking the highway over." Replied a crew member: "We're not interested in the instrument ma'am. It's the man inside we're worried about." The shocked woman drove away and never bothered them again.

## SUMMERVIEW

- Headquartered in Pincher Creek.
- Total area: 298.5 sq. miles
- Total services: 149
- Total pipe: 165.6 miles

**Directors Past and Present:** Pat Watson, John Mitchell, Paul Tschetter, Fred Ames, Ed Janzen, Jack Smith, Dave Claypool, Bud Jenkins, Art Doram, Bob Burles, Larry Dwyer, Reno Welsch, Scott Hammond, Leonard McGlynn, Horst Puch, Harry Welsch, John MacLeod, Garry Janzen, Lawrence Winters, Gary Lewis, Gerald Lewis, Kerm Stav.

**Manager:** Ed Janzen.

Schoolchildren designed this co-op's logo—a circle with a gas flame in the centre set against a background of mountains and sky. "We teach our children to be very co-op minded, so we think the co-op will be here for a long, long time," say directors, who proudly note they will serve the Oldman Dam upon its completion in the early 1990s. This co-op already serves the Three Rivers Dam.

## SUNSHINE

- Headquartered in Blackie.
- Total area: 1600.64 sq. miles
- Total services: 1293
- Total pipe: 973.8 miles

**Directors Past and Present:** John Green, Blain Middleton, O.M. (Pat) Roe, Milton Ryan, Fred Payce, Ervin Brown, Gordon Mackay, George Gooch, Gilbert Vooys, Gordon Leadbeater, Ralph Oberholtzer, Barry Bricker, Gordon Newman, David Wark, Allan Hurl, Wayne M. Stier, Murray Phillips, Verlyn Culp, Don Gottenberg, Don Young, Grant Cooke, Fred Geschwendt, Dan McNiven, Alvin Winch, Lloyd Groenveld.

**Managers:** Walter Harvey, Larry Grandahl.

Among several co-ops to inadvertently build their original systems with faulty PE 3306 pipe—it had to replow 400 miles of the stuff—Sunshine rebounded from near bankruptcy in 1976 to financial independence in the 1980s. Says former manager Walter Harvey: "Despite all the difficulties, we are now free of debt, have a nice building, reliable staff—all our troubles are over and behind us. And I'm awfully glad to be able to say this."

To commemorate its tenth anniversary in 1984, Sunshine published a twenty-four-page history. Among its many recollections is this one from original director John Green aptly summing up the trials and tribulations of forming a co-op:

*Mistakes, misunderstandings, reinterpretations, people problems, red tape and writing were all frustrating. Contracts, easements, absentee land owners, rerouting, looping and taps were all demanding. Accidents, crop and damage claims, testing, faulty equipment, bad pipe, leaks, replowing and deadlines became worrisome. Financial arrangements, loans, grants, liens, insurance, performance bonds—name it, we had trouble with it. These devils, many a story in themselves, were all erased by ultimate success. We fumbled our way through.*

## SWAN RIVER

- Headquartered in Kinuso.
- Total area: 203 sq. miles
- Total services: 561
- Total pipe: 68.17 miles

**Directors Past and Present:** Bill Karpa, Warren Rybok, Denny Garrett, Rick Pratt, Art Emes, Lorne Larson, June Roe, Bill Berezowsky, Lorne Cornell, Milton Sloan, Norm Gall, James Sprowl, Gilbert Nygaard, Ken Killeen, Dick Churchill.

**Manager:** Jean Sheldon.

Unlike most gas co-ops, this one is not predominantly farmer-owned. Indeed, founder Bill Karpa is the only grain farmer among the directors. The rest are teachers, oil field workers, social workers, electricians, plumbers, and gasfitters who work in the nearby town of Slave Lake. Says Karpa: "A number of our directors can step in as servicemen in emergencies."

Adds office administrator Jean Sheldon: "The rural population here uses gas strictly for house heating."

Crossing the Swan River posed the toughest construction problem for this co-op. Says Sheldon: "The Swan is a terrible and unpredictable river. Its banks are always changing, and it often floods."

## THREE HILLS

- Headquartered in Three Hills.
- Total area: 163.9 sq. miles
- Total services: 207
- Total pipe: 110.9 miles

**Directors Past and Present:** Fred Penner, Horton Dolsen, Lawrence Braconnier, Ray Dau, Dean Lytle, Roy Davidson, Clarence Becker, Vern Kester, Leo Stankievech, Jim Stewart, Vern Crawford, Eldon Brodner, Joe DeBeaudraup, Ray Johnson, Aarne Luomo, Roy Butler, Art Krahn, Les Crawford, Robert Bicknell, Harvey Olsen, Ken Leaf.

**Managers:** Horton Dolsen, Art Krahn.

Although formed in 1966 with the help of then-Three Hills MLA Roy Davidson, this co-op wasn't economically feasible until the Prairie Bible Institute (PBI) agreed to become a customer in 1968. The PBI has never regretted its decision, and when asked its opinion about becoming part of the Town of Three Hills said annexation would be fine as long as the co-op continued to supply its gas. With its reputation for good service and low rates, the co-op has grown from only 29 members to more than 200 today.

## THREE RIVERS

- Headquartered in Whitecourt.
- Total area: 543.51 sq. miles
- Total services: 681
- Total pipe: 370.2 miles

**Directors Past and Present:** B. Hanson, W.G. Smith, F. Selleck, William Heslop, F. Pischinger, I. McGregor, F. Starman, R. Shuck, F. Tschigerl, D.D. Stockwell, E.B. Selleck, R. Thompson, D. Haines, K. Charles, I. Von Wackerbarth, P.E. Pritchard, R. Huntley, R. Krause, C. Gould, J. Lilley, William Fischer, C. McIlwaine, W. Ball, W. Jackson, T. Birkbeck, J. Bates, G. Merrifield, R. Merrifield, A. Meilicke, P. Baxter, D. Hoybak, D. Thomas, R. McCallum, R. Worobec, N. Latka, James McCallum.

**Managers:** Ted Selleck, Roy Merrifield.

Fire destroyed this co-op's office and records on January 2, 1980. It was a bad start to the New Year, but with the help of suppliers, the bank, and the Utilities department, directors were soon able to reconstruct co-op files. Fortunately, nobody was in the office when the fire, caused by a faulty wall heater, occurred.

This co-op is one of the only ones (Pembina River is another) to use the budget billing method. Every year it estimates each customer's gas consumption for the next twelve months, divides by twelve, and bills the customer the same amount each month. At year end, customers are either charged or reimbursed for the difference between estimated and actual use.

## TIROL

- Headquartered in Tilley.
- Total area: 264.16 sq. miles
- Total services: 514
- Total pipe: 212.21 miles

**Directors Past and Present:** Leo Skanderup, John Hollenzer, Frank Stevens, Dave Friesen, Gordon Nielsen, William Sinclair, Dale Patterson, Jack Hutchison, Cleo Dunne, Walter Olafson, Joseph Volek, Robert Holt, Keith Benson, Edwin Bronsch, Reinhold Hirch, Ralph Kristianson, John Straub, Alfred Tessman, Frank Virovec, Frank Zahenaiko, James Burton, Chris Christensen, Leo Corriveau, Robert Daniels, Lawrence Dolter, Helmut Entrup, William Garden, John Hollinda, Norman Jasperson, Steve Johasz, Albert Lester, William Lester, Clayton McNalley, Marvin Miller, William Mortensen, Steve Mrakava, Alfred Nygaard, Clarence Rosdal, Halvar Rosdal, Reinhold Schiemann, Rasmus Skriver, Mike Skuban, John Suchy, Robert Thomsen, Ben Valerian, John Voroney, Jack Lester, M. Skrove, Don Friesen, Carl Hendriksen, Jorden Jacobson.

**Joint Managers:** Ruth Colbens, Keith Shuttleworth.

Among the pioneer co-ops, Tirol was bound to experience a few glitches. For example, the co-op decided to test its system for leaks by pumping odorant, nicknamed "skunk juice," into the lines. Unfortunately, the line wasn't yet connected at one person's home, and the odorant, which smells like rotten eggs, wafted inside the house, rendering it uninhabitable for weeks.

Moreover, its first batch of pipe was faulty. Recalls one director: "Gas lines started to break as soon as they were pressured up. Pipes were bursting—it was quite a mess. We ended up in a conflict with the pipemaker, an eastern firm. And for a time, the provincial government stepped in and took over our co-op."

## TRIPLE W

- Headquartered in Wrentham.
- Total area: 934.45 sq. miles
- Total services: 830
- Total pipe: 520.48 miles

**Directors Past and Present:** Ted Rudd, Roy Nelson, Wayne Bartlett, Elda Mueller, R.K. Bailie, Vince Bobinec, Jerry Kubik, David Waldner, Joseph Wurz, Jacob Hofer, Stan LaValley, John Entz, George Wurz, Gordon Mackenzie, Jack Ashmore, Ernie Reid, Bill Thomas, Clayton Soice, Forest Greeno, Peter Waldner, Oscar Mueller, Otto Cronkhite, Glen Svenson, Ray Depew, Ed Fenz, George Kleinsasser, George D. Minion, Jacob Waldner, Donald M. Duncan, Peter B. Coppieters, Peter M. Coppieters, Nim Sugimoto, Alvin Bullock, Calvin Hancock, Harold Pittman, Ken Culler, Lindy Smith, Frank Vas, Dale Morrison, Peter Entz, Bob Edwards, Ernie Nottingham, Bob Duncan, August Kaupp, Harry Swanson, Dennis Lagler, Jack Kearns, Allan Jones, George Mandel, Andy Gross, Collin Holt, Doug Mueller, Bill Duncan, Bruce Atkins, Murray Doenz, Derek Baron, Carson Mueller, Andrew Wipf, Bob Thomas.

**Manager:** Beryl Brantner.

Unofficial manager Beryl Brantner remembers fondly the early days of this pre-act co-op. "It was exciting getting orders written on the back of calendars or information scribbled on old envelopes or whatever else Ted Rudd, our first chairman, had handy. I often told him not to wash his hands until I had a chance to check them for important notes."

"There were so many times in the height of the mass confusion that I'd get phone calls from people needing an answer almost immediately. It's a tough situation. I was never really the manager, but just stumbled through."

Among the most memorable excuses for non-payment of a gas bill, says Brantner, came from a fellow who claimed to have received a telegram saying, "Mother died. Send money so we can bury her."

## WAINEDGE

- Headquartered in Wainwright.
- Total area: 710.94 sq. miles
- Total services: 400
- Total pipe: 366.81 miles

**Directors Past and Present:** Don Redmond, Gordon Donaldson, Bryan Perkins, Glen Berg, Robert Rajotte, Ray Belanger, Les Johnson, Ralph Patterson, Everett Tuffe, Allan Hicox, Raleigh Kett, Mark Perkins, Clayton Tondu, Tom Pederson, Ken Wasmuth, Jim Fraser.

**Managers:** Ralph Gilbert, Lawrence Hoover, Allan Johnson.

Muskeg caused plenty of trouble for this co-op, say directors. Pipelines floated and had to be re-laid. And at least one plow cat had to be winched from the mud, a rescue that took hours.

The provincial government has encouraged this co-op to amalgamate with nearby Co-op # 52. "But local autonomy is important here and our members don't want to," say directors.

## WASHOUT CREEK

- Headquartered in Buck Lake.
- Total area: 8.61 sq. miles
- Total services: 15
- Total pipe: 7.05 miles

**Directors Past and Present:** Charlie Parker, Lloyd Alcock, Ernest Parker, Paul Rainer, Faye Parker, Gordon Borle, L. Misku, F. Foster, Harry Foster, A.J. Rainer, P.B. Rainer, Jim Foster.

**Manager:** Charlie Parker.

Even though it is the smallest gas co-op, Washout Creek boasts one of the lowest gas rates in Alberta at 37 cents per gigajoule.

## WEST PARKLAND

- Headquartered in Stony Plain.
- Total area: 465.33 sq. miles
- Total services: 3218
- Total pipe: 847.8 miles

**Directors Past and Present:** Ed Fuhr, Ron Morris, Henry Schutz, Ken Porter, Ed Ulmer, Russell Scheideman, R. Miskey, C. White, Hilding Dekinder, Gerald Schoepp, Al Olson, Jerry Goebel, Keith Waters, Peter Mik, P.C. Carey, P. Florkewich, D. Kondruck, M. Velichko, Art Boje, H. Wagner, Tim Stevenson, Albert Schultz, Wm. Seehagel, Wm. Reimer, Wm. Goebel, Ron Martin, John Lemckert, Cy Trudel, F. Florkewich, Wayne Donner, Pat Davis, Orest Oginski, Bunnie Grant, Cameron MacDonald, Denis Dubrule, Vern Kibblewhite.

**Managers:** Reinhold Miskey, Don Griffiths, Larry Nelson, Al Taylor, Dennis Lenner.

Area residents tried three times to form a co-op before the Rural Gas Program was announced. Says founding director Ken Porter: "The program was just what we needed to get us going."

With about 80 per cent of its customers being acreage owners or summer village residents, this co-op has higher than average turn over and is constantly showing new members how to read meters.

## WEST THORHILD

- Headquartered in Thorhild.
- Total area: 9 sq. miles
- Total services: 42
- Total pipe: 30.46 miles

**Directors Past and Present:** Bob Remley, Bill Ewasiw, Nick Babiak, Jerry Baver, Stan Kaminski, George Quaghebeur, Herb Holgate, Ed Wiess, Zenny Mandziuk, David Chaba, Ron Mykyte, Fred Skowronski.

**Managed by Board.**

The Superior Natural Gas Company had offered to serve some of the residents in the area when Helmut Entrup, speaking at a local Unifarm meeting, persuaded people to form a co-op in 1971.

Directors feared a long construction delay when their home-made plow failed to lay pipe deep enough on its test run. Luckily, a few adjustments to the angle of the plow shaft solved the problem and the co-op was on its way.

## WINTERING HILLS

- Headquartered in Hussar.
- Total area: 188.51 sq. miles
- Total services: 85
- Total pipe: 114.11 miles

**Directors Past and Present:** Ray Snyder, Leonard Armstrong, George Kaiser, Albert Kaiser, Joe Merkel, George Thompson, Gordon Sandum, Peter Isaak, Gordon Armstrong, Rick Laursen, Gordon Schaffer.

**Manager:** Peter Isaak.

Among the biggest challenges faced by this co-op was persuading absentee American landowners to sign easements. Says one director: "Some of these Americans had had bad experiences with oil companies over right-of-ways."

Servicemen Roy Clark and Leonard Armstrong once played a harmless prank on a government inspector, who was a nice but humourless man. Clark was standing in a trench completing a repair to a gas line when the inspector walked up. "Have you got a lighter, Len?" called out Clark. "I want to test this pipe and I can't find a match." Recalls Armstrong: "The inspector nearly exploded when he heard that."

## YELLOWHEAD

- Headquartered in Edson.
- Total area: 892.30 sq. miles
- Total services: 1235
- Total pipe: 478.56 miles

**Directors Past and Present:** Ernie Fahrion, Vic Maris, Louis Baudin, Paul Miluch, Jeff Emmons, Clarence Love, George Seibel Sr., Ed Sobush, Roy Mellersh, Alvin Acorn, Nick Romaniuk, Eric Karlzen, Tom Haddock, Wanda Fossheim, Dietre Hiese, Joe Kistenfeger, Martin Theile, Ed Birkenhagen, Leonard Plante, Francis Mellersh, Earl Oliver, Dorothy Rurka, John Van Woudenberg, Frank Resek, Carl Tews, Roger Pelletier, Carl Stitzenberger, James Lawrence, Ken Nelson, Norman Fowler, Hank Fousert, Albert Dykema, Pam Pambrun, Phyllis Daniels.

**Managers:** Vic Maris, Don Rutherford, Richard Thorne, Gordon Zweitzer.

This co-op, which stretches about 130 miles from end to end, broke trail for the others in two important areas: it was the first to obtain special grants to cover the extra costs of building in tough terrain; and, it was the first to continue serving customers in an annexed portion of its franchise.

Among this co-op's commercial customers are a coal mine and the Canadian National Railway, which uses natural gas heating in winter to prevent its switching stations from freezing.

# The Counties

## COUNTY OF SMOKY LAKE NATURAL GAS UTILITY

- Total area: 981.61 sq. miles
- Total services: 1480
- Total pipe installed: 800 miles

**Councillors past and present:** John Boyko, Bill Kuryliw, Donald Tkachuk, W.M. Cherniwchan, John Chorwonak, Henry Melnyk, Orest Sobzda, Nick Darichuk, Fred Moschansky, Peter Habiak, Jeff Wade, Alex Makowichuk, George Baibchuk, Dennis Holowaychuk, Dareld Cholak, Joe Dombowsky, Bob Novosiwsky.

**Manager:** Cary Smigerowsky.

At the request of area farmers, this county plunged into the rural gas business in 1974 by launching a massive canvassing drive that resulted in an 80 per cent sign-up. With this excellent number, the county was ready to begin building in July 1975. It purchased a plow and by February 1976, had buried some 150 miles of plastic and aluminum pipe. Huge boulders and sandstone bedrock were among the major construction obstacles. Distance was another. Remembers one former councillor: "Because we were a county system, we had to include everyone in the area, whatever the cost. So one farmer's line was 6 miles long, and he only used gas for a hot water heater."

## COUNTY OF THORHILD

- Total area: 812.65 sq. miles
- Total services: 1170
- Total pipe installed: 685 miles

**Councillors past and present:** Steve Schwetz, Ted Bewcharski, Reg Nikiforuk, John Small, Davie Barnes, Peter Goruk, David Petroski, Walter Wolansky, Marris Yurkiw, William Skuba, Charles Crosswell, L. Kuzik, D. Delorme, Steve Presdyk, Stanley Olchowy, Jerry Bauer, John Boychuk, Nick Lagowski, Kathy Clark, Leo Larose, Randy Ewasko, William S. Kasliw.

**Manager:** Bill Kostiw.

Reeve Steve Schwetz, secretary/treasurer Peter Wolosechuk, and councillor William Skuba were holidaying at the Fairmont Hotsprings with their wives in 1970 when they began discussing the comforts of natural gas and what a boon it would be for the county. By 1974, county council had sorted through all of the legalities and was ready to canvass the countryside for contracts and easements. Steve Malanchuk, the county's first gas serviceman, and John Kaban, its first manager, did most of the canvassing.

Recalls Malanchuk: "The name on one land title was simply "Sundog." The place was a two-room log house, unfurnished except for mattresses on the floor and people everywhere. In the middle of the yard was a "hippie" on his knees, like he was worshipping Allah. After this Sundog fellow finally signed the easement, they gave me some coffee. I drank it and could barely make it out of the house, I got so dizzy. I'm sure they put marijuana in it."

## COUNTY OF TWO HILLS

- Total area: 1090.17 sq. miles
- Total services: 1239
- Total pipe installed: 865 miles

**Councillors past and present:** John Dudar, John Bober, Vince Romaniuk, Victor Chrapko, Walter Verenka, Bill Stewart, Nick Dushenski, Fred Hasiuk, Robert Bachelet, Dan Ursuliak, Bill Kokotailo, Alexander Boida, M. Stefaniuk.

**Managers:** Ed Bragg, Eugene Dmytriw.

When a group of area farmers was unable to sign up enough co-op members, they asked county council to take over. The county hired a few local people to canvass the area and in 1976 began construction. Unlike Smoky Lake, which did its own construction, Two Hills hired ICG to engineer, manage, and inspect the project. Despite rock, gravel pits, and some large trees, crews plowed some 700 miles of pipe within two years. Councillors say today the system is running well, with money in the bank.

## COUNTY OF VERMILION RIVER

- Total area: 1977.43 sq. miles
- Total services: 2337
- Total pipe installed: 1633 miles

**Councillors past and present:** Frank Wheat, Art Nicholson, Gordon Davidson, F. Wolters, L.A. Kenzie, W.B. Graham, J.C. Anderson, Don Wilson, Harold Nickless, A.M. Bell, D. Cherry, C.G. Goldsmith, F. Vanwageningen, R. Vanee.

**Manager:** Dave Stewart.

When the Vermilion River Gas Co-op couldn't sign enough members, the county took over, purchased equipment, hired crews, and contracted CU Engineering to design a system. Construction began in May 1979; the first gas was turned on in March 1980, and the entire system completed by 1983. The system is in good financial shape, thanks partly to several lucrative oil company customers whose wells, gas heaters, and treating plants are powered by natural gas. Several out-of-province visitors have inspected this system, including a Saskatchewan Power official and representatives from the People's Republic of China.

# Towns and Villages

## TOWN OF CASTOR

**Councillors past and present:** Mike Bain (mayor), Kenneth Wetter (mayor), John Wright.

Before gas, residents of this farm community in eastern Alberta used coal from several local mines which are now closed.

Interest in gas was generated in 1962, when residents became aware of the convenience and costs in other towns supplied with gas. Palmer Engineering was hired to drill a well and when gas was located, proceeded to design and build an all steel system. Work began in the summer of 1963. No real problems were encountered in construction and the system was completed in late fall.

Most town residents took gas immediately and have since been provided with virtually trouble-free service. Today the system supplies 510 residential and commercial consumers.

Many local farmers now retire in Castor because all conveniences, including natural gas, are available at virtually the same costs as in the larger cities.

## TOWN OF DAYSLAND

**Councillors past and present:** Allen Pryor (mayor), Sam Worth, Bill Stevens, George Cramton, Les Dolanz, Joe Swoboda, John Josephison, Art Ginter (secretary/treasurer), Graeme Davidson, Ina Wendt (mayor), Joe Adams, Joe Longhe, Gary Meyer, Don Surdiak, Avril Crossley (administrator), Dave Gordash (assistant), Al Wallace (manager).

Daysland, which is located 40 km southwest of Camrose, has served its 370 customers since gas was turned on in 1967. Al Wallace has been involved with this town's gas system since its inception in 1965. He supervised construction and upon completion in March 1967, was hired to manage the system, a job he still held in 1989. Originally, gas was supplied through 10 km of pipeline from two wells near town. In 1972 the wells failed, so the town installed another 2.5 km of pipeline to connect the system to Nova. Two years later the town began sharing lines and facilities with Ankerton Gas Co-op, which served the surrounding area.

## TOWN OF DEVON

**Councillors past and present:** George H. Thompson (mayor), J.W. Somers, George C. Powell, William T. Currie, John J. Bowen, William P. Henderson, Dale Fisher (mayor), Dick Steinhauer, Don Szyndrowski, Denis Paquette, Bob McDonald, Dianne Tharp, Gary Browning.

Devon, located just southwest of Edmonton, was Canada's first "Model Oil Town." Built in the late 1940s in the first oil boom, the streets and services were all built by Imperial Oil Ltd. for its workers in the oil industry.

In 1950 the newly incorporated town bought the natural gas system from Imperial. The steel pipe used in construction was the heavy walled pipe that was being used in the oil industry. Early residents hooked up to gas as soon as it was available as they were well aware of its application and economics.

The gas franchise grew with the town to match the corporate boundaries and service is now provided to about 1300 outlets including schools, a hospital, coal research centre, and light industrial customers. Gas and water meters are read at the same time and billing is done from the town office, also bought from Imperial Oil. Service is provided by trained staff around the clock and service vehicles are equipped for any emergency.

Insurance was a serious problem until the town joined the federation of Alberta Gas Co-ops. Having joined the federation, the town made use of other benefits such as gas industry training, related information at conventions, problem solving, and a joint voice with others in the same business.

Town-operated gas systems can be used as a marketing tool to entice industry into the town.

# TOWN OF HIGH PRAIRIE

In 1959 a natural gas system was installed by Northland Utilities serving some 500 customers who lived within the boundaries of the Town of High Prairie. The source of the natural gas was two wells located 18 miles north of High Prairie. A transmission line was installed connecting the town users to each of the two wells. One well was owned by Imperial Oil (ESSO Petroleum) and the other by a consortium headed by Husky Oil. Both wells were located in the Hudson Bay—Union Heart River field. The franchise granted by the Town of High Prairie was for a period of 10 years, to 1969. The franchise was further extended for 5 years. During the 5-year period, Northland Utilities sold the natural gas system to Northwestern Utilities Ltd.

During the early 1970s, Mayor Fred J. Dumont and the town council explored many avenues to raise the necessary funds to purchase the distribution and transmission system from Northwestern Utilities. The usual funding source for municipalities, the Alberta Municipal Financing Corporation, could not, under existing laws, approve debentures for municipalities for the purchase of utility systems.

Given that Palmer Engineering had done a study of the system's operation telling town council that ownership of this utility was comparable to a "money tree" in terms of its profitability, the town sought and received authority to borrow the necessary funds from the Royal Bank of Canada. Mayor Dumont and the town secretary/treasurer met in Toronto with Royal Bank executives to secure the loan.

The purchase of a system back in the 70s was a complex and difficult project. First a hearing was held by the Public Utilities Board to set the price of the system. Northwestern Utilities used their expertise to put forth a solid case to the P.U.B. for a sale price many times more than the figure provided to the town by its own consulting firm. A third group of experts in evaluation techniques provided a figure which was acceptable to the P.U.B. and the Town of High Prairie. Secondly, the town had to prove to the P.U.B.'s satisfaction that a reliable supply of natural gas was available. Experts from Northwestern Utilities stated that both wells would become water-logged in a short span of time. The town's consultant predicted that the wells would continue to serve the needs of consumers for many years. In view of the fact that other wells, then tapped, could be accessed if Northwestern's predictions were correct, finally allowed the P.U.B. to rule in favour of the town.

The final negotiations were held at Northwestern's head office building in Edmonton and the bank draft was handed over and reluctantly accepted. In February of 1974, the town was the proud owner of a natural gas utility. To this day the original wells are still producing enough natural gas to serve an expanded system of 1120 residential, commercial, and industrial customers. During the late 70s the Prairie River Gas Co-op was established to serve out-of-town customers and initially used the town's gas supply. Later the Prairie River Gas Co-op built a transmission line to several wells located south of the town. Both systems were interconnected and a natural gas exchange agreement was reached thus ensuring long-term reliability of supply for both the co-op and the town.

The purchase of the system, however difficult, provided a blueprint to other municipalities to assist them to "wrestle away" franchises from other large corporations. The system has indeed proven to be a "money tree." In spite of the dramatic increases in natural gas prices, the town has managed to turn a yearly profit. By 1990 the system was paid for in full and the town had accumulated a surplus of over one-half million dollars. At the same time, the Town of High Prairie has been able to maintain one of the lowest natural gas rates in Alberta. The town operates with qualified staff and also now provides support and service, not only to the Prairie River Co-op, but to a nearby Indian Reservation.

## TOWN OF LAC LA BICHE

**Councillors past and present:** Michael Maccagno (mayor), Lionel Vincent (deputy mayor), Floyd McMillan, Eli Tkachuk, James Hamar, Harry Lobay, Ernie Shanks, Alcide "Sid" Baglot (manager).

"Make no little plans: they have no magic to stir men's blood and probably themselves will not be realized. Make big plans: Aim high in hope and work." So reads the inscription on the souvenir program from this system's opening ceremonies held September 26, 1960. It's advice town councillors have taken to heart in operating one of Alberta's oldest town-owned systems.

Northland Utility built the system in 1959 and sold it to the town the following year. In 1966 and 1977 council extended the system's franchise area to serve farmers east and west of town. The system has always run smoothly and in 1990 Mayor Michael Maccagno was at work on a book chronicling the system's success.

## TOWN OF MANNING

**Councillors past:** Delphine Harbourne (mayor), Robert Schmidt, Alvis Dechant, Robert Banach, Darrell Smith, Frank Moreside, Eldwyne Jones.

This system was running well and was fully paid off by 1988 although it had been built of 3306 plastic and had to be completely replaced in 1981. Town councillors credit the system's success to a wide array of organizations and individuals including Alberta Consumer and Corporate Affairs, Alberta Parks and Recreation, and MLA Al "Boomer" Adair. Work on the system began in 1973 with a feasibility study by Omega Techno Ltd. and ended October 17, 1975, with a gas turn-on ceremony. Construction highlights included the crossing of the Notikewin River, accomplished by local contractor Robert Schmidt and his crew in only two days. This system was originally supplied by the Manning Gas Co-op, which has since amalgamated with the North Peace Gas Co-op. As of 1990, the Town of Manning was the North Peace Gas Co-op's biggest customer.

## NEW TOWN OF RAINBOW LAKE

**Councillors past and present:** Norm Milne (chairman), Jack Scott (deputy chairman and chairman), Jim Kirwan, Frank Wilson, Jean Lederer, Al Freckelton (deputy chairman), Darcy Wilson, Ernie Hunt, Gary Whelan.

Even the most ardent supporters of the Rural Gas Program doubted a town as far north as this one (72 miles west of High Level) would ever enjoy the convenience of natural gas. But in 1980 a determined town manager, Doreen Bello, wrote to the provincial government about the feasibility of getting service. It was a daunting prospect considering the lack of supply, but the government responded by building a $1.1-million, 18-mile transmission line into Rainbow Lake in 1981. This enabled the town to build its 55 000 foot system. By December, 85 per cent of the residents were burning gas. By 1990 there were 348 primary connections and 103 secondary ones. Doug Brown, who was hired to oversee the construction, now maintains and operates the system.

## TOWN OF REDWATER

Esso Resources built the original system in 1950 to service its employees living in town. Later Esso sold the system to Redwater Utilities, which in turn sold to the Town of Redwater in 1976. By 1990 the system had 775 residential and 130 commercial subscribers and was still owned and operated by the town. Gas supply which was originally bought from an Esso Resources well is now taken from a Nova line.

## TOWNS OF SEDGEWICK-KILLAM

**Councillors past and present: Sedgewick:**
Howard Smith (mayor), A. Edwards, Norm
Culbert, Lawrence Kneeland (secretary), Ken
Offord (chairman), Robert Hansen (mayor),
Jeannette Harris, Harry Raine (secretary/treasurer).
**Killam:** Gordon Hilker (mayor), Arnold Saunders,
Eddie Dammann, Sid James (secretary), Brian
Sorenson (deputy chairman), John Felgate, Tony
Schnettler, Vera Engel (secretary/treasurer), Jack
Warner (mayor).

In 1964 these two towns, east of Camrose,
previously reliant on propane, decided to jointly
build a natural gas system. They hired Palmer
Engineering to design a system and secure a gas
supply and Campion Pipelines of Edmonton to
build the system. Al Wallace, a pipeliner with
experience in rural Alberta and Ontario, supervised
construction and was subsequently hired to
manage the system, a job he still held in 1989.

Construction began in May 1965 and a turn-on
ceremony was held November 1, 1965 after the
job was completed. Until 1974, the towns were
relying on two gas wells for their gas supply. The
wells depleted, a 10 km pipeline was built to a
Nova pipeline. This new source is now shared by
the Iron Creek Gas Co-op. Jointly these two towns
serve around 900 customers.

## TOWN OF SMOKY LAKE

**Councillors past and present:** George Kozub
(mayor), Nick Palamarek (secretary/treasurer), Harry
Leskiw, George Rredy, John Kaban, Steve W.
Romanchuk, N.W. Purych, Frank Stockl, Maurice
Lalonde (chairman), Peter Goruk (mayor), Walter
DeSilva, Elmer Oshan, Ken Osepchuk.

By chance, in 1943, a British American (BA)
official called in at the town office to ask for
directions to the BA drilling rig. Rather than give
the confusing directions, Nick Palamarek, the town
secretary/treasurer, went with him to show the
way. As they drove, they discussed the well being
drilled, and the possibility of it serving the Town
of Smoky Lake. Afterwards Nick wrote to Head
Office in Regina, and received a courteous reply,
stating that "in the event of any development of a
town gas system, BA would be glad to serve the
community." Nick filed the letter and forgot it.

Twenty years later, in 1963, the gas system idea
was revived by council. Approximately 97 per cent
of the proprietary electors were in favour of a self-
liquidating town-owned natural gas system. The
provincial government of the day was not in favour
of municipally-owned gas systems so the Public
Utilities Board ruled the vote invalid on a technicality.
A second vote was taken with the same result.

Debentures were issued to cover the installation
cost of $197 000, estimated by Bruce Palmer, the
engineer who had been engaged to plan the
specifications and estimates. The construction of
the Smoky Lake town system was completed in
November '63. However BA refused to deal with
the town council and supply gas for their system.
Nick Palamarek produced his letter of intent. The
BA company lawyer declared it was illegal—the
writer had no authority in the matter 20 years before.

The Minister of Mines and Minerals pleaded ignorance,
stating that he was not aware that the transmission
line was laid to the No. 1 and No. 2 Edwand BA gas
wells. He failed to remember that he had signed
documents for some of the rights-of-way for the natural
gas transmission line.

The matter was taken to Michael Maccagno, Liberal
MLA in opposition. It was brought before the Alberta
Legislature. The British American Oil Co. Ltd. had
broken the law by refusing to comply with By-law No.
170 and was in danger of being cited for contempt of

the law. The Town of Smoky Lake engaged Arnold Moire, a highly noted lawyer. The publicity by Michael Maccagno, Arnold Moire, and the *Edmonton Journal* brought public pressure on the British American Oil Co. Ltd. for having unethical, restrictive business practices.

BA yielded to the pressures by the press, the government, and the public, and offered to sell Edwand No. 1 well to the Town of Smoky Lake for $100 000. This placed the town in a problem situation again since By-law No. 170 did not authorize town council to make such a purchase. The provincial government came to the rescue. A special act was presented and passed by the Alberta Legislature. The passage of "The Town of Smoky Lake Gas Utility Act" enabled the town to purchase the BA Edwand No. 1 and the right to drill a stand-by well without the need of receiving the consent of the proprietary electors or local authority board.

In 1971 the town tried to drill another well on a different section. The well was a wildcat—drill stems were flying out like toothpicks. It was two weeks before it could be sealed off and cemented in. That well cost the town $105 000. Several other wells have since been drilled, only one of which was usable, and that is sitting idle until it is needed.

The town draws all of its gas from three wells owned and operated 100 per cent by the Town of Smoky Lake Gas Utility. "The Smoky Lake town owned self-liquidating natural gas system has provided a viable financial potential for the town, to attract people and industry into the town of Smoky Lake." (Extract from local history book.)

## TOWN OF SUNDRE

**Councillors past and present:** Louis Lund (mayor), E.A. Halvorson, R.W. Martyn, R. Christopher, A.W. Nelson, H. Chemelli, N.S. Ellithorpe. (**Gas committee members:** E. Trevor Morgan, N.S. Ellithorpe, E. Vennard, J. Howton, R. Macleod, V. Richter.) Terry Leslie (mayor), Gwen Fletcher, R.W. (Bill) Scott, Ken Guenther, Jerry Convery, Tim Williams, Wm. (Bill) Cooper, Harvey Doering.

Town councillors began investigating the feasibility of obtaining natural gas service in 1961. After looking at the systems owned by Lac La Biche and Milk River, council held a plebiscite in 1962 and obtained unanimous approval to proceed. Council hired engineers Pryde, Flovin and Associates Ltd. and contractor Canadian Well Services who completed construction by the fall of 1962. As of 1989, the system has 785 residential and commercial customers.

## TOWN OF VALLEYVIEW

In 1960 town council approached Northland Utilities for gas service but was turned down for the usual reason—it would be economically unfeasible. Undaunted, council pursued other options and by 1963 had raised enough funds through debentures to finance the building of a transmission and distribution system supplied from a number of local wells. Interestingly this "economically unfeasible" system has done so well that several organizations have offered to purchase it, including the nearby East Smoky Natural Gas Co-op and a major utility. "We have a lot of takers," says town employee Joyce Craig. "Generally, our system breaks even or generates some extra revenue for the town every year." Valleyview now serves 775 customers.

## TOWN OF WAINWRIGHT

Supply has never been a problem for this gas system. Local man Charles Taylor discovered oil and gas in the area in 1914 and formed the Gratton Oil Company, which eventually sold its leases to the Northwest Company, a subsidiary of Imperial Oil. Several companies have since drilled wells and/or operated refineries in the area, including British Petroleums of Vancouver, Wainwell Oils Ltd., American Northland Oils, Petro Canada, and Husky Oil. In 1989, over 400 people were employed in the local oil and gas fields.

In 1927 a large portion of the town was serviced with natural gas from wells in the Fabyan area. The wells and system were owned by a Mr. Campbell whose sons sold the system to the town in 1965, but retained ownership of the wells. The town has owned and operated the system ever since with gas now supplied by Interprovincial Gas Co. from wells in the Fabyan area.

The town of Wainwright is nearing completion of a program to replace all old mains and services (steel) with polyethylene plastic. All new construction to serve the growing town is with PE plastic.

## VILLAGE OF ANDREW

Andrew-area MLA George Topolnisky was already a natural gas veteran when the Alberta government launched its Rural Gas Program. In 1965 Topolnisky, then Mayor of the Village of Andrew, joined with fellow councillors Peter Palamarchuk and George Pesaruk in investigating the feasibility of obtaining natural gas service for the village. When price quotations by Plains Western proved too high, the councillors decided to build their own system and hired Palmer Engineering to build a 10-mile pipeline from a gas well southeast of Andrew. Construction began in October 1966 and by the end of the year gas was flowing through the $180 000 system to 116 members. By 1990, the municipally-owned system had 312 connections and was fully paid for. Topolnisky recalls that securing a gas supply, selling debentures, and freeze-ups were among the major problems in the early days. "My background in building a municipal-owned system served me in good stead when the province undertook its Rural Gas Program," says Topolnisky, who while he was in Cabinet had the responsibility of Rural Development.

One advantage to the town owning a gas system is that profits earned would stay in the community and could be earmarked to support public projects such as community halls and pools or simply to reduce heating costs.

## VILLAGE OF BOYLE

**Councillors past and present:** John Nayowski (mayor), Pete Hupka, Lou Fetaz, Clint Berg, George Opryshko, Walter Harrynuck (mayor), Fred Lamiuk, Ken Nayowski, Malcolm Herrman.

The first discussions on natural gas were held in 1963, but interest wasn't revived until neighbouring Lac La Biche acquired its system. A plebiscite was held in 1966 and the residents were in favour of the idea.

Palmer Engineering was hired first to do a feasibility study, and then as consulting engineer. A gas well was offered by Continental to the village for about $25 000, "as is." When the price dropped to $15 000 a year later, the village bought it.

Debentures were issued and the Social Credit government was approached. In previous years, the government had been buying debentures from municipal systems to promote gas for Albertans. But the village received a letter saying, "No more debentures." The debentures were eventually sold locally, a very difficult task. The rest of the money was borrowed from the bank.

A half section of land was bought and a second well drilled as one was insufficient for the system. The cost of this well, which came in at 2000 feet, was between $25 000 and $30 000. In 1987 the village hooked up to the Nova system and since that time, gets its gas supply from both sources.

At the 1989 convention of the Federation of Alberta Gas Co-ops, this village's gas system was commended for being among the best in the province. Indeed, the system has been trouble-free since its construction in 1967 to present day.

## VILLAGE OF CHAUVIN

**Councillors past and present:** Harold Hjelmeland (mayor), Robert Taylor, Robert Delemont, George Gibb, Belva Goede (mayor), Perry McMann, Bert Newton (mayor), Alf Pollard, Phil Sevigny.

In the early days, the villagers went to the coulees of the Battle River and cut trees for wood for fuel. The village council at one time stipulated that chimneys had to be high enough, so that in the event of a chimney fire, burning debris would not fall on the neighbours' roofs. Later oil and propane became the most used fuels. In the late 1950s, the council tried to buy gas for the village from local wells, but the company couldn't ensure a reliable supply, so it wasn't able to hook up to those wells.

In 1972 Northwestern Utilities proposed supplying the village with gas, but most residents said they wanted a village-owned system instead. Hence, village council hired Palmer Engineering to plan a system and to arrange for gas supplies from Nova. Construction, financed through debentures and government grants, began late in the fall of 1973 and was built entirely in the winter. Frozen ground was ripped out which created a huge clean-up job in the spring of 1974. Residents were nevertheless happy with the system—no more running out of propane.

Village councillor Phil Sevigny recalls that during construction of the Co-op 52 system in nearby Provost, the contractor accidentally tore up part of the Chauvin system. Says Sevigny, "They ripped out the gas line, regulator building, everything. It was 2 or 3 in the morning before the gas was on again." There were no hard feelings, however, as Chauvin became a Co-op 52 member later that year and has been supplied by the co-op ever since that time.

## VILLAGE OF FORESTBURG

**Councillors past and present:** Tage Knudsen (mayor), Robert McNabb, Clarence Oberg, Eldon Oberg (mayor), Charter Smith, Doris Farvolden, Earl Ross, Rick Forster. **Managers:** Ian Laing, Peter Tschaja.

Although now convinced of the advantages of natural gas, village residents once turned down gas service in favour of continued reliance on coal. Residents in fact turned down a proposed by-law in 1963; the manager of the local coal mine was very much opposed. However in 1967 attitudes towards gas had changed enough that council decided to try again. Bruce Palmer of Palmer Engineering was hired to design a gas system and find a gas supply. Anchor Construction began work in August 1967 and the last gas outlet was turned on in September 1968. The initial gas source was two gas wells purchased from Hudson Bay Oil Co. for the sum of $70 000. Unfortunately one well went dry and the other contained too high a concentration of hydrogen sulphide and had to be abandoned. The new swimming pool was the first to be turned on—and off. Sulphates in the gas reacted with the copper tubing and corroded the heater. Luckily it was the end of the season, as the heater had to be replaced.

The village then acquired another supply of gas from Hudson Bay Oil Co. and in 1967 a Voyageur well was also connected. In 1973 the South Flagstaff Gas Co-op installed a transmission line from the Nova system and connected it to the Forestburg system. Forestburg has a unique system in place. It can now supply the village and gas co-op with gas from any one of three supplies if the weather turns extremely cold or something happens to one system.

Having the convenience of clean burning natural gas has enticed area farmers to retire among friends in the village. Also employees of Luscar, Manolta Coal, and Alberta Power who mine the coal and operate the huge Battle River Power Generating station, call Forestburg their home. A town today without natural gas would be by-passed by nearly everyone.

## VILLAGE OF GALAHAD

**Councillors past and present:** Lois Brausen (mayor), Allan Dietz, Irwin Keith, Howard Vincentt (mayor), Lionel Sanche (mayor), Terry Chapman.

Since the early homesteading days, coal mines have been in operation in the area. Many local people were employed at the mines and therefore received free coal. Some have received coal until recently when the last tipple, west of Galahad, closed. There was little use of oil or propane in the area.

Mayor Lois Brausen and Councillor Allan Dietz put the idea of a gas system to a council vote in 1973. However, progress stalled until 1975 when the South Flagstaff Co-op began operations and agreed to install and operate a system for the village. Gas was turned on in the fall of 1975. Eventually the village took over operations and now does its own meter reading and bill collecting. The co-op continues to service the system in what remains a mutually beneficial relationship.

## VILLAGE OF HALKIRK

**Councillors past and present:** Don Thomson (mayor), Jean Anderson, George Rowland, Dorothy Anderson (secretary/treasurer), Don Engel (mayor), Gordon Taylor, Ross Elsasser (mayor).

Before natural gas, coal was the main fuel in this small village taken from large mines in the area. Mayor Don Thomson and Councillors Jean Anderson and George Rowland were the driving force behind getting gas service for the village in 1973. About 95 per cent of village residents signed on for gas service as soon as the project was announced. Construction began in the summer of 1974 and was complete by that November. Councillor Anderson credits the co-operation of the nearby Paintearth Gas Co-op for the village's ability to afford its own gas system as the co-op and village shared the expense of gas, engineers, and contractors.

Gas has been a great boon to Halkirk as 75 per cent of the residents are seniors who have been able to retire with its greater convenience and economy.

On a sad note, one family of four who were heating their home with coal had not cleaned their chimney because they were expecting to reline the chimney as soon as a gas furnace was installed. Cleaning chimneys was an annual chore with coal. The family, father, mother, and two children, were asphyxiated by the coal gas.

## VILLAGE OF THORHILD

**Councillors past and present:** Dave Yachimec (mayor), J.W. Rowland, Peter Macyk, Joe Wilflingsider, Mrs. W. LaBelle, Ray Schwetz (mayor), Charlie Simpson (deputy mayor), Mort Harkness, Michael Senych, Mike Prodaniuk.

Village council arranged to buy gas from a Gulf Oil well in 1966 and hired Palmer Engineering to design and build a system, which was turned on January 6, 1967. Construction continued throughout the winter, which meant frequently thawing frozen ground with burning straw and coal. The Gulf well supplied not only the village but several other villages, serviced by Superior Gas Co., and beginning in 1971, the West Thorhild Gas Co-op. In 1972 and 1974, the system was connected to two other wells owned by Gulf. By 1980 all wells ceased production and the entire system was connected to a Nova pipeline.

The village is proud of its system and has refused purchase offers from ICG who now buy gas from the village.

## ELK POINT GAS

In 1947, the Elk Point Chamber of Commerce elected local surgeon A.G. Ross and businessman Paul Stepa to look into natural gas service for the community. Together with John Falkenbergh, the men immediately began selling shares for the proposed Elk Point Natural Gas Syndicate. Stepa recalls promoting the idea by day in his barber shop and pool hall and signing up shareholders in the evening along with Dr. Ross. By 1948, the men had generated enough interest to lease 20 000 acres and drill the first well, which was still producing in 1989. Elise (Mac) Mailleaux, owner of the nearby St. Paul Foundry, ran the operation and connected the syndicate's first 27 shareholders.

In 1949 the Elk Point Gas Company Ltd. was formed and given the franchise for the village of Elk Point and surrounding area. Hook-ups were completed on November 11, 1949. Recalls Stepa, who entered the insurance business in 1953 and is now retired: "Just before the Armistice Parade was due to start, my pool hall and barber shop were hooked up and the gas turned on. We installed the heater and went to the parade. When we came back it was nice and warm."

Materials were scarce after the war, and Mailleaux had to order meters from Edmonton and used boiler pipe from Montreal to build the system. Gas suppliers weren't easy to come by either; the company lost about $11 000 when its second well came up dry.

Over the years the company has drilled 13 wells, four of which were producing in 1989. Elk Point now purchases half its gas from Westmin Resources. Stepa's daughter, Lillian Demchuk, remembers vividly the drilling of well number three on Nick Slywka's farm. "I recall almost a carnival atmosphere as people gathered to see the soaring flames before the well was capped. This was a lucky break as another dry well would have spelled financial disaster for the company."

More than 40 years after its founding, the Elk Point Gas Company is a healthy little company providing quality service to its customers. Dr. Ross, whose idea it was to found the company, loved the little utility and before his death at age 72 said he sometimes wished he had quit medicine to become a company serviceman.

# *Federation Directors*

The Federation of Alberta Gas Co-ops present Board of Directors. From L-R. Back Row: Len Gabert, John Ogilvie, John Krall, Richard Biggs, Bill Gray. Front Row: John Dudar, Alex Onody, Henry Tomlinson, Walter Nasse.

## ZONE 1

**Ed Pimm**: farmer, Peace River. Board member from November 1971 to November 1974; was board vice-chairman when he resigned.

**Mel Longson**: farmer, Beaverlodge. Board member from November 1974 to May 1976. Also a director of the UFA.

**Jim Rasmussen**: farmer, Peace River. Board member from July 1976 to November 1986. A strong advocate for building systems big enough for grain dryers.

**John Krall**: farmer, Nampa. Board member from November 1986 - . Vice-chairman of East Peace Gas Co-op. Years of experience on various provincial boards and in banking.

## ZONE 2

**Henry Tomlinson**: former hog farmer, Spruce Grove. Board member from November 1973 - . Chairman since June 1975. Former chairman of Ste. Anne Gas Co-op. Totally dedicated to the Rural Gas Program.

## ZONE 3

**John Shaw**: farmer, Gibbons. Board member from 1969 to November 1978. Former chairman of North Edmonton Gas Co-op.

**Dan Geiblehaus**: farmer, Vegreville. Board member from November 1978 to November 1980. Former director of Lamco Gas Co-op, and director of provincial hog marketing board.

**Dick Wunder**: farmer, Grassland. Board member from November 1980 to November 1982. Former councillor for County of Athabasca. Later involved in Saskatchewan's rural gas system.

**Steve Schwetz**: farmer, Wasketenau. Board member from November 1982 to November 1986. Reeve of County of Thorhild for thirty years. Successfully pressed to have county systems removed from PUB rate setting jurisdiction.

**John Dudar**: retired farmer, Myrnam. Board member from 1986. Former reeve of County of Two Hills. Encourages counties to retain and operate systems.

## ZONE 4

**Fernand Belzil**: farmer, St. Paul. Board member from November 1973 to December 1975. Represented north-east area during formative years of federation.

**Leo Dechaine**: farmer, St. Lina. Board member from March 1976 to November 1981. Former director of St. Paul Lakeland Gas Co-op.

**Walter Wolanski**: farmer, Redwater. Board member from November 1981 to November 1984. Director of North Edmonton Gas Co-op.

**Bill Gray**: retired Edmonton City Police, Bruderheim. Board member from January 1985 -. Advocate for better training, first class service.

## ZONE 5

**George Ekman**: farmer, Castor. Board member from 1972 to June 1975. Chaired the organization during formative years when finances nearly non-existent and problems plentiful. Former chairman of Paintearth Gas Co-op.

**Charles Archibald**: retired farmer, Rosalind. Board member from July 1975 to November 1975 and from April 1976 to June 1980. Former director of Ankerton Gas Co-op, vice-president of Unifarm and on numerous other provincial committees. Stressed need for greater government financial assistance to overcome large distances and high costs in some areas.

**Merv Giem**: farmer, Ferintosh. Board member from November 1975 to March 1976. A director of UFA farm supply co-op and director of Battle River Gas Co-op.

**Len Gabert**: farmer, Castor. Board member from November 1980 - . Secretary/treasurer since September 1988. Advocates need to market and expand. "Run your business as big business, because that's what it is."

## ZONE 6

**John Moran**: farmer, Huxley. Board member from November 1973 to March 1975. First chairman of Crossroads Gas Co-op.

**Angus Park**: farmer, Trochu. Board member from July 1975 to November 1976. A director and chairman of Crossroads Gas Co-op. Stressed importance of directors taking responsibility for running gas system for owner-members.

**Cecil Flake**: farmer, Markerville. Board member from November 1976 to November 1988. Director/manager of Burnt Lake Gas Co-op. Was co-ordinator of ten trade shows for federation conventions.

**Richard Biggs**: farmer, Lousana. Board member from November 1988-. New trade show co-ordinator and energetic newcomer.

## ZONE 7

**George Comstock**: farmer, Rosebud. Board member from November 1973 to November 1978. Director/manager of Rosebud Gas Co-op. Federation secretary/treasurer from May 1975 to August 1988. Well-known and respected throughout Alberta for his humour and ability.

**Garnet Ovans**: rancher, Cochrane. Board member from November 1978 to November 1984. Chairman/manager of Cochrane Lake Gas Co-op. Great organizational and technical ability honed during years with military.

**Ed Murray**: farmer, Crossfield. Board member from November 1978 to February 1989. Manager of Rockyview Gas Co-op. Brought manager's viewpoint to the board. Hardworking member of sub-committees.

**John Ogilvie**: retired businessman, Priddis. Board member from April 1989 - . Chairman of Meota Gas Co-op. A wealth of experience.

## ZONE 8

**Sam Alberts**: farmer, Brooks. Board member from November 1973 to November 1979. Director/manager of Dinosaur Gas Co-op from 1973 to 1984. Federation treasurer from November 1973 to May 1975. An excellent photographer.

**Milt Ryan**: farmer, Blackie. Board member from November 1979 to November 1985. Director/chairman of Sunshine Gas Co-op, former director of Gem Gas Co-op. Good background in irrigation requirements.

**Walter Nasse**: farmer, Bassano. Board member from 1985 - . Chairman/manager of Bassano Gas Co-op. Represents technical, practical, administrative view of small co-ops.

## ZONE 9

**Alex Onody**: farmer, Bow Island. Board member from November 1973 - . Vice-chairman of federation since June 1975. Represents the views of southern co-ops, particularly on irrigation issues.

## PAST DIRECTORS

Fernand Belzil, Jon Van Bergen, George Ekman, Helmut Entrup, Art Larson, Gordon Nielson, Dale Paterson, Ed Pimm, Lawrence Scheibner, John Shaw, Bill Sinclair, Leo Skanderap, John Voroney, Ernie Walde.

# INDEX

# PHOTO CREDITS

Typesetting and Design:
Pièce de Résistance Ltée., Edmonton, AB
Maps: Government of Alberta;
Photographed by Bill McKeown/Westfile
Lithography:
Color Graphics Alberta, Ltd., Edmonton, AB
Printing:
Quality Color Press Inc., Edmonton, AB

Reidmore Books gratefully acknowledges the assistance and the cooperation of the following individuals, agencies, and corporations in providing the visuals used in this book:

**Abbreviations**
FOAGC: Federation of Alberta Gas Co-ops Ltd.
GAC: Glenbow Archives, Calgary
PAA: Provincial Archives of Alberta

Entries are by page number, coded as follows:
T = Top B = Bottom C = Centre L = Left R = Right

**Front Cover:**
T-PAA/A 6592
C-Courtesy, Alberta Government Photographic Services
B-Courtesy, Canadian Western Natural Gas
**Back Cover:**
GAC/NA-1446-20

**Endsheet:**
Birch Hills Gas Co-op
**Author's Photo:**
L. Amanda Bailey
**Text:**
xi   PAA/A5027
xii  Courtesy, Steve Shwetz.
xiii PAA/A5934
1    PAA/B1439
3    GAC/NA-1446-22
4    GAC/NA-1446-17
5    L-PAA/PA 2110/1     R-Fay Orr
6    Courtesy, Canadian Western Natural Gas
7    Courtesy, Nova Photo Library/201.82 (242584)
8    PAA/PA 6312
10   Tom Adams
11   Courtesy, FOAGC
12   PAA/BL 2032/1
13   PAA/PA 1633/6
14   Tom Adams
15   BL, BR-Tom Adams
16   Tom Adams
17   Meota Gas Co-op
19   Leo Skanderup
20   John Hollenzer/Tirol Gas Co-op Limited
21   Helmut Entrup
22   L-Gem Gas Co-op     R-K. Anderson/SR&B Co-op
23   Courtesy, FOAGC
25   Battle River Gas Co-op Ltd.

26  Glen Skocdopole
27  Courtesy, Alberta Government Photographic
    Services
28  PAA/PA 1655/13
29  PAA/J 1494
30  PAA/A 2465
31  PAA/J 692/3
32  PAA/J 712/6
33  TL-PAA/PA 5089      BR-Courtesy, Alberta
    Government Photographic Services
35  Courtesy, Canadian Utilities Ltd.
38  TL, BR-Mathieson Photo Service Ltd, Calgary
39  Courtesy, Alberta Government Photographic
    Services
40  PAA/J4721
41  Tom Christie
45  Courtesy, Nova Photo Library
46  BL-Courtesy, Alberta Government Photo-
    graphic Services      TR-Tom Christie
47  Courtesy, Alberta Government Photographic
    Services
48  BL-Tom Christie      BR-Courtesy, Alberta
    Government Photographic Services
49  Tom Christie
50  Tom Christie
51  Bob Bellis Photography
53  Benjamin Natural Gas Co-op
54  TR-Cochrane Lake Gas Co-op      B-Alex
    Onody
56  TL-Peyre Family/Prairie River Gas
    Co-op      TR-Chief Mountain Gas Co-op
57  Chinook Gas Co-op
58  Forty Mile Gas Co-op Ltd.
59  Chinook Gas Co-op
60  Minco Gas Co-op
61  Benjamin Natural Gas Co-op
62  County of Vermilion
64  Jerry Koustrup/Big Country Gas Co-op
65  TR-Kardy Terhorst/Pembina River Co-
    op      BR-Lac La Biche District Gas Co-op
66  Dry Country Gas Co-op Ltd.
67  North Peace Natural Gas Co-op
68  Courtesy, Alberta Government Photographic
    Services
69  Yellowhead Natural Gas Co-op
70  East Smoky Gas Co-op
71  Battle River Gas Co-op
72  TL-Courtesy, Alberta Government Photo-
    graphic Services      B-East Peace Co-op

73  North Peace Natural Gas Co-op
74  Courtesy, Alberta Government Photographic
    Services
75  Foothills Natural Gas Co-op Ltd.
76  Fay Orr
77  East Smoky Gas Co-op
78  Birch Hills Natural Gas Co-op
79  Albert Wanuch/Paddle Prairie Natural Gas
    Co-op
80  Easy Smoky Gas Co-op
81  County Council of Thorhild
82  The Signal/Rycroft, AB
83  Courtesy, Alberta Government Photographic
    Services
84  Fay Orr
85  Fay Orr
86  North Peace Natural Gas Co-op
87  Fay Orr
88  Fay Orr
89  L-Chin Coulee Gas Co-op Ltd.      BR-Triple
    W Natural Gas Co-op
90  TL-Don Olesky      B-Chief Mountain Gas
    Co-op
92  Allan Wallace/Ankerton Gas Co-op
93  Cochrane Lake Gas Co-op Ltd.
94  East Central Gas Co-op
95  PAA/J 3672/2
97  Tom Christie
98  Alberta Government Photographic Serv-
    ices/Courtesy, John Nesom
99  Courtesy, FOAGC
100 Susan Francis, PC Research
102 Evergreen Gas Co-op
103 TL,BR-Courtesy, FOAGC
104 Courtesy, FOAGC
105 T,BR-Courtesy, FOAGC
106 TL-Courtesy, FOAGC      B-Prairie River Gas
    Co-op
107 Fay Orr
108 Courtesy, FOAGC
109 Ken Gerber/Ankerton Gas Co-op
153 Courtesy, FOAGC

We have made every effort to correctly identify and
credit the sources of all photographs and illustrations
used in this textbook. Reidmore Books appreciates any
further information or corrections, acknowledgement
would be given in subsequent editions.